COMPUTATIONAL LEARNING THEORY

Cambridge Tracts in Theoretical Computer Science

Managing Editor Professor C.J. van Rijsbergen, Department of Computing Science, University of Glasgow

Titles in the series

1. G. Chaitin *Algorithmic Information Theory*
2. L.C. Paulson *Logic and Computation*
3. M. Spivey *Understanding Z*
4. G. Revesz *Lambda Calculus, Combinators and Logic Programming*
5. S. Vickers *Topology via Logic*
6. A. Ramsay *Formal Methods in Artificial Intelligence*
7. J-Y. Girard, Y. Lafont & P. Taylor *Proofs and Types*
8. J. Clifford *Formal Sematics & Pragmatics for Natural Language Processing*
9. M. Winslett *Updating Logical Databases*
10. K. McEvoy & J.V. Tucker (eds) *Theoretical Foundations of VLSI Design*
11. T.H. Tse *A Unifying Framework for Structured Analysis and Design Models*
12. G. Brewka *Nonmonotonic Reasoning*
13. G. Smolka *Logic Programming over Polymorphically Order-Sorted Types*
15. S. Dasgupta *Design Theory and Computer Science*
17. J.C.M. Baeten (ed) *Applications of Process Algebra*
18. J.C.M. Baeten (ed) & W.P. Weijland *Process Algebra*
23. E.-R. Olderog *Nets, Terms and Formulas*
30. M. Anthony & N. Biggs *Computational Learning Theory*

COMPUTATIONAL LEARNING THEORY

An Introduction

MARTIN ANTHONY & NORMAN BIGGS

Deoartment of Statistical and Mathematical Sciences
London School of Economics

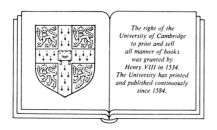

The right of the
University of Cambridge
to print and sell
all manner of books
was granted by
Henry VIII in 1534.
The University has printed
and published continuously
since 1584.

CAMBRIDGE UNIVERSITY PRESS

Cambridge

New York   Port Chester   Melbourne   Sydney

Published by the Press Syndicate of the University of Cambridge
The Pitt Building, Trumpington Street, Cambridge CB2 1RP
40 West 20th Street, New York, NY 10011-4211, USA
10 Stamford Road, Oakleigh, Victoria 3166, Australia

First published 1992

Printed in Great Britain at the University Press, Cambridge

Library of Congress cataloguing in publication data available

British Library cataloguing in publication data available

ISBN 0 521 41603 5 hardback

Contents

Notation

Chapter 1: Concepts, Hypotheses, Learning Algorithms

   1.1 Introduction 1

   1.2 Concepts 2

   1.3 Training and Learning 3

   1.4 Learning by Construction 5

   1.5 Learning by Enumeration 6

      Further Remarks 7

      Exercises 8

Chapter 2: Boolean Formulae and Representations

   2.1 Monomial Concepts 9

   2.2 A Learning Algorithm for Monomials 11

   2.3 The Standard Notation for Boolean Functions 13

   2.4 Learning Disjunctions of Small Monomials 14

   2.5 Representations of Hypothesis Spaces 15

      Further Remarks 17

      Exercises 17

Chapter 3: Probabilistic Learning

   3.1 An Algorithm for Learning Rays 19

   3.2 Probably Approximately Correct Learning 20

   3.3 Illustration — Learning Rays is Pac 23

   3.4 Exact Learning 24

      Further Remarks 26

      Exercises 27

Chapter 4: Consistent Algorithms and Learnability

    4.1 Potential Learnability 29

    4.2 The Finite Case 30

    4.3 Decision Lists 31

    4.4 A Consistent Algorithm for Decision Lists 33

    Further Remarks 35

    Exercises 36

Chapter 5: Efficient Learning – I

    5.1 Outline of Complexity Theory 38

    5.2 Running Time of Learning Algorithms 40

    5.3 An Approach to the Efficiency of Pac Learning 41

    5.4 The Consistency Problem 44

    5.5 A Hardness Result 44

    Further Remarks 48

    Exercises 49

Chapter 6: Efficient Learning – II

    6.1 Efficiency in Terms of Confidence and Accuracy 51

    6.2 Pac Learning and the Consistency Problem 52

    6.3 The Size of a Representation 55

    6.4 Finding the Smallest Consistent Hypothesis 57

    6.5 Occam Algorithms 59

    6.6 Examples of Occam Algorithms 61

    6.7 Epac Learning 64

    Further Remarks 67

    Exercises 69

Chapter 7: The VC Dimension

    7.1 Motivation 71

    7.2 The Growth Function 73

    7.3 The VC Dimension 74

    7.4 The VC Dimension of the Real Perceptron 77

    7.5 Sauer's Lemma 79

    Further Remarks 84

    Exercises 84

Chapter 8: Learning and the VC Dimension

    8.1 Introduction 86

    8.2 VC Dimension and Potential Learnability 86

    8.3 Proof of the Fundamental Theorem................................ 89

    8.4 Sample Complexity of Consistent Algorithms 94

    8.5 Lower Bounds on Sample Complexity 96

    8.6 Comparison of Sample Complexity Bounds 101

    Further Remarks.. 103

    Exercises... 103

Chapter 9: VC Dimension and Efficient Learning

    9.1 Graded Real Hypothesis Spaces.................................. 105

    9.2 Efficient Learning of Graded Spaces 108

    9.3 VC Dimension and Boolean Spaces.............................. 111

    9.4 Optimal Sample Complexity for Boolean Spaces................ 113

    9.5 Efficiency With Respect to Representations..................... 115

    9.6 Dimension-based Occam Algorithms 117

    9.7 Epac Learning Again... 120

    Further Remarks... 121

    Exercises... 122

Chapter 10: Linear Threshold Networks

    10.1 The Boolean Perceptron 123

    10.2 An Incremental Algorithm 125

    10.3 A Finiteness Result 127

    10.4 Finding a Consistent Hypothesis 130

    10.5 Feedforward Neural Networks 131

    10.6 VC Dimension of Feedforward Networks 134

    10.7 Hardness Results for Neural Networks 137

    Further Remarks 140

    Exercises 141

References... 143

Index 150

Preface

Computational Learning Theory is one of the first tentative attempts to construct a mathematical model of a cognitive process. It may be described as a macro-theory, because it provides a framework for studying a variety of algorithmic processes such as those currently in use for training artificial neural networks. There is every reason to suppose that better versions of the model will be produced, but the current state of the theory is sufficiently respectable to warrant a short introductory account, as provided in this book. We concentrate on 'probably approximately correct' learning, because this area is well-developed and appears to be fundamental for the general theory.

The book is intended to introduce the main ideas at a level suitable for a wide range of postgraduate students. It may also be useful for advanced undergraduate courses in mathematics or computing science. We have tried to keep the prerequisites to a minimum by including relevant background material from logic, probability, and complexity theory. The first five chapters, in particular, are suitable for students with a fairly modest mathematical background. The book should also be of interest to research workers in theoretical computer science, mathematics, and neural computing.

The book has developed from a course of postgraduate lectures given by one of us (NLB) at the London School of Economics in October-December 1990. In preparing the lectures, the notes of a course given by Professor Lenny Pitt at the University of Illinois in Summer 1990 were very helpful. We are happy to acknowledge the influence of those notes on the content and organisation of the book. We are also grateful to friends and colleagues for reading and commenting upon various drafts of the book. In particular, we should like to thank Graham Brightwell and John Shawe-Taylor for their advice, and Roger Astley of Cambridge University Press for his efficient handling of the project.

London, September 1991.

Notation

Throughout this book, we use $\ln x$ to denote the natural logarithm of x, and $\lg x$ to denote the logarithm of x to base 2. For any real number x, $\lceil x \rceil$ denotes the ceiling of x, the least integer greater than or equal to x. Further, we use the standard notation for intervals on the real line; for example, $[0,1)$ is the set of all real numbers x such that $0 \le x < 1$. For any finite set S, the cardinality of S will be denoted by $|S|$. Algorithms are often presented in a 'pseudo-code' rather like the Pascal programming language, and the commands used are fairly self-explanatory. The symbol $\square$ denotes the end of an example, proof, or statement. Frequently used symbols are listed below, together with page references and, where appropriate, brief descriptions of their meaning.

Σ	alphabet	2
$\mathbf{R}$	the set of real numbers	2
Σ^n	set of strings of length n in elements of Σ	2
Σ^*	set of non-empty finite strings in elements of Σ	2
X	example space	2
c	concept	2
C	concept space	3
H	hypothesis space	3
h	hypothesis	3
$\mathbf{x}$	sample	3
m	length of sample	3
$\mathbf{s}$	training sample	3
t	target concept	4
L	learning algorithm	4
$u_1, \bar{u}_1, \ldots$	literals	9
$\vee$	*or* connective	13
$\wedge$	*and* connective	13
$\langle u_i \rangle$	elementary boolean function	13
$\langle \phi \rangle$	boolean function represented by formula ϕ	13
$\langle \phi \vee \psi \rangle, \langle \phi \rangle \vee \langle \psi \rangle$	disjunction of boolean functions	13

$\langle \phi \wedge \psi \rangle, \langle \phi \rangle \wedge \langle \psi \rangle$	conjunction of boolean functions	13
DNF	disjunctive normal form	13
CNF	conjunctive normal form	13
M_n	monomials defined on $\{0,1\}^n$	14
$M_{n,k}$	monomials on $\{0,1\}^n$ having at most k literals	14
$D_{n,k}$	disjunctions of small monomials	14
$\Omega \to H$	representation of H	16
Ω	set of states	16
ω	state	16
h_ω	hypothesis represented by ω	16
α_i	weights	16
θ	threshold	16
r_θ	ray	17
μ	probability distribution	20
$\mathrm{er}_\mu(h,t)$	error of h with respect to t	21
$\mathrm{er}_\mu(h)$	error of h (when target understood)	21
μ^m	product probability distribution	22
$S(m,t)$	set of training samples of length m for t	22
δ	confidence parameter	22
ϵ	accuracy parameter	22
$m_0(\delta, \epsilon)$	sufficient sample length	22
$H[\mathbf{s}]$	set of hypotheses consistent with $\mathbf{s}$	29
B_ϵ	set of hypotheses with error at least ϵ	29
$DL(K)$	space of decision lists based on K	32
(f_i, c_i)	term of decision list	32
$O(\ )$	O-notation	38
NP	the complexity class NP	39
Π	a problem	39
n	example size	40
$\bigcup H_n$	hypothesis space graded by example size	40
$R_L(m,n)$	worst-case running time of L	40
$m_L(T, \delta, \epsilon)$	sample complexity of L on T	42
$m_0(T, \delta, \epsilon)$	upper bound on sample complexity of L on T	42
C_n	space of clauses on $\{0,1\}^n$	44
C_n^k	conjunctions of k clauses in C_n	44
C^k	graded space of conjunctions of k clauses	45
G	graph	45
V	vertex-set of graph	45
E	edge-set of graph	45
χ	graph-colouring	45

$\mathbf{s}(G)$	training sample corresponding to graph	45
δ^{*}	the quantity $\ln(\delta^{-1})$	51
$\|\omega\|$	size of representation ω	56
$(U, \mathbf{S})$	instance of *SUBCOVER* or *MINIMUM COVER*	57
Ω_r	set of representations of size r	59
r	representation size	59
H_r	set of hypotheses with minimal representation size r	59
$\bigcup H_r$	hypothesis space graded by representation size	59
$H_{n,r}$	hypotheses of H_n with representation size r	65
$\bigcup H_{n,r}$	doubly-graded hypothesis space	65
DNF_n	boolean functions on $\{0,1\}^n$, with DNF representation	67
DNF	graded space of all boolean functions	67
P_n	real perceptron on n inputs	72
$\Pi_H(\mathbf{x})$	number of classifications of $\mathbf{x}$ by H	73
$E_{\mathbf{x}}$	examples in sample $\mathbf{x}$	73
$H\|E$	restriction of H to domain E	73
Π_H	growth function of H	73
$\mathrm{VCdim}(H)$	VC dimension of H	74
$\mathrm{conv}(S)$	convex hull of S	77
o	the origin	78
$\Phi(d,m)$		80
$(\mathbf{x}, \mathbf{b})$	training sample	86
$\mathrm{er}_{\mathbf{s}}(h)$	observed error of h on $\mathbf{s}$	86
$\mathrm{er}_{\mathbf{x}}(h)$	observed error of h on $\mathbf{x}$ (when target understood)	87
χ_A	characteristic function of A	87
J	interval union space	88
Q_m^{ϵ}	set of bad training samples	88
R_m^{ϵ}	set of bad training/testing samples	90
$LE(p,m,s)$	tail of binomial distribution	91
G_m	swapping group	91
$\Gamma(\mathbf{z})$		92
$GE(p,m,s)$	tail of binomial distribution	97
$\Omega(\ )$	Ω-notation	102
P	graded real perceptron space	105
$\mathbf{R}_+^n$	non-negative quadrant	105
$\mathbf{R}_+^n + v$	translate of non-negative quadrant	106
Q_n	space of n-dimensional quadrants	106
q_v	quadrant	106
Q	quadrant space	106
B_n	space of n-dimensional boxes	106

B	space of boxes	106
B_n^r	r-fold unions of n-dimensional boxes	115
I_n	n-dimensional box union space	115
J_r	r-fold unions of intervals	115
$L(m, H_r)$	effective hypothesis space	118
BP_n	boolean perceptron on n inputs	123
Θ_n	boolean perceptron with threshold 1	124
ν	constant in incremental algorithm	126
L_ν	incremental algorithm	126
α^t	weight vector for Θ_n which realises t	127
c_t	separation constant in perceptron	127
$I(t, \nu)$	number of invocations of incremental algorithm	128
N	set of nodes	131
A	set of arcs	131
(N, A)	directed graph	131
J	set of input nodes	131
z	output node	131
$w(r, s)$	weight on arc	131
f_r	activation function	132
$S_l(\mathbf{x})$	number of states mutually l-distinguishable by $\mathbf{x}$	134
W	number of weights and thresholds	135
P_n^k	parallel linear threshold machine	137
P^k	graded hypothesis space of parallel machine	140

Chapter 1: Concepts, Hypotheses, Learning Algorithms

1.1 INTRODUCTION

There are many types of activity which are commonly known as 'learning'. In this book we shall study a mathematical model of one such process. This particular model appears to be useful because it captures the essence of certain activities which were formerly described only in vague terms, and it enables non-trivial mathematical assertions to be proved.

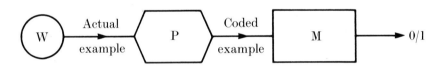

Figure 1.1: Diagram of a framework for learning

The schematic diagram in Figure 1.1 depicts a general framework for our discussion of 'learning'. The circle W represents a 'real world' containing a set of objects which we shall refer to as examples. The box P is a pre-processor, which takes an example and converts it into a coded message, such as a string of bits. This coded version of the example is then presented to M, a machine whose purpose is to recognise certain examples. The output of M is a single bit, either 1 (if the example is recognised as belonging to a certain set), or 0 (if not). The machine can be in one of many states. For example, M might be in a state in which it will recognise examples of the letter **A**, coded as a string of bits in which the 1's correspond to the positions of black pixels on a grid; other states of M might enable it to recognise examples of other letters. The learning process we consider involves making changes to the state of M on the basis of examples presented to it, so that it achieves some desired classification. For instance, we might be able to change the state of M in such a way that the more positive and negative examples of the letter **A** that are presented, the better will M recognise future examples of that letter.

1.2 CONCEPTS

In this section, we formalise the notion that a 'concept' can be described by a set of examples. Let Σ be a set, which we shall call the *alphabet* for describing examples. In this book, Σ will be either the *boolean* alphabet $\{0, 1\}$, or the *real* alphabet **R**. We denote the set of n-tuples of elements of Σ by Σ^n and the set of all non-empty finite strings of elements of Σ by Σ^*.

Let X be a subset of Σ^*. We define a *concept*, over the alphabet Σ, to be a function

$$c : X \rightarrow \{0, 1\}.$$

In some cases X will be the whole of Σ^*; while in other cases X will be taken as Σ^n for one specific value of n, which will be clear from the context. Occasionally X will be a proper subset of some Σ^n, and when this is so we shall make the point explicitly.

The set X will be referred to as the *example space*, and its members as *examples*. An example $y \in X$ for which $c(y) = 1$ is known as a *positive example*, and an example for which $c(y) = 0$ is known as a *negative example*. The union of the set of positive examples and the set of negative examples is the domain of c. So, provided that the domain is known, c determines, and is determined by, its set of positive examples. Sometimes it is helpful to think of a concept as a set in that way.

Example 1.2.1 Let $\Sigma = \{0, 1\}$ and define $p : \Sigma^* \rightarrow \{0, 1\}$ as follows: if $y = y_1 y_2 \ldots y_n$ then

$$p(y) = \begin{cases} 1, & \text{if an odd number of } y_i\text{'s are 1;} \\ 0, & \text{otherwise.} \end{cases}$$

This is known as the *parity* concept. The string 1101010 is a negative example of p, and 001101 is a positive example. □

Example 1.2.2 The boolean concept *palindrome* is defined by taking the positive examples to be just those strings which read the same backwards as forwards. □

Example 1.2.3 Let $\Sigma = \mathbf{R}$ and define $u : \Sigma^n \rightarrow \{0, 1\}$ as follows:

$$u(y_1 y_2 \ldots y_n) = \begin{cases} 1, & \text{if } y_1^2 + \ldots + y_n^2 \leq 1; \\ 0, & \text{otherwise.} \end{cases}$$

This concept is the *n-dimensional unit ball*. □

1.3 TRAINING AND LEARNING

There are two sets of concepts inherent in the framework for learning described by Figure 1.1. First, there is the set of concepts derived from the real world which it is proposed to recognise. This set might contain concepts like 'the letter **A**', 'the letter **B**', 'the letter **C**', and so on, each of which can be coded to determine a set of positive and negative examples. When a set of concepts is determined in this way, we shall use the term *concept space* for it. The other set of concepts inherent in Figure 1.1 is the set which the machine M is capable of recognising. We shall suppose that M can assume various states, and that in a given state it will classify some inputs as positive examples (output 1), and the rest as negative examples (output 0). Thus a state of M determines a concept, which we may think of as a hypothesis. For this reason, the set of all concepts which M determines will be referred to as its *hypothesis space*.

The aim of the learning process is to produce a hypothesis which, in some sense, corresponds to the concept under consideration. The details of when and how this might be done are the central concern of this book. Generally speaking, we are given two sets of concepts, C (the concept space) and H (the hypothesis space), and the problem is to find, for each $c \in C$, some $h \in H$ which is a good approximation to c. In realistic situations hypotheses are formed on the basis of certain information which does not amount to an explicit definition of c. In our framework we shall assume that this information is provided by a sequence of positive and negative examples of c.

If sufficient resources are available, we could build a very large machine and take a very long time to provide it with a marvellous program which would ensure that $h = c$ or that h is as close an approximation to c as we might wish. But in practice there are constraints upon our resources, and we have to be content with a hypothesis h which 'probably' represents c 'approximately', in some sense to be defined.

Let $X \subseteq \Sigma^*$ be the example space, where as always Σ is $\{0,1\}$ or $\mathbf{R}$. A *sample* of *length* m is just a sequence of m examples, that is, an m-tuple $\mathbf{x} = (x_1, x_2, \ldots, x_m)$ in X^m. The sequence may contain the same value more than once, although in most applications there will be no loss in assuming that the examples are distinct. A *training sample* $\mathbf{s}$ is an element of $(X \times \{0,1\})^m$, that is,

$$\mathbf{s} = ((x_1, b_1),\ (x_2, b_2),\ \ldots,\ (x_m, b_m)),$$

where the x_i are examples and the b_i are bits. We shall think of a training sample as a sequence of examples, together with some additional information contained in the associated sequence of bits. This additional information could be provided by a 'teacher', so that the label b_i specifies whether x_i is a positive or negative example of some given concept. We shall insist that there are no contradictory labels, so that if $x_i = x_j$ then $b_i = b_j$. This is equivalent to the assumption that s is a function, defined by $s(x_i) = b_i$ $(1 \leq i \leq m)$. We say that s is a *training sample for the target concept t* if $b_i = t(x_i)$, $(1 \leq i \leq m)$. For example, the following is a training sample for the 'palindrome' concept:

$$(0010, 0), \ (1001001, 1), \ (111, 1), \ (010101, 0), \ (1110111, 1).$$

We can now be rather more specific about the nature of the learning process which we propose to study. Suppose we are given a concept space C and a hypothesis space H, over the same alphabet Σ. A *learning algorithm for* (C, H), sometimes referred to as a (C, H)-*learning algorithm*, is a procedure which accepts training samples for functions in C and outputs corresponding hypotheses in H. Of course, in order to qualify as an algorithm the procedure must be effective in some sense, and we shall need to discuss this point in more detail in due course. If we ignore the problem of effectiveness, a learning algorithm is simply a function L which assigns to any training sample s for a target concept $t \in C$ a function $h \in H$. We write $h = L(s)$.

Note that the hypothesis $L(s)$ is a function defined on the whole example space X, whereas s is a function defined on the finite subset $E \subseteq X$ comprising the examples in the sample $(x_1, x_2, \ldots, x_m)$. A hypothesis h in H is said to be *consistent* with s, or to *agree* with s, if $h(x_i) = b_i$ for each $1 \leq i \leq m$. We do not, in general, make the assumption that $L(s)$ is consistent with s, but when this condition does hold for all s we shall say that L itself is *consistent*. In that case the function $L(s)$ is simply an extension of s, and the diagram in Figure 1.2 is commutative.

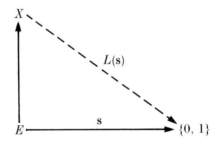

Figure 1.2: Learning as extending a function

In general, not every extension of a training sample will be a valid generalisation because the target concept is only partially defined by the sample. Furthermore, a training sample may be unrepresentative or misleading. For instance, if, under a suitable encoding, the example space consists of all animals and the target concept is 'cat', it could happen that a sample consists entirely of tail-less cats. In practice we must expect that unrepresentative samples are unlikely and that the majority of samples are sufficiently representative so that most extensions are reasonably valid. We shall return to this point in Chapter 3, when we discuss the probabilistic model of learning which is the main topic of this book.

1.4 LEARNING BY CONSTRUCTION

In this section and the next one we shall describe two very simple and very general learning algorithms. As might be expected, the simplicity and generality of the algorithms is offset by their impracticality in all but the most trivial situations. Indeed, much of the rest of the book is devoted to the construction of algorithms which offer provably more efficient methods of learning.

When the example space X is known, a target concept t is determined by its set X^+ of positive examples, and so one way of learning t is to construct this set explicitly. Specifically, we can begin with the empty set and run through the training sample adding each positive example when and if it is presented. In more formal language, suppose that a training sample $\mathbf{s}$, of length m, for the target concept t is given, and define $L(\mathbf{s})$ as follows.

> *set $h(x) = 0$ for all x in X;*
> `for i:= 1 to m do`
>   `if` $b_i = 1$ `then` *set $h(x_i) = 1$;*
> $L(\mathbf{s}) := h$

In this case there are already some pertinent questions about how such a procedure might be implemented, and whether it can reasonably be regarded as an algorithm, especially if X is infinite. Also, we should have to explain exactly how to define an appropriate hypothesis space, so that the hypotheses can be represented in some suitable way.

If we set aside, for the moment, the problem of effectiveness, there remain some other points which are worthy of note. Clearly, the output hypothesis $L(\mathbf{s})$ is equal to the target concept t if and only if $\mathbf{s}$ contains all positive examples of t. Because $\mathbf{s}$ is a finite sequence, this means that only concepts with a finite number of positive examples can be learned with total success. For example, the 'parity' concept is defined over the whole of $\{0,1\}^*$, and so the algorithm can never complete the task of constructing the set of positive examples. If we restrict 'parity' to strings of a fixed length n, then the algorithm can succeed, but the number of positive examples is 2^{n-1}, and so m must be at least that large.

The algorithm does have a couple of more pleasant properties. First, it is consistent, in the sense of Section 1.3; that is, the output hypothesis $L(\mathbf{s})$ classifies all the examples occurring in $\mathbf{s}$ correctly. Secondly, it has the property that each component of the training sample is presented just once, and is not referred to again thereafter. This is a very strong version of what is usually referred to as the 'on-line' property. In practice it means that the examples can be presented to the learner in turn, as they occur, without the necessity of having a 'memory' which stores them for future use. Formally, we shall say that a learning algorithm is a *memoryless on-line* algorithm if, for any given training sample $\mathbf{s}$, it produces a sequence of hypotheses $h_0, h_1, \ldots, h_m$, such that h_{i+1} depends only on h_i and the current labelled example (x_i, b_i).

1.5 LEARNING BY ENUMERATION

The following method of learning is certainly not a memoryless on-line algorithm. We suppose that the hypothesis space H is countable, and that an explicit enumeration of it is given:

$$H = \{h^{(1)}, h^{(2)}, h^{(3)}, \ldots \}.$$

Suppose $\mathbf{s}$ is a training sample for a target concept t. The method is to compare each hypothesis in turn with each component of $\mathbf{s}$ in turn, rejecting the hypothesis on the first occasion that it disagrees with a labelled example. After rejecting a hypothesis, the next one is tested in the same way. The process is stopped when a hypothesis is found to agree with the entire training sample.

```
r:= 1; i:= 1;
repeat
if h^(r)(x_i) ≠ b_i
    then begin r:= r+1; i:= 1 end
    else i:= i+1
until i = m+1;
L(s):= h^(r)
```

If H contains a hypothesis which agrees with the target concept on the training sample, then the algorithm will terminate when it finds the first such hypothesis. Otherwise it will not terminate. If H is finite we can make a trivial modification so that the algorithm terminates with a **not found** message when the entire hypothesis space has been tested without success. But in practice we must avoid using an unreasonably large hypothesis space: for example, if we try to test all possible hypotheses $h : \{0,1\}^n \to \{0,1\}$ we have a hypothesis space of size 2^{2^n} (Exercise 4). These remarks indicate that, for this to be a practical method of learning, some restrictions must be imposed upon the the hypothesis space H and, in particular, on its relationship with the concept space C.

This last consideration, concerning the relationship of the hypothesis space to the concept space, is pertinent for any learning algorithm, and leads to the notion of 'inductive bias'. This is the assumption that the learner has some preconceived idea about what method of classification the teacher is using; that is, the learner knows, or has some indication of, the concept space. The simplest way to model such an assumption is to insist that $H = C$, and in that case we shall speak of a learning algorithm for H, rather than for (H, H). In the next few chapters almost all the algorithms discussed will be of this type.

FURTHER REMARKS

The origins of *Computational Learning Theory* are fairly recent. For many years there have been studies of *Machine Learning* (as in Michalski *et al.* (1983)), *Pattern Recognition* (see Duda and Hart (1973)), and *Inductive Inference* (see Angluin and Smith (1983)), but they do not cover exactly the kind of problem discussed in this book. The foundation of Computational Learning Theory as described in this book may be credited to L.G. Valiant (1984a, 1984b). Since 1988 there have been annual ACM meetings on the subject, known as COLT'88 and so on. The proceedings of these meetings provide a comprehensive review of current progress in the field, and many of the papers are cited in the list of references at the end of the book.

The idea of inductive bias, in the sense of using a restricted hypothesis space for learning, is common in research in Artificial Intelligence: see, for example, Utgoff (1986). A discussion relevant to the learning models described in this book can be found in Haussler (1987, 1988).

There are many variants of the process of 'supervised learning from examples' which is the main topic of this book, and a number of them have been investigated by mathematicians and computer scientists in recent years. In particular, Angluin has studied models which allow the 'learner' to ask questions, rather than simply accept the examples provided by the 'teacher'; see Angluin (1988), for example. One type of question is the *membership query*: Is y a positive example of the target concept? Another is the *equivalence query*, where the learner asks if the current hypothesis is the correct one, and if the answer is *no*, a counterexample is returned.

Finally, it is worth remarking that, in this new and rapidly-developing field of Computational Learning Theory, the notation and terminology is not yet standardised. We hope that our choices are not too bizarre, but certainly they do not coincide with every other publication in this field.

EXERCISES

1. What is the number of positive examples of the palindrome concept, when the example space is $\{0,1\}^n$?

2. Let w be the concept defined on $\{0,1\}^n$ by $w(y) = 1$ if and only if y contains at most two 1's. Show that the number of positive examples of w is a quadratic function of n.

3. Suppose that, in a finite 'learning by enumeration' situation, we are sure that the hypotheses are enumerated in such a way that the one we want is in the first half. If we can check one million hypotheses per second, and the example space is $\{0,1\}^9$, how long will it take, in the worst case?

4. Given that the number of subsets of a set with N elements is 2^N, show that the number of functions from $\{0,1\}^n$ to $\{0,1\}$ is 2^{2^n}.

Chapter 2: Boolean Formulae and Representations

2.1 MONOMIAL CONCEPTS

One of the simplest of boolean concept spaces is the set of *monomial* concepts. In Section 2.3 we shall describe a general framework which encompasses many concept spaces, including the monomials, but for the time being a simple-minded approach will be sufficient.

What is a chair? One attempt to describe the concept 'chair' would be to make a list of properties, and to decide which of them must be attributes of a chair, which of them must not be, and which of them are irrelevant. A very primitive list might be something like the following.

> Four legs – yes
> Tail – no
> Flat seat – yes
> Coloured brown – irrelevant
> Alive – no

This list defines a function $chair : \{0,1\}^5 \to \{0,1\}$ as follows.

$$chair(y_1 y_2 y_3 y_4 y_5) = \begin{cases} 1, & \text{if } y_1 = 1, y_2 = 0, y_3 = 1, y_5 = 0; \\ 0, & \text{otherwise.} \end{cases}$$

It is conventional to represent the function *chair* as $\langle u_1 \bar{u}_2 u_3 \bar{u}_5 \rangle$, indicating that the value of the function is 1 if and only if the first bit is 1, the second is 0, the third is 1, and the fifth is 0. The fourth bit is irrelevant. The expressions $u_1, \bar{u}_2$ and so on are known as *literals*, the expression $u_1 \bar{u}_2 u_3 \bar{u}_5$ is a *monomial formula*, and the angled brackets are simply a way of emphasising that the formula enclosed within the brackets represents a function. This notation will be formalised in Section 2.3.

Another way of representing monomials is by means of a 'machine' whose main components are four-way switches, with positions labelled a, b, c, d. The input to a switch is a single bit, 0 or 1, and the output depends upon the position of the switch according to the following table.

Position	Input $= 0$	Input $= 1$
a	0	1
b	1	0
c	1	1
d	0	0

The machine in Figure 2.1 receives an input $y = y_1 y_2 y_3 y_4 y_5$, and each bit y_i is fed into a switch which operates according to the table above. The outputs from the five switches are then sent to a 'multiple AND unit', which outputs 1 if and only if all five of them are 1. For example, when the machine in the state defined by the switch positions *abacb* it computes the function *chair* defined above.

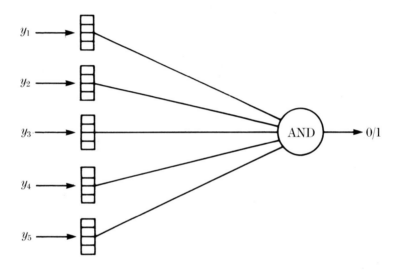

Figure 2.1: A machine which can represent monomials in five variables

The machine is capable of representing any monomial function of five variables, by choosing an appropriate setting of the switches. When the ith switch is in position a, this corresponds to the presence of the term u_i in the monomial; position b corresponds to the presence of $\bar{u}_i$, and position c to absence of both terms. Position d is included for completeness; it corresponds to the situation where both u_i and $\bar{u}_i$ are present. When any one of the switches is in position d the corresponding function is identically zero. Strictly speaking the identically-zero function is not a monomial, but it is often convenient to include it.

2.2 A LEARNING ALGORITHM FOR MONOMIALS

There is a very simple learning algorithm for monomials. We shall describe how it works in terms of the 'formula' representation; there is a parallel description in terms of the machine.

The algorithm operates sequentially, using the following basic idea. Suppose the target monomial is the simplified description of the function *chair*, that is, $\langle u_1 \bar{u}_2 u_3 \bar{u}_5 \rangle$, and the current hypothesis is $h = \langle u_1 \bar{u}_2 u_3 u_4 \bar{u}_5 \rangle$. If the labelled example $(10100, 1)$ is presented, this provides the new information that the target monomial is satisfied when $y_4 = 0$; that is, there is a positive example which is not brown. Thus our hypothesis is wrong because it contains the literal u_4, which indicates that all positive examples should be brown ($y_4 = 1$). Clearly the literal u_4 must be deleted.

This idea is the basis for a simple algorithm due to Valiant (1984b). We begin with no information, so we must assume that every one of the $2n$ literals $u_1, \bar{u}_1, \ldots, u_n, \bar{u}_n$ can occur in the target monomial. Each positive example $y = y_1 \ldots y_n$ enables us to discard those literals u_j for which $y_j = 0$, and those literals $\bar{u}_j$ for which $y_j = 1$. Suppose we are given a training sample **s** containing the labelled examples (x_i, b_i) $(1 \le i \le m)$, where each example x_i is an n-tuple of bits $(x_i)_j$. If we let h_U denote the monomial formula containing the literals in the set U, the algorithm can be expressed as follows.

```
set U = {u₁, ū₁, ..., uₙ, ūₙ};
for i:= 1 to m do
    if bᵢ = 1 then
        for j:= 1 to n do
            if (xᵢ)ⱼ = 1 then delete ūⱼ if present in U
                         else delete uⱼ if present in U;
L(s):= hᵤ
```

We call this algorithm the *standard learning algorithm* for monomials. Note that it is a memoryless on-line algorithm, in the sense described in Section 1.4.

Example 2.2.1 Suppose that $n = 7$, the target concept is $\langle u_1 \bar{u}_2 u_4 u_7 \rangle$, and the training sample is

$$(1001111, 1), \ (0110110, 0), \ (1011101, 1), \ (1011001, 1).$$

The initial hypothesis is $\langle u_1 \bar{u}_1 \ldots u_7 \bar{u}_7 \rangle$, which represents the identically-zero function, and (as we have already remarked) is conveniently regarded as a 'monomial' in this context. The sequence of hypotheses generated by the algorithm is:

$$\langle u_1 \bar{u}_2 \bar{u}_3 u_4 u_5 u_6 u_7 \rangle, \ \langle u_1 \bar{u}_2 \bar{u}_3 u_4 u_5 u_6 u_7 \rangle, \ \langle u_1 \bar{u}_2 u_4 u_5 u_7 \rangle, \ \langle u_1 \bar{u}_2 u_4 u_7 \rangle.$$

So in this case the training sample is good enough to ensure total success. Note that the negative example is not used.   □

There is an equivalent description of the computation by the sequence of states of a 'machine' like the one in Figure 2.1, with seven switches instead of five. In this example the initial state is *ddddddd*, and the subsequent ones are *abbaaaa, abbaaaa, abcaaca, abcacca*.

It is clear that, if the training sample contains all positive examples of the target concept, then the algorithm will output the correct answer. But this condition is not necessary for success, as Example 2.2.1 shows. Each positive example which provides new information results in the deletion of at least one literal, and so n positive examples may suffice, if they are well-chosen. In any case, the algorithm is consistent: its output agrees with each member of the training sample, as we now show.

Theorem 2.2.2 The standard learning algorithm for monomials is consistent.

Proof At each stage some (possibly none) of the literals are deleted from the current hypothesis. It is clear that literals which occur in the target monomial t are never deleted.

Any negative example of t 'falsifies' some literal in t, which is not deleted. It follows that *all* negative examples of t (and, in particular, those in the sample) are correctly classified by $L(\mathbf{s})$.

On the other hand, if $h_U(x) = 1$ and $V \subseteq U$ then $h_V(x) = 1$. After each positive example x in $\mathbf{s}$ is presented, the deletion procedure ensures $h_U(x) = 1$, and therefore the classification of x is subsequently correct. This shows that the final hypothesis $L(\mathbf{s})$ correctly classifies all the positive examples in $\mathbf{s}$.   □

This simple algorithm is quite efficient — a remark which will be elaborated in due course. At this point it is worth noting that one reason why it needs a fairly small number of examples is because the hypothesis space, which, in this case, is the same as the concept space, is very limited. The number of concepts defined on $\{0,1\}^n$ which can be represented as monomials is 3^n, because there are only three possibilities for each one of the 'terms': either u_i is present, or $\bar{u}_i$ is present, or neither is present. (Here we disregard the identically-0 function.) On the other hand, the total number of concepts which can be defined on $\{0,1\}^n$ is 2^{2^n}, which is much larger.

2.3 THE STANDARD NOTATION FOR BOOLEAN FUNCTIONS

There is a standard method of representing boolean functions $\{0,1\}^n \to \{0,1\}$ by means of formulae. The symbols required are the literals $u_1, \bar{u}_1, \ldots, u_n, \bar{u}_n$, the logical connectives $\vee$, meaning *or*, and $\wedge$, meaning *and*, and the parentheses ( ). Each one of the literals u_i and $\bar{u}_i$ defines an elementary function by the rules

$$\langle u_i \rangle(y) = \begin{cases} 1, & \text{if } y_i = 1; \\ 0, & \text{if } y_i = 0; \end{cases}$$

$$\langle \bar{u}_i \rangle(y) = \begin{cases} 1, & \text{if } y_i = 0; \\ 0, & \text{if } y_i = 1. \end{cases}$$

The angled brackets are used to emphasise the distinction between the symbol and the function it represents.

Simple rules of formation enable us to build up more complicated functions. If $\langle \phi \rangle$ and $\langle \psi \rangle$ are functions (in particular, if they are elementary functions) then the *disjunction*, denoted $\langle \phi \vee \psi \rangle$ or $\langle \phi \rangle \vee \langle \psi \rangle$, and the *conjunction*, denoted $\langle \phi \wedge \psi \rangle$ or $\langle \phi \rangle \wedge \langle \psi \rangle$, are the functions defined as follows.

$$\langle \phi \vee \psi \rangle(y) = \begin{cases} 1, & \text{if } \langle \phi \rangle(y) = 1 \text{ or } \langle \psi \rangle(y) = 1; \\ 0, & \text{otherwise.} \end{cases}$$

$$\langle \phi \wedge \psi \rangle(y) = \begin{cases} 1, & \text{if } \langle \phi \rangle(y) = 1 \text{ and } \langle \psi \rangle(y) = 1; \\ 0, & \text{otherwise.} \end{cases}$$

These rules, together with the usual conventions about the use of parentheses, allow the formation of functions like

$$\langle (\bar{u}_1 \wedge u_4) \vee (u_1 \wedge u_2 \wedge \bar{u}_3) \rangle.$$

There is a convention that the symbol $\wedge$ for conjunction may be omitted if the meaning is clear, so that the function above is usually written as $\langle \bar{u}_1 u_4 \vee u_1 u_2 \bar{u}_3 \rangle$. The values of such functions are defined recursively by the rules of construction, and if necessary the familiar method of 'truth tables' can be used for explicit evaluation.

A very useful property of this notation is that every boolean function $\{0,1\}^n \to \{0,1\}$ can be represented by such a formula. In fact, there are many different ways of representing a given function, but there are two 'normal forms' which are particularly convenient. The *disjunctive normal form* or *DNF* is a disjunction

$$\mu_1 \vee \mu_2 \vee \ldots \vee \mu_r,$$

where each μ_i is a monomial, that is, a conjunction of literals, as in Section 2.1. (Note that the convention about suppressing the $\wedge$ symbol is applied there.) The *conjunctive normal form* or *CNF* is a conjunction

$$\gamma_1 \wedge \gamma_2 \wedge \ldots \wedge \gamma_s,$$

where each γ_i is a *clause*, that is, a disjunction of literals.

By placing restrictions on the size and number of the components of the two normal forms we obtain several important hypothesis spaces. We have already studied the set of functions which can be represented by monomials defined on $\{0,1\}^n$; this space will be denoted by M_n. The space of functions represented by monomials which have at most k literals will be denoted by $M_{n,k}$, and the space of functions which can be represented by a disjunction of monomials in $M_{n,k}$ will be denoted by $D_{n,k}$. Other hypothesis spaces defined in a similar way will be used in subsequent chapters: there is a list of the notations used at the beginning of the book.

2.4 LEARNING DISJUNCTIONS OF SMALL MONOMIALS

In this section we think of n as being a 'large' positive integer, and k as being fixed and relatively 'small'. The space $D_{n,k}$, comprising all those boolean functions of n variables which can be expressed as the disjunction of monomials of length at most k, is significantly larger, and consequently more expressive, than M_n. (See Exercise 7 for an explicit estimate of $|D_{n,k}|$.) However, it is simple enough to admit a straightforward consistent learning algorithm.

The learning algorithm, due to Valiant (1984a), begins with the initial hypothesis which is the disjunction of all monomials of length at most k. As in the monomial learning algorithm, each step is based on a simple logical deduction involving a comparison between the current labelled example and the current hypothesis. Specifically, at each step some of the monomials may be deleted, according to the following rule. Suppose we are presented with a negative example $(y, 0)$, but the current hypothesis h produces the value $h(y) = 1$. This means that at least one of the monomials comprising h must evaluate to 1, and since that is in error, all such monomials should be deleted.

As usual, we shall suppose that a training sample s of length m is given. The algorithm may be described as follows.

> set $h =$ *disjunction of all monomials of length at most k* ;
> `for i:= 1 to m do`
>   `if` $b_i = 0$ `and` $h(x_i) = 1$
>   `then` *delete monomials* μ *for which* $\mu(x_i) = 1$;
> $L(\mathbf{s}) := h$

Example 2.4.1 Suppose we are working in $D_{3,2}$ and the target concept is $\langle \bar{u}_1 \vee (u_2 \bar{u}_3) \rangle$. There are three negative examples, 101, 111 and 100, and the other five examples are positive. The collection of all relevant monomial formulae is:

$$u_1,\ u_2,\ u_3,\ \bar{u}_1,\ \bar{u}_2,\ \bar{u}_3,\ u_1u_2,\ u_1u_3,\ u_2u_3,$$

$$\bar{u}_1u_2,\ \bar{u}_1u_3,\ \bar{u}_2u_3,\ u_1\bar{u}_2,\ u_1\bar{u}_3,\ u_2\bar{u}_3,\ \bar{u}_1\bar{u}_2,\ \bar{u}_1\bar{u}_3,\ \bar{u}_2\bar{u}_3.$$

In the algorithm only the negative examples are effective. Suppose these are presented, in the order 101, 111, 100. The presentation of $(101,0)$ results in the deletion of all those monomials which are 1 on 101, that is: $u_1, u_3, \bar{u}_2, u_1u_3, \bar{u}_2u_3$ and $u_1\bar{u}_2$. The subsequent presentation of $(111,0)$ results in the deletion of u_2, u_1u_2 and u_2u_3, and the presentation of $(100,0)$ results in the deletion of $\bar{u}_3, u_1\bar{u}_3$ and $\bar{u}_2\bar{u}_3$. Thus, provided the training sample contains the three negative examples, the output hypothesis is the disjunction of all the remaining monomials, that is

$$h = \langle \bar{u}_1 \vee \bar{u}_1u_2 \vee \bar{u}_1u_3 \vee u_2\bar{u}_3 \vee \bar{u}_1\bar{u}_2 \vee \bar{u}_1\bar{u}_3 \rangle.$$

Here we see clearly that the output is not the simplest representation of the target concept in the hypothesis space $D_{3,2}$. The formula does indeed represent exactly the same function as the given formula, $\langle \bar{u}_1 \vee (u_1\bar{u}_3) \rangle$, but it is much longer. In some cases, such considerations are important, and we shall return to this issue later in the book. □

2.5 REPRESENTATIONS OF HYPOTHESIS SPACES

The learning algorithms discussed in this chapter rely on the simplifying assumption that the concept space is the same as the hypothesis space. In effect, we have been concerned with 'learning' only in situations where the target concepts have some artificial description in terms of formulae or machines. Although this assumption may seem rather restrictive, it is natural in a mathematical development of the subject.

If we are asked to construct a machine to compute a boolean function of n variables, there is a well-known technique which produces a network of 'gates' — a boolean circuit, in the accepted terminology. The construction of a suitable circuit is closely linked to the construction of a formula representing the function, and the size of the machine is related to the length of the formula. Since neither the formula nor the machine is unique, it is important that we try to find a good solution, if not the best.

The machines needed in this area of Computational Learning Theory have the additional feature that they can take on a number of different states, and so a machine represents a set of functions, rather than a single function. A state of the machine is a representation of a function, and the set of all such functions comprises the hypothesis space defined by the machine. This is analogous to defining a hypothesis space in terms of a specific class of formulae, such as the space $D_{n,k}$ discussed above.

In order to model both interpretations of a hypothesis space, it is convenient to define a *representation* to be a surjection $\Omega \to H$, where Ω is a set and H is a hypothesis space. The set Ω may be the set of states of a machine, or the set of formulae constructed by some specific rules of formation. The surjection assigns to each state or formula ω a corresponding function h_ω.

Example 2.5.1 Let Ω be the set of monomial formulae in five variables and $H = M_5$. For each formula $\omega \in \Omega$ there is a boolean function $h_\omega \in M_5$, defined by the rules outlined in Section 2.1. For example, if $\omega = u_1 \bar{u}_2 u_3 u_5$, then h_ω is the function $\langle u_1 \bar{u}_2 u_3 \bar{u}_5 \rangle$, which is just the function *chair* used as an illustration in Section 2.1. $\square$

Example 2.5.2 Figure 2.2 is a diagram of a *linear threshold machine* with five boolean inputs and a single active node. The arcs carrying the inputs have associated weights $\alpha_1, \alpha_2, \alpha_3, \alpha_4, \alpha_5$ and the weighted sum $\alpha_1 y_1 + \alpha_2 y_2 + \alpha_3 y_3 + \alpha_4 y_4 + \alpha_5 y_5$ of the inputs is applied to the active node. This node outputs 1 if the weighted sum is at least θ, and 0 otherwise.

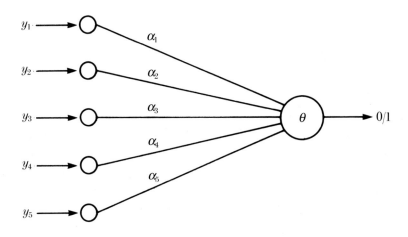

Figure 2.2: A linear threshold machine

In this case the representation $\Omega \to H$ is defined as follows. The set Ω is the real space $\mathbf{R}^6$, that is, the set of 6-tuples $\omega = (\alpha_1, \alpha_2, \alpha_3, \alpha_4, \alpha_5, \theta)$. The function h_ω is given by

$$h_\omega(y_1 y_2 y_3 y_4 y_5) = \begin{cases} 1, & \text{if } \alpha_1 y_1 + \alpha_2 y_2 + \alpha_3 y_3 + \alpha_4 y_4 + \alpha_5 y_5 \geq \theta; \\ 0, & \text{otherwise.} \end{cases}$$

$\square$

Example 2.5.3 Let $\Omega = \mathbf{R}$ and for each real number θ define the real concept r_θ by

$$r_\theta(y) = \begin{cases} 1, & \text{if } y \geq \theta; \\ 0, & \text{otherwise.} \end{cases}$$

The concept r_θ is known as a *ray*; the set of positive examples is the right half-line with end-point θ.   □

FURTHER REMARKS

Of course, there can be more than one learning algorithm for any given hypothesis space. In particular, there are alternative algorithms for the space M_n of monomials. We shall describe one of these, a 'greedy' algorithm due to Haussler (1988), in Chapter 6.

The brief presentation of the algebra of boolean expressions given in Section 2.3 is amplified in many texts on Discrete Mathematics and Computer Science. The existence of the disjunctive normal form may be established by a process rather like 'learning by construction', as follows. Let $\langle \phi \rangle$ be a boolean function of n variables. For each positive example y of $\langle \phi \rangle$, form the monomial

$$\mu^y = \langle l_1 \wedge l_2 \wedge \ldots \wedge l_n \rangle,$$

where

$$l_i = \begin{cases} u_i, & \text{if } y_i = 1; \\ \bar{u}_i, & \text{if } y_i = 0. \end{cases}$$

Then $\mu^y(y) = 1$ and $\mu^y(z) = 0$ if $z \neq y$. Thus, if $x_1, x_2, \ldots, x_k$ are *all* the positive examples of $\langle \phi \rangle$ then

$$\langle \phi \rangle = \langle \mu^{x_1} \vee \mu^{x_2} \vee \ldots \vee \mu^{x_k} \rangle.$$

We remark that this procedure produces a rather long DNF formula representing $\langle \phi \rangle$, and so is of little practical use.

We refer the reader to Kearns *et al.* (1987b) for further description of some of the standard boolean spaces considered in Computational Learning Theory.

EXERCISES

1. Write down the sequence of hypotheses generated when the training sample

$$(11100101, 1), (00100011, 0), (11001001, 1)$$

is input to the monomial learning algorithm. If the target concept is $\langle u_2 \bar{u}_4 u_8 \rangle$, write down an additional labelled example which will result in complete success.

2. Describe the process in Exercise 1 in terms of the states of a machine with switch positions a, b, c, d as defined in Section 2.1.

3. In each of the following cases find a DNF formula which defines the same function as the given one:

$$\langle u_1 \wedge (\bar{u}_2 \vee u_3) \rangle;$$

$$\langle (u_1 \vee u_4) \wedge (u_2 \vee u_3) \rangle;$$

$$\langle (u_1 \vee u_2) \wedge (u_1 \vee u_3) \rangle;$$

4. Write down DNF formulae for the *parity* and *palindrome* concepts on the example space $\{0,1\}^5$.

5. What is the output from the algorithm for learning $D_{3,2}$ when the training sample is

$$(100,0), \ (010,1), \ (011,0)?$$

What is the simplest formula in $D_{3,2}$ which defines the same function?

6. Give an explicit example of a boolean function of three variables which is not in $D_{3,2}$.

7. Prove that

$$1 + \binom{2n}{1} + \binom{2n}{2} + \ldots + \binom{2n}{k} \le (2n)^k,$$

for $n \ge k > 1$. Deduce that $|M_{n,k}|$ is bounded above by $(2n)^k$, and that $|D_{n,k}|$ is bounded above by $2^{(2n)^k}$.

8. Show that the *exclusive-or* function $xor : \{0,1\}^2 \to \{0,1\}$ defined by

$$xor(y_1 y_2) = \begin{cases} 1, & \text{if exactly one of } y_1, y_2 \text{ is } 1; \\ 0, & \text{otherwise;} \end{cases}$$

does not belong to the hypothesis space of the two-input linear threshold machine.

9. For which of the three Examples discussed at the end of Section 2.5 is the representation $\omega \mapsto h_\omega$ an injection?

Chapter 3: Probabilistic Learning

3.1 AN ALGORITHM FOR LEARNING RAYS

As an introduction to one of the most important ideas in Computational Learning Theory, we shall discuss a very simple algorithm for learning in a real hypothesis space.

Recall that for each real number θ the ray r_θ is the concept defined on the example space $\mathbf{R}$ by

$$r_\theta(y) = 1 \iff y \geq \theta.$$

An algorithm for learning in the hypothesis space $H = \{r_\theta \mid \theta \in \mathbf{R}\}$ is based on the idea of taking the current hypothesis to be the 'smallest' ray containing all the positive examples in the training sample. A suitable default hypothesis when there are no positive examples in the sample will be the identically-0 function. For convenience, we therefore consider this to be a ray, and call it the *empty ray*. It will be denoted r_∞, where ∞ is merely a symbol taken to be greater than any real number. Then, for a given training sample $\mathbf{s} = ((x_1, b_1), \ldots, (x_m, b_m))$, the output hypothesis $L(\mathbf{s})$ should be r_λ, where

$$\lambda = \lambda(\mathbf{s}) = \min_{1 \leq i \leq m} \{x_i \mid b_i = 1\},$$

and $\lambda = \infty$ if the sample contains no positive examples.

A simple modification of an algorithm which computes the minimum of a finite set is sufficient for our purposes. This yields the following memoryless on-line algorithm.

```
set λ = ∞;
for i:= 1 to m do
    if b_i = 1 and x_i < λ then set λ = x_i;
L(s):= r_λ
```

For example, if the training sample is

$$(3.6578, 1), \ (2.5490, 0), \ (3.4156, 1), \ (3.5358, 1), \ (3.3413, 1), \ (4.4987, 1),$$

then the corresponding sequence of hypotheses is

$$r_\infty, \; r_{3.6578}, \; r_{3.6578}, \; r_{3.4156}, \; r_{3.4156}, \; r_{3.3413}, \; r_{3.3413}.$$

It is easy to see that if the training sample is for a target hypothesis r_θ then $L(\mathbf{s})$ will be a ray r_λ with $\lambda = \lambda(\mathbf{s}) \geq \theta$. Because there are only finitely many examples in a training sample, and the example space is uncountable, we cannot expect that $\lambda = \theta$. However, it seems that as the length of the training sample increases, so should the likelihood that there is small error resulting from using r_λ instead of r_θ.

In practical terms, this property can be characterised as follows. Suppose we run the algorithm with a large training sample, and then decide to use the output hypothesis r_λ as a substitute for the (unknown) target hypothesis r_θ. In other words, we are satisfied that the 'learner' has been adequately trained. If λ is not close to θ, this indicates that positive examples close to θ are relatively unlikely and did not occur in the training sample. Consequently, if we now classify some more examples which are presented according to the same distribution, then we shall make few mistakes as a result of using r_λ instead of r_θ.

In the next section we shall set up the definitions required to formalise this property, and in Section 3.3 we shall prove that the algorithm does indeed have the property.

3.2 PROBABLY APPROXIMATELY CORRECT LEARNING
We proceed to develop the ideas introduced at the end of the previous section. Consider a model in which a training sample $\mathbf{s}$ for a target concept t is generated by drawing the examples $x_1, x_2, \ldots, x_m$ from X 'at random', according to some fixed, but unknown, probability distribution. A learning algorithm L produces a hypothesis $L(\mathbf{s})$ which, it is hoped, is a good approximation to t. More fully, we require that, as the number m of examples in the training sample increases, so does the likelihood that the error which results from using $L(\mathbf{s})$ in place of t is small.

In order to formalise these ideas it is necessary to review some elementary probability theory. A *probability space* is a set X, together with a family $\mathbf{A}$ of subsets of X and a function μ, the *probability distribution* or *probability measure*, from $\mathbf{A}$ to the unit interval $[0, 1]$. The family $\mathbf{A}$ is required to be closed under the operations of taking complements, finite intersections, and countable unions. An element A of $\mathbf{A}$ is known as an *event*, and the value of $\mu(A)$ is known as the *probability* of A. The function μ is required to satisfy the following conditions:

$$\mu(\emptyset) = 0; \quad \mu(X) = 1;$$

for any pairwise disjoint sets $A_1, A_2, \ldots \in \mathbf{A}$, $\mu\left(\bigcup_{i=1}^{\infty} A_i\right) = \sum_{i=1}^{\infty} \mu(A_i)$.

In the cases of direct concern here, X is an example space, and the examples are either boolean or real. In the boolean case X is finite or countable, and we can take **A** to be the family of all subsets of X. In the real case we can take **A** to be any family large enough to contain all those sets which we need to consider; it turns out that it is sufficient to use the family of Borel sets in $\mathbf{R}^n$. In both boolean and real cases we shall use the appropriate family without explicit reference to the details.

From now on, then, we shall simply speak of a 'probability distribution μ on X', by which we mean a function μ defined on the appropriate family **A** and satisfying the axioms given above. It must be emphasised that, in the applications we have in mind, we make no assumptions about μ, beyond the conditions stated in the definition. The situation we are modelling is that of a world of examples presented to the learner according to some fixed but unknown distribution. The 'teacher' is allowed to classify the examples as positive or negative, but cannot control the sequence in which the examples are presented.

We shall continue to assume that the target concept belongs to a hypothesis space H which is available to the learner. Given a target concept $t \in H$ we define the *error* of any hypothesis h in H, with respect to t, to be the probability of the event $h(x) \neq t(x)$. That is,

$$\mathrm{er}_\mu(h, t) = \mu\{x \in X \mid h(x) \neq t(x)\}.$$

We refer to the set on the right-hand side as the *error set*, and we assume that it is an event, so that a probability can be assigned to it. In order to streamline the notation, we suppress the explicit reference to t when it is clear from the context, and we write $\mathrm{er}_\mu(h)$ in place of $\mathrm{er}_\mu(h, t)$.

Example 3.2.1 Let $X = \{0, 1\}^3$, and suppose the target concept is $\langle u_1 \rangle$. The error set for the hypothesis $\langle u_1 \bar{u}_2 \rangle$ contains just two examples, 110 and 111. So

$$\mathrm{er}_\mu(\langle u_1 \bar{u}_2 \rangle) = \mu\{110, 111\}.$$

For example, if μ is the uniform distribution on X (each of the eight possible examples has probability 1/8), then the error is 1/4. On the other hand, if for some reason examples with $y_2 = 1$ are relatively unlikely, then the error will be correspondingly smaller.   □

When a given set X is provided with the structure of a probability space, the product set X^m inherits a probability space structure from X. The details need not concern us; it is sufficient to remark that the construction allows us to regard the components of an m-tuple $(x_1, x_2, \ldots, x_m)$ as 'independent' variables, each distributed according to the probability distribution μ on X. The corresponding probability distribution on X^m is denoted by μ^m. Informally, for a given $Y \subseteq X^m$ we shall interpret the value $\mu^m(Y)$ as 'the probability that a random sample of m examples drawn from X according to the distribution μ belongs to Y'.

Let $S(m, t)$ denote the set of training samples of length m for a given target concept t, where the examples are drawn from an example space X. Any sample $\mathbf{x} \in X^m$ determines, and is determined by, a training sample $\mathbf{s} \in S(m, t)$: if $\mathbf{x} = (x_1, x_2, \ldots, x_m)$, then $\mathbf{s} = ((x_1, l(x_1)), (x_2, t(x_2)), \ldots, (x_m, t(x_m)))$. In other words, there is a bijection $\phi : X^m \to S(m, t)$ for which $\phi(\mathbf{x}) = \mathbf{s}$. Thus, we can interpret the probability that $\mathbf{s} \in S(m, t)$ has some given property P in the following way. We define

$$\mu^m \{\mathbf{s} \in S(m, t) \mid \mathbf{s} \ has \ property \ P\}$$

to mean

$$\mu^m \{\mathbf{x} \in X^m \mid \phi(\mathbf{x}) \in S(m, t) \ has \ property \ P\}.$$

It follows that, when the example space X is equipped with a probability distribution μ, we can give a precise interpretation to

(i) the error of the hypothesis produced when a learning algorithm L is supplied with $\mathbf{s}$; and

(ii) the probability that this error is less than ϵ.

The first quantity is just $\mathrm{er}_\mu(L(\mathbf{s}))$. The second is the probability, with respect to μ^m, that $\mathbf{s}$ has the property

$$\mathrm{er}_\mu(L(\mathbf{s})) < \epsilon.$$

Putting all this together we can formulate the notion that, given a *confidence* parameter δ and an *accuracy* parameter ϵ, the probability that the error is less than ϵ is greater than $1 - \delta$. The result is one of the most important definitions in this book. It was formulated first by Valiant (1984a) and, using this terminology, by Angluin (1988).

We say that the algorithm L is a *probably approximately correct* learning algorithm for the hypothesis space H if, given

- a real number δ $(0 < \delta < 1)$;
- a real number ϵ $(0 < \epsilon < 1)$;

then there is a positive integer $m_0 = m_0(\delta, \epsilon)$ such that

- for any target concept $t \in H$, and
- for any probability distribution μ on X;

whenever $m \geq m_0$, $\mu^m \{\mathbf{s} \in S(m, t) \mid \mathrm{er}_\mu(L(\mathbf{s})) < \epsilon\} > 1 - \delta.$

The term 'probably approximately correct' is usually abbreviated to the acronym *pac*.

The fact that m_0 depends upon δ and ϵ, but not on t and μ, reflects the fact that the learner may be able to specify the desired levels of confidence and accuracy, even though the target concept and the distribution of examples are unknown. The reason that it is possible to satisfy the condition for any μ is that it expresses a relationship between two quantities which involve μ: the error er_μ and the probability with respect to μ^m of a certain set.

Pac learning is, in a sense, the best one can hope for within this probabilistic framework. Unrepresentative training samples, although unlikely, will on occasion be presented to the learning algorithm, and so one can only expect that it is *probable* that a useful training sample is presented. In addition, even for a representative training sample, an extension of the training sample will not generally coincide with the target concept, so one can only expect that the output hypothesis is *approximately* correct.

3.3 ILLUSTRATION — LEARNING RAYS IS PAC

We can now give a formal verification that the algorithm of Section 3.1 has the pac property.

Theorem 3.3.1 The algorithm L given in Section 3.1 for learning rays is probably approximately correct.

Proof Suppose that $\delta, \epsilon, r_\theta$, and μ are given. Let $\mathbf{s}$ be a training sample of length m for r_θ and let $L(\mathbf{s}) = r_\lambda$. Clearly, the error set is the interval $[\theta, \lambda)$. For the given value of ϵ, and the given μ, define

$$\beta_0 = \beta_0(\epsilon, \mu) = \sup\{\beta \mid \mu[\theta, \beta) < \epsilon\}.$$

Then it follows (Exercise 4) that $\mu[\theta, \beta_0) \leq \epsilon$ and $\mu[\theta, \beta_0] \geq \epsilon$. Thus if $\lambda \leq \beta_0$ we have

$$\mathrm{er}_\mu(L(\mathbf{s})) = \mu[\theta, \lambda) \leq \mu[\theta, \beta_0) \leq \epsilon.$$

The situation $\lambda \leq \beta_0$ is illustrated in Figure 3.1.

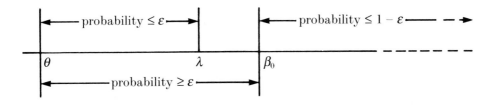

Figure 3.1: In this situation the error of the output is at most ϵ

The event that $\mathbf{s}$ has the property $\lambda \leq \beta_0$ is just the event that at least one of the examples in $\mathbf{s}$ is in the interval $[\theta, \beta_0]$. Since $\mu[\theta, \beta_0] \geq \epsilon$ the probability that a single example is not in this interval is at most $1 - \epsilon$. Therefore the probability that none of the m examples comprising $\mathbf{s}$ is in this interval is at most $(1 - \epsilon)^m$. Taking the complementary event, it follows that the probability that $\lambda \leq \beta_0$ is at least $1-(1-\epsilon)^m$. We noted above that the event $\lambda \leq \beta_0$ implies the event $\mathrm{er}_\mu(L(\mathbf{s})) \leq \epsilon$, and so

$$\mu^m\{\mathbf{s} \in S(m, r_\theta) \mid \mathrm{er}_\mu(L(\mathbf{s})) \leq \epsilon\} \geq 1 - (1 - \epsilon)^m.$$

Note that the right-hand side is independent of the target function r_θ (and μ). In order to make it greater than $1 - \delta$ we can take

$$m \geq m_0 = \left\lceil \frac{1}{\epsilon} \ln \frac{1}{\delta} \right\rceil.$$

For then it follows that

$$(1 - \epsilon)^m \leq (1 - \epsilon)^{m_0} < \exp(-\epsilon m_0) < \exp(\ln \delta) = \delta.$$

This calculation shows that the algorithm is pac.   □

It should be noted that the inequality $\mathrm{er}_\mu(L(\mathbf{s})) \leq \epsilon$ is used in the foregoing proof, whereas our definition of pac learning required the inequality to be strict. However, it is easy to see that the difference is not significant.

The proof of the theorem provides an explicit formula for the length of sample (that is, the amount of training) sufficient to ensure prescribed levels of confidence and accuracy. Suppose we require $\delta = 0.001$ and $\epsilon = 0.01$. Then the value of m_0 is $\lceil 100 \ln 1000 \rceil = 691$. So if we supply at least 691 labelled examples of any ray, and take the output ray as a substitute for the target, then we can be 99.9% sure that at most 1% of future examples will be classified wrongly, provided they are drawn from the same source as the training sample.

3.4 EXACT LEARNING

When the example space X is finite the notion of pac learning has some additional ramifications. We begin by observing that any probability distribution μ on a finite set X is determined by its values on the singleton sets $\{x\}$, using the additivity axiom. For convenience we write $\mu(x)$ instead of $\mu(\{x\})$. If there are some examples for which $\mu(x) = 0$, with probability 1 these will not occur in a finite random sample, and can be ignored. In other words, we can, if necessary, redefine X so that $\mu(x) > 0$ for all $x \in X$. Since X is finite, the quantity

$$\epsilon_\mu = \min_{x \in X} \mu(x)$$

is well-defined and strictly positive.

Suppose that we have an algorithm L which is pac for a hypothesis space H defined on X. In the notation of Section 3.2, we have, given δ, ϵ, μ, and t with their usual meanings,

$$m \geq m_0 \implies \mu^m \{ \mathbf{s} \in S(m,t) \mid er_\mu(L(\mathbf{s})) < \epsilon \} > 1 - \delta.$$

Suppose the accuracy ϵ is chosen to be no greater than ϵ_μ. Then the condition $er_\mu(L(\mathbf{s})) < \epsilon$ implies that the error set for $L(\mathbf{s})$ is empty, because there are no examples which have probability less than ϵ. Thus the condition implies that $L(\mathbf{s}) = t$: that is, the output hypothesis is *exactly* equal to the target t.

The conclusion of the preceding argument is that a pac learning algorithm on a finite example space is 'probably exactly correct', which is apparently rather stronger than being probably approximately correct. But there is a snag. The sample length m_0 in the definition of pac learning depends upon the parameters δ and ϵ, but is independent of μ (and t). The argument given above involves choosing ϵ in terms of ϵ_μ, and so the value of m_0 required for exact learning will depend upon δ and μ. This conflicts with our original aim of providing performance guarantees which are independent of μ, the possibly unknown distribution of examples in an unhelpful world.

Example 3.4.1 We shall establish the 'probably exactly correct' property of the standard monomial learning algorithm on the boolean example space $\{0,1\}^n$, for fixed n, by an explicit argument.

The key observation is that the algorithm yields the correct hypothesis provided that *all* positive examples have been included in the training sample. As the length of the training sample increases, so does the probability that it contains all positive examples; consequently so does the probability that the output is correct. Precisely, let ϵ_μ be the least value of $\mu(x)$ taken over the set $X \subseteq \{0,1\}^n$ of examples with non-zero probability. Then the probability that a training sample of length m does not contain a given example is at most $(1 - \epsilon_\mu)^m$. The probability that there is one of a given set of p examples which is not in the training sample is therefore $p(1 - \epsilon_\mu)^m$. In particular, if X^+ is the set of positive examples for a given target concept t, the probability that there is a member of X^+ which is not in the sample is at most $|X^+|(1 - \epsilon_\mu)^m$.

We need to choose m so that

$$|X^+|(1 - \epsilon_\mu)^m < \delta.$$

Using the facts that $|X^t| \le |X| \le 2^n$, and $1 - \epsilon_\mu < \exp(-\epsilon_\mu)$, it follows that it is sufficient to choose

$$m \ge \left\lceil \frac{n}{\epsilon_\mu} \ln 2 + \frac{1}{\epsilon_\mu} \ln \frac{1}{\delta} \right\rceil.$$

Note that the sample length is independent of t, but does depend upon the distribution μ through the parameter ϵ_μ.   □

FURTHER REMARKS

In Valiant's original description of learning, it was assumed that the learning algorithm had access to an 'oracle' which generated labelled examples of the target concept, drawn according to the distribution on the example space. In such a model, the input to the algorithm consists solely of the parameters δ and ϵ: the algorithm itself then uses the oracle to generate sufficiently many labelled examples to ensure that the output hypothesis is pac. This model is commonly known as the *oracle* model, while the model described in this book is the *functional* model. Haussler *et al.* (1988) have shown that these versions of the learning model, and a number of other variants, are, to all intents and purposes, equivalent. (We are being deliberately vague here. Later in the book we discuss 'efficient' learning: the paper referenced above shows that the spaces learnable efficiently in one model are learnable efficiently in the others.)

Suppose that L is a memoryless on-line learning algorithm for some space H, and that we input some training sample s for a hypothesis t of H. We may allow s to be chosen arbitrarily: that is, it need not be drawn according to some distribution on the example space, but may, for example, be a sequence chosen maliciously by a 'teacher' trying to impart as little information as possible to the learner. Suppose that L updates its current hypothesis each time it makes a *mistake* on an example in s. In other words, L adjusts its current hypothesis after presentation of a labelled example with which its current hypothesis disagrees. We say that L has *absolute mistake bound k* if on *any* training sample, of any length, L makes at most k mistakes. The *mistake-bounded learning* model provides a general framework for studying this situation; see, for example, Littlestone (1988). A number of researchers have studied mistake-bounded learning and its variants, and have related them to the pac model described here and to other models of learning: see, for example, Littlestone (1988), Angluin (1988), Haussler, Littlestone and Warmuth (1988) and Blum (1990).

There are many types of error that can occur during a practical implementation of a particular learning algorithm, and a number of these have been formalised (see Sloan (1988) for a discussion). For example, Angluin and Laird (1987) have produced algorithms for pac learning in the presence of random *misclassification* errors, while Kearns and Li (1988) studied this model and the stronger one of learning in the presence of *malicious* errors, obtaining results on the feasibility of pac learning in such circumstances.

More severe variants of pac learning are obtained by allowing the learning algorithm and the sufficient sample length m_0 to depend in some way either on the probability distribution μ or on the target concept t. This is not artificial: in many learning problems, something is known of the distribution or the target. The resulting definitions of learnability are less attractive than the concept-free and distribution-free pac definition, but they are often more easily satisfied. Much work has been done on such 'non-uniform' pac learning. As a sampling, we refer the reader to the papers by Ben-David *et al.* (1989), Benedek and Itai (1988), Linial *et al.* (1989), Kearns *et al.* (1987a), Li and Vitanyi (1989), Baum (1990), Natarajan (1988) and Bartlett and Williamson (1991).

EXERCISES

1. Write down the sequence of hypotheses generated by the algorithm for learning rays, when the training sample is

$$(6.1436, 1),\ (1.5987, 0),\ (4.2381, 1),\ (5.7462, 1),\ (4.3964, 1),\ (4.2167, 1).$$

2. What length of training sample for the ray learning algorithm will guarantee with 99.5% confidence that at most 0.25% of examples drawn from the same distribution as the sample will be misclassified?

3. Modify the ray learning algorithm of this chapter to obtain a ray learning algorithm which makes no use of the empty ray, but starts instead with λ initialized to some large real number *large*. Is this algorithm consistent?

4. Prove that if β_0 is as defined in Section 3.3, then $\mu[\theta, \beta_0) \leq \epsilon$ and $\mu[\theta, \beta_0] \geq \epsilon$. [Hint: For the first part, use the fact that $\mu\left(\bigcup_n [\theta, \beta_0 - 1/n)\right) = \lim_n \mu[\theta, \beta_0 - 1/n).$]

5. Given real numbers $\alpha \leq \beta$ the *interval* concept $c_{\alpha,\beta}$ is defined by

$$c_{\alpha,\beta}(y) = \begin{cases} 1, & \text{if } \alpha \leq y \leq \beta; \\ 0, & \text{otherwise.} \end{cases}$$

Let H be the hypothesis space of all intervals, together with the identically-0 function (which can be thought of as the empty interval). The following is a learning algorithm for H.

```
empty:= true;
for i:= 1 to m do
      if b_i = 1 then
                  if empty then begin
                                    set α = x_i and β = x_i;
                                    empty:= false end
                          else begin
                                    if x_i > β then set β = x_i;
                                    if x_i < α then set α = x_i end
      if empty then L(s):=empty interval
            else L(s):= c_{α,β}
```

Prove that L is pac, with a suitable value of $m_0(\delta, \epsilon)$ being $\lceil (2/\epsilon) \ln(2/\delta) \rceil$.

6. Modify the algorithm in Exercise 5 to obtain a consistent learning algorithm for the space of interval concepts which makes no use of the identically-0 function.

Chapter 4: Consistent Algorithms and Learnability

4.1 POTENTIAL LEARNABILITY

Learning in the pac sense is a property of an algorithm. Given any algorithm, we can try to prove directly that it is pac, but that might require a very specific argument. Consequently it is desirable to approach the problem more generally. In this chapter we shall describe a property of a hypothesis space H which ensures that any *consistent* algorithm for learning H by H is probably approximately correct, and we shall prove that many spaces H have this property.

We shall continue to use the notation introduced in previous chapters; in particular, H is a hypothesis space of functions defined on an example space X. Recall that a learning algorithm L for H is consistent if, given any training sample $\mathbf{s}$ for a target concept $t \in H$, the output hypothesis $h = L(\mathbf{s}) \in H$ agrees with t on the examples in $\mathbf{s}$. That is, $h(x_i) = t(x_i)$ ($1 \leq i \leq m$). For a given $\mathbf{s} \in S(m,t)$, it is convenient to denote by $H[\mathbf{s}]$ the set of all hypotheses consistent with $\mathbf{s}$:

$$H[\mathbf{s}] = \{h \in H \mid h(x_i) = t(x_i)\ (1 \leq i \leq m)\}.$$

Thus L is consistent if and only if $L(\mathbf{s}) \in H[\mathbf{s}]$ for all training samples $\mathbf{s}$. It turns out that in order to ensure that a consistent learning algorithm is pac, it is sufficient to put a condition on the sets $H[\mathbf{s}]$.

As in Chapter 3 we assume that there is an unknown probability distribution μ on X. Suppose we fix, for the moment, a target concept $t \in H$. Given $\epsilon \in (0,1)$ the set

$$B_\epsilon = \{h \in H \mid \mathrm{er}_\mu(h) \geq \epsilon\}$$

may be described as the set of ϵ-*bad* hypotheses for t. A consistent algorithm for H produces an output in $H[\mathbf{s}]$, and the pac property requires that such an output is unlikely to be ϵ-bad; in other words, we insist that a hypothesis is unlikely to be bad if it is correct on the training sample. This leads to the following definition.

We say that the hypothesis space H is *potentially learnable* if, given real numbers δ and ϵ ($0 < \delta, \epsilon < 1$), there is a positive integer $m_0 = m_0(\delta, \epsilon)$ such that, whenever

$m \geq m_0$,

$$\mu^m\{\mathbf{s} \in S(m,t) \mid H[\mathbf{s}] \cap B_\epsilon = \emptyset\} > 1 - \delta,$$

for any probability distribution μ on X and any $t \in H$.

Theorem 4.1.1 If H is potentially learnable, and L is a consistent learning algorithm for H, then L is pac.

Proof It is sufficient to recall the observation that if L is consistent, then $L(\mathbf{s})$ is in $H[\mathbf{s}]$. Thus the condition $H[\mathbf{s}] \cap B_\epsilon = \emptyset$ means that the error of $L(\mathbf{s})$ is less than ϵ, as required for pac learning.   □

4.2 THE FINITE CASE

The definition of potential learnability is quite complex, and it might be argued that it merely obscures the description of pac learning. Our task now is to justify the definition by showing that it has significant implications.

Theorem 4.2.1 Any finite hypothesis space is potentially learnable.

Proof Suppose that H is a finite hypothesis space and δ, ϵ, t, and μ are given. We shall prove that the probability of the event $H[\mathbf{s}] \cap B_\epsilon \neq \emptyset$ (the complement of the event in the definition) can be made less than δ by choosing the length m of $\mathbf{s}$ to be sufficiently large.

Since B_ϵ is defined to be the set of ϵ-bad hypotheses it follows that, for any $h \in B_\epsilon$,

$$\mu\{x \in X \mid h(x) = t(x)\} = 1 - \mathrm{er}_\mu(h) \leq 1 - \epsilon.$$

Thus

$$\mu^m\{\mathbf{s} \mid h(x_i) = t(x_i) \ (1 \leq i \leq m)\} \leq (1 - \epsilon)^m.$$

This is the probability that any one ϵ-bad hypothesis is in $H[\mathbf{s}]$. The probability that there is some ϵ-bad hypothesis in $H[\mathbf{s}]$, that is

$$\mu^m\{\mathbf{s} \mid H[\mathbf{s}] \cap B_\epsilon \neq \emptyset\},$$

is therefore less than $|H|(1 - \epsilon)^m$. This is less than δ provided

$$m \geq m_0 = \left\lceil \frac{1}{\epsilon} \ln \frac{|H|}{\delta} \right\rceil,$$

because in that case

$$|H|(1 - \epsilon)^m \leq |H|(1 - \epsilon)^{m_0} < |H|\exp(-\epsilon m_0) \leq |H|\exp(\ln(\delta/|H|)) = \delta.$$

Taking the complementary event we have the required conclusion.   □

It is clear that this is a useful theorem. It covers all boolean cases, where the example space is $\{0,1\}^n$ (or a subset thereof) with n fixed. In any such situation a consistent algorithm is automatically pac. For example, the algorithms for learning monomials and disjunctions of small monomials presented in Chapter 2 are pac. Furthermore, the proof tells us how many examples are sufficient to achieve prescribed levels of confidence and accuracy. For the monomial algorithm, we know that the size $|M_n|$ of the hypothesis space is 3^n (Section 2.2). Therefore

$$m_0 = \left\lceil \frac{1}{\epsilon} \ln \frac{|M_n|}{\delta} \right\rceil = \left\lceil \frac{1}{\epsilon}(n \ln 3 + \ln(1/\delta)) \right\rceil$$

is a sufficient number of examples to ensure that, with probability greater than $1 - \delta$, the output of the algorithm has error less than ϵ.

More generally we observe that, for any finite hypothesis space whatsoever, there is a consistent learning algorithm: the method of learning by enumeration, described in Section 1.5. Thus it is an immediate corollary of Theorem 4.2.1 that, given any finite hypothesis space H, there is a learning algorithm for H which is pac.

At this point the reader might well wonder what all the fuss is about. We have set up a complicated condition, only to prove that it is always satisfied in the finite case, which is most important in practice. But practical considerations impose the additional constraint that the number of examples should be 'manageable', and this is not necessarily the case with the method of learning by enumeration. Suppose, for example, that the hypothesis space is the set B_n of all boolean functions of n variables. Then we have $|B_n| = 2^{2^n}$, and so the bound for the sample length is

$$m_0 = \left\lceil \frac{2^n}{\epsilon} \ln \frac{2}{\delta} \right\rceil.$$

Even for applications of moderate size, when $n \approx 50$ say, this is unreasonably large, due to the presence of the term 2^n. In such cases, Theorem 4.2.1 is of little use in practice. This crucial problem will be studied at length in the next chapter.

4.3 DECISION LISTS

One way of describing complex concepts is to build them up from smaller units. This is just how we defined the space $D_{n,k}$ in Section 2.4: the units are the 'small' monomials with length at most k, and they are put together by the operation of disjunction. In this section we shall describe another method of construction, which can be applied to any given set of building blocks.

Let K be any set of boolean functions on $\{0,1\}^n$, n fixed. Following Rivest (1987), a boolean function f with the same domain as K is said to be a *decision list* based on K if it can be evaluated as follows. Given an example y, we first evaluate $f_1(y)$ for some fixed $f_1 \in K$. If $f_1(y) = 1$, we assign a fixed value c_1 (either 0 or 1) to $f(y)$; if not, we evaluate $f_2(y)$ for a fixed $f_2 \in K$, and if $f_2(y) = 1$ we set $f(y) = c_2$, otherwise we evaluate $f_3(y)$, and so on. The procedure is illustrated in Figure 4.1.

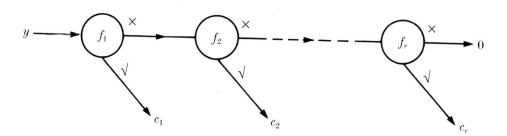

Figure 4.1: Diagrammatic representation of a decision list

The evaluation of a decision list f can be thought of as a sequence of `if then else` commands:

if $f_1(y) = 1$ then *set* $f(y) = c_1$
        else if $f_2(y) = 1$ then *set* $f(y) = c_2$
           . . .
           . . .
           else if $f_r(y) = 1$ then *set* $f(y) = c_r$
                 else *set* $f(y) = 0.$

More formally, we may define $DL(K)$, the space of *decision lists based on* K, to be the set of finite sequences

$$f = (f_1, c_1), (f_2, c_2), \ldots, (f_r, c_r),$$

such that $f_i \in K, c_i \in \{0,1\}$ $(1 \le i \le r)$. The values of f are defined by

$$f(y) = \begin{cases} c_j, & \text{if } j = \min\{i \mid f_i(y) = 1\} \text{ exists}; \\ 0, & \text{otherwise}. \end{cases}$$

There is no loss of generality in requiring that all terms f_i occurring in a decision list are distinct, because repetitions of a given function $g \in K$ can be removed without affecting the evaluation. Thus the length of a decision list based on a finite set K is at most $|K|$, and $|DL(K)|$ is bounded by a function of $|K|$. (See Exercise 10 for details.)

Example 4.3.1 Suppose that $K = M_{3,2}$, the space of monomials of length at most two in three boolean variables. The decision list

$$(\langle u_2 \rangle, 1), \ (\langle u_1 \bar{u}_3 \rangle, 0), \ (\langle \bar{u}_1 \rangle, 1)$$

may be thought of as operating in the following way on the example space $\{0,1\}^3$. First, those examples for which $\langle u_2 \rangle$ is satisfied are assigned the value 1: these are $010, 011, 110, 111$. Next the remaining examples for which $\langle u_1 \bar{u}_3 \rangle$ is satisfied are assigned the value 0: the only such example is 100. Finally, the remaining examples for which $\langle \bar{u}_1 \rangle$ is satisfied are assigned the value 1: this accounts for 000 and 001, leaving only the example 101 which is assigned the value 0.   □

It is worth remarking that the disjunction of two functions in K is a special case of a decision list based on K. Explicitly, $f \vee g$ is represented by the decision list

$$(f, 1), \ (g, 1).$$

This means that a decision list is a generalisation of a disjunction. In particular, the space $D_{n,k}$ is contained in $DL(M_{n,k})$; in fact it is a proper subset. Another consequence is that, for a given n, *any* boolean function of n variables is in some $DL(M_{n,k})$ for k sufficiently large. (Indeed, this is true for $k = n$ by the existence of the disjunctive normal form.) Further details concerning these remarks can be found in the Exercises at the end of the chapter.

4.4 A CONSISTENT ALGORITHM FOR DECISION LISTS

In this section we shall describe a learning algorithm for $DL(K)$ which works when K is any finite set. The algorithm is consistent, but is not a memoryless on-line algorithm. Of course, the learning by enumeration algorithm has similar properties, and it remains to be seen whether the algorithm described here is a significant improvement. This point will be discussed at length in Chapter 5.

The algorithm may be described as follows. Let **s** be a training sample of labelled examples (x_i, b_i) $(1 \le i \le m)$. At each step in the construction of the required decision list some of the examples have been deleted, while others remain. The procedure is to run through K seeking a function $g \in K$ and a bit c such that, for all remaining examples x_i, whenever $g(x_i) = 1$ then b_i is the constant boolean value c. The pair (g, c) is then selected as the next term of the sequence defining the decision list, and all the examples satisfying g are deleted. The procedure is repeated until all the examples in **s** have been deleted.

Let $\{g_1, g_2, \ldots, g_p\}$ be an enumeration of K. The algorithm is as follows.

```
set I = {1,2,...,m}; j:= 1;
repeat
if for all i ∈ I, gⱼ(xᵢ) = 1 implies bᵢ = c
        then begin select (gⱼ,c) ;
                    delete from I all i for which gⱼ(xᵢ) = 1;
                    j:= 1 end
        else j:= j+1;
until I = ∅
```

Example 4.4.1 Take $K = M_{5,2}$, and suppose that K is listed in 'dictionary' order, based on the ordering $u_1, u_2, u_3, u_4, u_5, \bar{u}_1, \bar{u}_2, \bar{u}_3, \bar{u}_4, \bar{u}_5$ of the literals. The first few entries in the dictionary are: the identically-1 monomial $\langle\rangle$, $\langle u_1 \rangle$, $\langle u_1 u_2 \rangle$, $\langle u_1 u_3 \rangle$. Suppose the training sample is

$$x_1 = 10000, \quad b_1 = 0;$$
$$x_2 = 01110, \quad b_2 = 0;$$
$$x_3 = 11000, \quad b_3 = 0;$$
$$x_4 = 10101, \quad b_4 = 1;$$
$$x_5 = 01100, \quad b_5 = 1;$$
$$x_6 = 10111, \quad b_6 = 1.$$

To begin, we select the first item from the dictionary which satisfies the required conditions. Clearly $\langle\rangle$ will not do, because all the examples satisfy it but some have label 0 and some have label 1. Also $\langle u_1 \rangle$ will not do, because (for example) x_1 and x_4 both satisfy it but $b_1 \neq b_4$. However, $\langle u_1 u_2 \rangle$ is satisfied only by x_3, and $b_3 = 0$, so we select $(\langle u_1 u_2 \rangle, 0)$ as the first term in the decision list, and delete x_3. The subsequent steps are as follows:

select $(\langle u_1 u_3 \rangle, 1)$, delete x_4 and x_6;
select $(\langle u_1 \rangle, 0)$, delete x_1;
select $(\langle \bar{u}_1 u_4 \rangle, 0)$, delete x_2;
select $(\langle\rangle, 1)$, delete x_5.

In this case the required decision list is

$$(\langle u_1 u_2 \rangle, 0), (\langle u_1 u_3 \rangle, 1), (\langle u_1 \rangle, 0), (\langle \bar{u}_1 u_4 \rangle, 0), (\langle\rangle, 1).$$

It is worth remarking that different orderings of $M_{5,2}$ may give different answers: see, for example, Exercise 5.   □

There is a slight air of mystery surrounding the example because it is not immediately clear why the search for g and c is always successful. In order to prove that the algorithm works, it is necessary to show that whenever we are given a training sample **s** *for a target concept in* $DL(K)$, then there will always be some pair (g, c) which has the required properties. The training sample given above was not initially known to be compatible with a concept in $DL(M_{5,2})$, although the successful completion of the algorithm shows that it is in fact of this form.

Proposition 4.4.2 Suppose that K is a hypothesis space containing the identically-1 function. Let t be a function in $DL(K)$ and let S be any finite set of examples. Then there is a $g \in K$ and a $c \in \{0, 1\}$ such that:

(i) the set $S^g = \{x \in S \mid g(x) = 1\}$ is not empty;
(ii) for all $x \in S^g, t(x) = c$.

Proof It is given that t is in $DL(K)$, so there is a representation of t as a decision list

$$t = (f_1, c_1), \ (f_2, c_2), \ \ldots, (f_r, c_r).$$

If $f_i(x) = 0$ for all $x \in S$ and all $i \in \{1, 2, \ldots, r\}$, then all the examples in S are negative examples of t. In this case we take g to be the identically-1 function and $c = 0$.

On the other hand, if there is some i such that the set of $x \in S$ for which $f_i(x) = 1$ is not empty, then let q be the least such value. Then it follows from the definition of a decision list that $t(x) = c_q$ for all x such that $f_q(x) = 1$. In this case we may select $g = f_q$ and $c = c_q$. □

It follows from Proposition 4.4.2 that, given any training sample for a function in $DL(K)$, there is a suitable choice of a pair (g, c) for the 'first term' of a decision list. Applying this result recursively, we see that the algorithm described above will always succeed.

FURTHER REMARKS

It is important to ensure that all the probabilities which occur in the definitions of this chapter are well-defined. There are no problems if the example space X is countable, but for real X we must place some measure-theoretic restrictions on the hypotheses spaces we consider. For any two hypotheses $t, h \in H$, we need to assign, as in Chapter 3, a probability to the error set $\{x \mid h(x) \neq t(x)\}$. This can be achieved if the hypotheses are *measurable* functions. To ensure that, for all m and all $t \in H$, the set

$$\{\mathbf{s} \in S(m, t) \mid H[\mathbf{s}] \cap B_\epsilon \neq \emptyset\}$$

has a well-defined probability (with respect to μ^m) some additional constraints must be imposed. It suffices to have H *universally separable*; we refer the reader to Pollard

(1984) and Blumer *et al.* (1989) for the details. We remark that most 'reasonable' hypothesis spaces have this property, and certainly the ones discussed in detail in this book do.

The theory of potential learnability can easily be extended to apply to algorithms which are 'nearly consistent'. For potential learnability, one wants to be able to guarantee that consistency on a training sample of sufficient length implies (with high probability) good approximation. The condition required for the extended definition is the following. For any fixed constant $\alpha < 1$, there is a positive integer $m_0(\alpha, \delta, \epsilon)$ such that if a hypothesis h disagrees with at most a fraction $\alpha\epsilon$ of a training sample of length m_0, then, with probability at least $1 - \delta$, h has actual error less than ϵ. This condition can be satisfied for any finite hypothesis space H; the proof follows quite easily using a bound of Angluin and Valiant (1979) on certain sums of binomial numbers.

EXERCISES

1. Prove by a direct argument that the space $H = \{r_\theta \mid \theta \in \mathbf{R}\}$ of rays is potentially learnable. (Note that this space is not finite.)

2. Show that for the hypothesis space $D_{n,k}$ ($n \geq k > 1$) it is sufficient to take the value

$$m_0(\delta, \epsilon) = \left\lceil \frac{k}{\epsilon} \ln 2n + \frac{1}{\epsilon} \ln \frac{1}{\delta} \right\rceil$$

in the definition of potential learnability.

3. Evaluate $f(y)$ when $f \in DL(M_{5,2})$ is the decision list

$$(\langle u_3 u_5 \rangle, 1), \ (\langle \bar{u}_2 \rangle, 0), \ (\langle u_1 \bar{u}_3 \rangle, 1)$$

and (i) $y = 10101$, (ii) $y = 01111$, (iii) $y = 01011$. What is the effect of interchanging the first two terms of the decision list?

4. Use the algorithm described in Section 4.4 to find a decision list in $DL(M_{6,2})$ consistent with the training sample

$$
\begin{aligned}
x_1 &= 100110, & b_1 &= 0; \\
x_2 &= 001100, & b_2 &= 1; \\
x_3 &= 110001, & b_3 &= 1; \\
x_4 &= 011011, & b_4 &= 1; \\
x_5 &= 111100, & b_5 &= 1; \\
x_6 &= 010010, & b_6 &= 0; \\
x_7 &= 000100, & b_7 &= 0.
\end{aligned}
$$

5. Suppose the space $M_{5,2}$ is ordered in such a way that all monomials of length one come first. Verify that the decision list algorithm, when applied to the training sample used in Example 4.4.1, produces a decision list involving only monomials of length one.

6. Prove that for all $n \geq k \geq 1$, $D_{n,k} \subseteq DL(M_{n,k})$. Deduce that any boolean function can be represented by a decision list.

7. Construct a boolean function of three variables which is not in the space $D_{3,2}$ but is in the space $DL(M_{3,2})$.

8. Construct a boolean function of three variables which is not in the space $DL(M_{3,2})$.

9. Prove that the algorithm described in Section 4.4 is consistent.

10. Prove that for any set K of boolean functions, $3^{|K|}|K|!$ is an upper bound on $|DL(K)|$.

11. The *complement* of a boolean function h is the boolean function $\bar{h}$ with $\bar{h}(x) = 1$ if and only if $h(x) = 0$. Prove that for any set K of boolean functions containing the identically-1 function,
$$h \in DL(K) \iff \bar{h} \in DL(K).$$
That is, $DL(K)$ is closed under complementation.

Chapter 5: Efficient Learning – I

5.1 OUTLINE OF COMPLEXITY THEORY

The subject known as *Complexity Theory* deals with the relationship between the size of the input to an algorithm and the time required for the algorithm to produce its output for an input of that size. In particular, it is concerned with the question of when this relationship is such that the algorithm can be described as 'efficient'. This book is intended to be intelligible to readers who have not studied Complexity Theory, but some knowledge of that subject will be helpful. In this section we shall describe the basic ideas in a very simplistic way. More details may be found in the books by Garey and Johnson (1979), Wilf (1986), and Cormen, Leiserson and Rivest (1990).

The *size* of an input to an algorithm can be measured in various ways. For the time being we shall be dealing mainly with boolean variables, and it will be sufficient to define the input size in terms of the number of bits which the input contains. However, it must be noted that more care is needed if we have to define a measure of size for real variables.

The 'running time' of an algorithm is, of course, dependent on the speed with which the underlying calculations can be carried out. Since the intention is to give a device-independent definition, it is usual to measure running time by the *number* of operations needed, rather than the actual *time* involved. Furthermore, we are only interested in the form of the dependence on input size, not the exact details, because the details will in any case vary with the implementation. For this purpose the mathematical O-notation, as explained below, is appropriate. Finally, the *worst-case* running time is generally employed: this means that we consider the maximum possible number of operations, taken over all inputs of a given size.

These ideas are encapsulated in the following definition. Let A be an algorithm which accepts inputs of varying size s. We say that *the running time of A is $O(f(s))$* if, for any input of size s, the number of operations required to produce the output of A is at most $Kf(s)$, where K is some constant.

For example, suppose we use the familiar long-multiplication algorithm to multiply two given binary integers of the same size. In this case, the size s is n, the number of bits in each integer. The operations involved are bit-multiplications, bit-additions, and carrying. The number of bit-multiplications is n^2, since each bit of the first integer must be mutliplied by each bit of the second integer. The number of bit-additions is about the same, and the carrying operations are less numerous, so we can say that the running time is $O(n^2)$.

There are good reasons for saying that an algorithm with running time $O(s^r)$, for some fixed integer $r \geq 1$, is 'efficient'. Such an algorithm is said to be a *polynomial time* algorithm, and problems which can be solved by a polynomial time learning algorithm are usually regarded as 'easy'. Thus, to show that a problem is easy, we should present a polynomial time algorithm for it. On the other hand, if we wish to show that a given problem is 'hard', it is enough to show that if this problem could be solved in polynomial time then so too could another problem which is believed to be hard. One standard problem which is believed to be hard is the following one.

> *SATISFIABILITY*
> **Instance** A boolean formula ϕ in n variables.
> **Question** Is there a positive example of $\langle \phi \rangle$?

When we say that *SATISFIABILITY* is 'believed to be hard', we mean that it belongs to a class of problems known as the *NP-complete* problems. This class of problems is very extensive, and contains many famous problems in Discrete Mathematics. Examples will be found in Section 5.4 and in later chapters of this book. Although it has not yet been proved, it is conjectured, and widely believed, that there is no polynomial time algorithm for any of the NP-complete problems. This is known as the 'P $\neq$ NP conjecture'.

We shall apply these ideas to Computational Learning Theory in the following way. Suppose that Π is a problem in which we are interested, and Π_0 is a problem which is known to be NP-complete. Suppose also that we can demonstrate that if there is a polynomial time algorithm for Π then there is one for Π_0. In that case our problem Π is said to be *NP-hard*. If the P $\neq$ NP conjecture is true, then proving that a problem Π is NP-hard establishes that there is no polynomial time algorithm for Π.

5.2 RUNNING TIME OF LEARNING ALGORITHMS

Most of the learning algorithms discussed in previous chapters deal with boolean concepts. In such cases the example space is $\{0,1\}^n$ for some fixed n, and the hypothesis space H_n is a set of functions defined on that example space. For each of these algorithms, the parameter n is arbitrary in the sense that the algorithm is defined for any n and, moreover, operates in essentially the same way for each value of n. For example, the standard learning algorithm for the space M_n of monomials is defined quite generally, although we need a specific 'machine' (like the one in Figure 2.1) in order to implement it for a given value of n.

We now wish to quantify the behaviour of learning algorithms with respect to n, and it is convenient to make the following definitions. We say that a union of hypothesis spaces $H = \bigcup H_n$ is *graded* by example size n, when H_n denotes the space of hypotheses defined on n-bit examples. By a *learning algorithm for* $H = \bigcup H_n$ we mean a function L from the set of training samples for hypotheses in H to the space H, such that when $\mathbf{s}$ is a training sample for $h \in H_n$ it follows that $L(\mathbf{s}) \in H_n$. That is, we insist that L preserves the grading.

Consider a learning algorithm L for a boolean hypothesis space $H = \bigcup H_n$, graded by example size. An input to L is a training sample, which consists of m n-bit vectors together with the m single-bit labels. The total number of bits in the input is therefore $m(n+1)$, and it would be possible to use this single number as the measure of input size. However, there is some advantage in keeping track of m and n separately, and so we shall use the notation $R_L(m,n)$ to denote the worst-case running time of L on a training sample of m n-bit vectors.

Example 5.2.1 Let L be the learning algorithm for monomials described in Section 2.2. The hypothesis space is the union $\bigcup M_n$. The main step in the algorithm requires the checking of each bit of each positive example, and possibly the deletion of some literals. In the worst case, every example in the training sample could be a positive example, and so we should have to carry out this step m times, each step involving the checking of n bits. The other parts of the calculation require comparatively few operations, so we can say that the running time $R_L(m,n)$ is $O(mn)$ in this case. □

Example 5.2.2 In Section 2.4 we described a learning algorithm for the space $D_{n,k}$ of disjunctions of small monomials. As usual, we regard k as fixed, and n as variable. Each step of the algorithm involves checking whether one of the m examples x in a training sample is positive or negative and, if it is negative, evaluating some monomials in $M_{n,k}$ on x. Initially the list of relevant monomials has length about $(2n)^k$ (Exercise 7 of Chapter 2) and at each stage some of them may be deleted. Since k is fixed the factor 2^k is a constant, and the running time is $O(mn^k)$.   □

Both algorithms discussed above are memoryless on-line algorithms, and this makes the calculation of the running-time very simple. If such an algorithm L requires at most $S_L(n)$ operations to process a single n-bit example, then its running time is

$$R_L(m, n) \leq mS_L(n).$$

For algorithms which are not of this kind, the calculation of running time may be more complicated.

Example 5.2.3 Recall the algorithm given in Section 4.4 for learning in the decision list space $DL(K_n)$. This is clearly not a memoryless on-line algorithm, because at each step it is necessary to check all the remaining examples against the list of pairs (g, c), where $g \in K_n$ and $c \in \{0, 1\}$. If there are initially m examples in the training sample, there will be $2|K_n|m$ checks at the first step, in the worst case. At least one example will be deleted, so the next step requires at most $2|K_n|(m - 1)$ checks. Repeating the same arguments, it follows that the total number of checks is at most

$$(m + (m - 1) + \cdots + 1)2|K_n| \; = \; m(m + 1)|K_n|.$$

Thus the running time is $O(m^2|K_n|)$. In particular, when K_n is the space $M_{n,k}$ of small monomials, for which the cardinality is bounded by $(2n)^k$, the running time is $O(m^2n^k)$.   □

5.3 AN APPROACH TO THE EFFICIENCY OF PAC LEARNING

A general approach to proving the pac property of a learning algorithm L was developed in Sections 4.1 and 4.2. In the context of a graded hypothesis space $H = \bigcup H_n$ of boolean functions, we may describe the procedure schematically as follows:

$$H_n \text{ finite} \Longrightarrow H_n \text{ potentially learnable};$$

$$H_n \text{ potentially learnable} \quad \text{and} \quad L \text{ consistent for } H_n \Longrightarrow L \text{ pac learns } H_n.$$

With regard to efficiency, the natural question is: given the required levels of confidence and accuracy, what conditions guarantee that the running time in which L pac learns H_n is polynomial in n?

At this point it is helpful to introduce a new piece of terminology to describe a familiar notion. Suppose that real numbers $0 < \delta, \epsilon < 1$ are given, and let L be a learning algorithm for a concept space C and a hypothesis space H. (The assumption $C = H$ is not required here.) We say that the *sample complexity* of L on a subset T of C is the least value $m_L(T, \delta, \epsilon)$ such that, for all target concepts $t \in T$ and all probability distributions μ,

$$\mu^m \{s \in S(m, t) \mid \mathrm{er}_\mu(L(s)) < \epsilon\} > 1 - \delta$$

whenever $m \geq m_L(T, \delta, \epsilon)$; in other words, a sample of length $m_L(T, \delta, \epsilon)$ is sufficient to ensure that the output hypothesis $L(s)$ is pac, with the given values of δ and ϵ. In practice we usually deal with a convenient upper bound $m_0 \geq m_L$, rather than m_L itself; thus $m_0(T, \delta, \epsilon)$ will denote *any* value sufficient to ensure that the pac conclusion, as stated above, holds for all $m \geq m_0$.

The full generality of the definition will be useful on occasions in subsequent chapters, but in most applications we shall take $T = C = H$. For example, using this terminology, Theorem 4.2.1 shows that, for a *consistent* learning algorithm on a *finite* space H, an upper bound for the sample complexity $m_L(H, \delta, \epsilon)$ is

$$m_0(H, \delta, \epsilon) = \left\lceil \frac{1}{\epsilon} \ln \frac{|H|}{\delta} \right\rceil.$$

The sample complexity provides the link between the running time $R_L(m, n)$ of a learning algorithm (that is, the number of operations required to produce its output on a sample of length m when the examples have size n) and its running time as a pac learning algorithm (that is, the number of operations required to produce an output which is probably approximately correct with given parameters). Since a sample of length $m_0(H_n, \delta, \epsilon)$ is sufficient for the pac property, the number of operations required is at most

$$R_L(m_0(H_n, \delta, \epsilon), n).$$

In the case of a consistent algorithm, this provides an answer to the question posed at the beginning of this section.

Theorem 5.3.1 Suppose that L is a consistent learning algorithm for the hypothesis space $H = \bigcup H_n$. If
   - $R_L(m, n)$ is polynomial in m and n, and
   - $\ln |H_n|$ is polynomial in n,

then, for given values of the confidence and accuracy parameters, the running time in which L will produce a probably approximately correct hypothesis is polynomial in n.

Proof Since L is consistent, an upper bound for the sample complexity of L on H_n is

$$\left\lceil \frac{1}{\epsilon} \ln \frac{|H_n|}{\delta} \right\rceil.$$

Thus it is only necessary to observe that, when the conditions hold, the expression $R_L(\lceil (1/\epsilon)\ln(|H_n|/\delta)\rceil, n)$ reduces to a polynomial function of n. $\qquad\square$

This result throws some light on the efficiency of the learning algorithms previously discussed. For example, the space of monomials has cardinality $|M_n| = 3^n$, and so $\ln|M_n| = n\ln 3$. The standard learning algorithm for monomials is consistent (Theorem 2.2.2) and has running time $O(mn)$. It follows that the algorithm pac learns M_n in time polynomial in n — specifically the running time is $O(n^2)$. Similarly, we have shown that there is a consistent learning algorithm for $D_{n,k}$ which has running time $O(mn^k)$, and we also know that $|D_{n,k}|$ is at most $2^{(2n)^k}$ (Exercise 7 of Chapter 2). It follows that $\ln|D_{n,k}|$ is bounded by a constant multiple of n^k, and the theorem implies that the algorithm pac learns $D_{n,k}$ with running time $O(n^{2k})$.

Theorem 5.3.1 does not however enable us to draw any conclusion about the efficiency of more 'general' learning algorithms. For example, the algorithm for learning by enumeration, given in Section 1.5, requires each one of the m labelled examples in a training sample to be checked against each one of the hypotheses in H_n. Thus it is a consistent algorithm whose running time $R_L(m, n)$ is $O(m|H_n|)$. In this case the first condition of Theorem 5.3.1 requires that $|H_n|$ itself (rather than its logarithm) have polynomial growth. This is a very restrictive condition, because even quite limited hypothesis spaces, like M_n and $D_{n,k}$, have cardinality which grows exponentially. Consequently, although the enumeration algorithm can be used for any finite space, there are many cases where Theorem 5.3.1 cannot be applied to show that it will produce a probably approximately correct hypothesis in polynomial time.

It is instructive to apply Theorem 5.3.1 to the learning algorithm for $DL(K_n)$, for which the running time is $O(m^2|K_n|)$. The first condition requires that the cardinality of the base space K_n is a polynomial function of n. In fact this is all that is needed, because the second condition follows automatically; that is, $\ln|DL(K_n)|$ is polynomial if $|K_n|$ is. To verify this, we observe that $|DL(K_n)| \leq 3^{|K_n|}|K_n|!$ (Exercise 10 of Chapter 4). Using the fact that $\ln(N!) \leq N\ln N$, we have

$$\ln|DL(K_n)| \leq |K_n|(\ln|K_n| + \ln 3),$$

and clearly this is bounded by a polynomial in n whenever $|K_n|$ is — for example when $K_n = M_{n,k}$.

5.4 THE CONSISTENCY PROBLEM

We are now ready to consider the implications for learning of the theory of NP-hard problems. Let $H = \bigcup H_n$ be a hypothesis space of boolean functions, graded by the example size n. The consistency problem for H may be stated as follows.

> $H-CONSISTENCY$
> **Instance** A training sample **s** of labelled n-bit vectors.
> **Question** Is there a hypothesis in H_n consistent with **s**?

We shall show that, in some non-trivial cases, this problem is NP-hard. In order to explain the practical implications of this result, we need to make a few general comments. First, if we consider only those instances of the problem in which the length of **s** is bounded by some fixed polynomial in n, then we have a *restricted* form of the consistency problem. It is such restricted forms which will arise in this book, and we shall see that in some cases these problems are NP-hard. Observe that if a restricted form of $H-CONSISTENCY$ is NP-hard then, in particular, $H-CONSISTENCY$ itself is NP-hard.

Another comment is that, in practice, we wish to produce a consistent hypothesis, rather than simply know whether or not one exists. In other words, we have to solve a 'search' problem, rather than an 'existence' problem. But these problems are directly related. Suppose, as above, that we consider only those **s** with length bounded by some polynomial in n. Then, if we can find a consistent hypothesis in time polynomial in n, we can answer the existence question by the following procedure. Run the search algorithm for the time (polynomial in n) in which it is guaranteed to find a consistent hypothesis if there is one; then check the output hypothesis explicitly against the examples in **s** to determine whether or not it is consistent. This checking can be done in time polynomial in n also. Thus if we can show that a restricted form of the existence problem is NP-hard, this means that there is no polynomial time algorithm for the corresponding search problem (unless P = NP).

5.5 A HARDNESS RESULT

Pitt and Valiant (1988) were the first to give an example of a hypothesis space H for which a restricted form of the consistency problem is NP-hard. The following is a slightly simplified account of their method. Let C_n, the space of *clauses*, be the set of boolean functions of n variables which can be represented by clause formulae; that is, by formulae like $u_2 \vee \bar{u}_3 \vee u_6$ which are disjunctions of literals. Let C_n^k be the space of boolean functions which can be represented as the conjunction of k clauses. We can think of C_n as being the hypothesis space of a machine 'dual' to the monomial machine, and C_n^k as the hypothesis space of a machine formed by putting k C_n-machines in parallel, and passing their individual outputs through a multiple

AND unit (Figure 5.1).

We shall show that, for fixed $k \geq 3$, the consistency problem for $C^k = \bigcup C_n^k$ is NP-hard. Thus it is unlikely that there is a polynomial time learning algorithm for C_n^k which produces a consistent hypothesis.

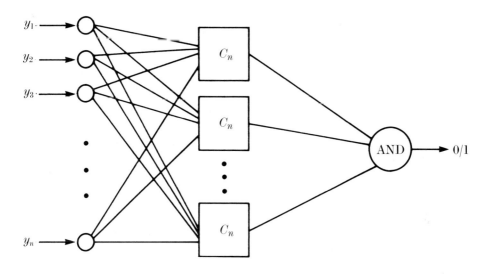

Figure 5.1: The C_n^k machine

The proof follows the standard technique, outlined in Section 5.1, of relating the problem to one which is known to be NP-complete — in this case the problem of k-colouring a graph with n vertices. Let G be a graph with vertex-set V and edge-set E, so that E is a subset of the set of 2-element subsets of V. A k-colouring of G is a function $\chi : V \rightarrow \{1, 2, \ldots, k\}$ with the property that, whenever $ij \in E$, then $\chi(i) \neq \chi(j)$. The existence problem for k-colourings is known to be NP-complete for each $k \geq 3$ (Garey and Johnson 1979).

Suppose we are given a graph $G = (V, E)$, with $V = \{1, 2, \ldots, n\}$. We construct a training sample $s(G)$, as follows. For each vertex $i \in V$ we take as a negative example the vector v_i which has 1 in the ith coordinate position and 0's elsewhere. For each edge $ij \in E$ we take as a positive example the vector $v_i + v_j$. For example, a graph G and the corresponding training sample $s(G)$ are shown in Figure 5.2.

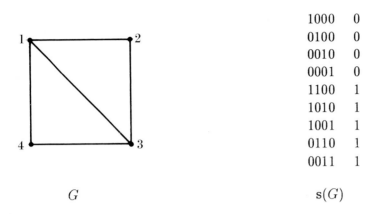

$$\begin{array}{cc} 1000 & 0 \\ 0100 & 0 \\ 0010 & 0 \\ 0001 & 0 \\ 1100 & 1 \\ 1010 & 1 \\ 1001 & 1 \\ 0110 & 1 \\ 0011 & 1 \end{array}$$

G s(G)

Figure 5.2: A graph and the corresponding training sample

Proposition 5.5.1 There is a function in C_n^k which is consistent with the training sample s(G) if and only if the graph G is k-colourable.

Proof Suppose that $h \in C_n^k$ is consistent with the training sample. By definition, h is a conjunction

$$h = h_1 \wedge h_2 \wedge \ldots \wedge h_k$$

of clauses. For each vertex i of G, $h(v_i) = 0$, and so there must be at least one clause h_f $(1 \le f \le k)$ for which $h_f(v_i) = 0$. Thus we may define a function χ from V to $\{1, 2, \ldots, k\}$ as follows:

$$\chi(i) = \min\{f \mid h_f(v_i) = 0\}.$$

It remains to prove that χ is a colouring of G; in other words, if i and j are two vertices for which $\chi(i) = \chi(j)$, then $ij \notin E$. Suppose that $\chi(i) = \chi(j) = f$, so that $h_f(v_i) = h_f(v_j) = 0$. Since h_f is a clause, every literal occurring in it must be 0 on v_i and on v_j. Now v_i has a 1 only in the ith position, and so $h_f(v_i) = 0$ implies that the only negated literal which can occur in h_f is $\bar{u}_i$. Since the same is true for $\bar{u}_j$, we conclude that h_f contains only some literals u_z, with $z \ne i, j$. Thus $h_f(v_i + v_j) = 0$ and $h(v_i + v_j) = 0$. Now if ij were an edge of G, then we should have $h(v_i + v_j) = 1$, because we assumed that h is consistent with s(G). Thus ij is not an edge of G, and χ is a colouring, as claimed.

Conversely, suppose we are given a colouring $\chi : V \to \{1, 2, \ldots, k\}$. For $1 \le f \le k$, define h_f to be the clause

$$\left\langle \bigvee_{\chi(i) \neq f} u_i \right\rangle,$$

and define $h = h_1 \wedge h_2 \wedge \ldots \wedge h_k$. We claim that h is consistent with $s(G)$.

First, given a vertex i suppose that $\chi(i) = g$. The clause h_g is defined to contain only those (not negated) literals corresponding to vertices *not* coloured g, and so u_i does not occur in h_g. It follows that $h_g(v_i) = 0$ and $h(v_i) = 0$.

Secondly, let ij be any edge of G. For each colour f, there is at least one of i, j which is not coloured f; denote an appropriate choice by $i(f)$. Then h_f contains the literal $u_{i(f)}$, which is 1 on $v_i + v_j$. Thus every clause h_f is 1 on $v_i + v_j$, and $h(v_i + v_j) = 1$, as required.   □

Example 5.5.2 The graph depicted in Figure 5.2 has a 3-colouring χ given by $\chi(1) = 1, \chi(2) = 2, \chi(3) = 3, \chi(4) = 2$. Thus there is function h in C_4^3 consistent with the corresponding training sample:

$$h = h_1 \wedge h_2 \wedge h_3 = \langle (u_2 \vee u_3 \vee u_4) \wedge (u_1 \vee u_3) \wedge (u_1 \vee u_2 \vee u_4) \rangle.$$

This graph does not have a 2-colouring, and so we can conclude that there is no function in C_4^2 which is consistent with the training sample.   □

The preceding proposition is the link between the k-colouring problem for graphs and the C^k-consistency problem. If we regard the positive integer k as being fixed in advance, then we can state these problems more formally as follows.

> *GRAPH k-COLOURING*
> **Instance** A graph G with n vertices.
> **Question** Does G have a k-colouring?

> $C^k - CONSISTENCY$
> **Instance** A training sample s of labelled n-bit vectors.
> **Question** Is there a function in C_n^k consistent with s?

The proof that $C^k - CONSISTENCY$ is NP-hard is indicated diagrammatically in Figure 5.3. First, given an instance G of *GRAPH k-COLOURING*, we can construct (in polynomial time) an instance $s(G)$ of $C^k - CONSISTENCY$. Note that the number of edges in a graph with n vertices is at most $n(n-1)/2$, and so the number of examples in $s(G)$ is at most $n + n(n-1)/2$, which is $O(n^2)$. Now suppose there is an algorithm (which we may think of as an 'oracle') that can provide answers to the $C^k - CONSISTENCY$ question. If the oracle operates in polynomial time, then we could answer the *GRAPH k-COLOURING* question in time polynomial in n, by the following procedure: given G, construct $s(G)$, and consult the oracle. Proposition 5.5.1 tells us that the answer given by the oracle is the same as the answer to the original question. Note that this argument shows that a restricted form of $C^k - CONSISTENCY$ in which m is $O(n^2)$ is NP-hard.

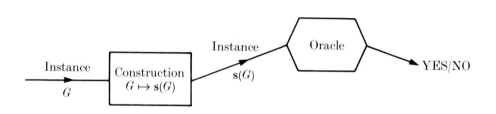

Figure 5.3. The relation between graph k-colouring and C^k-consistency

The foregoing proof that the consistency problem for C^k is NP-hard works only when $k \geq 3$, because the graph k-colouring problem is NP-complete only when $k \geq 3$. When $k = 1$, we have $C_n^1 = C_n$, and there is a polynomial time learning algorithm for C_n dual to the familiar one for the monomials (Exercise 6).

When $k = 2$ it can be shown, by transforming from a different NP-complete problem, that the consistency problem remains NP-hard. See Pitt and Valiant (1988) and Exercise 7 for the details. So we can summarise the results of this section by saying that the consistency problem for C^k is NP-hard if and only if $k \geq 2$.

FURTHER REMARKS
In this chapter we have discussed learning algorithms for graded spaces $H = \bigcup H_n$, where the hypothesis space and the concept space coincide. It is easy to define a learning algorithm for a graded concept space $\bigcup C_n$ by a (possibly different) graded hypothesis space $\bigcup H_n$: such an algorithm takes as input training samples for hypotheses in $C = \bigcup C_n$, and outputs hypotheses in $H = \bigcup H_n$, with the property that if s is a training sample of a hypothesis in C_n then $L(s) \in H_n$. In this vein, Haussler, Littlestone and Warmuth (1988) introduced the notion of *efficient prediction*, subsequently studied by Pitt and Warmuth (1988, 1990) and Haussler *et al.* (1988). Roughly speaking, the graded concept space $C = \bigcup C_n$ is efficiently predictable if there is *some* graded hypothesis space $H = \bigcup H_n$ such that there is a pac learning algorithm for $(\bigcup C_n, \bigcup H_n)$ with running time polynomial in n. (To be more precise,

H is required to have a 'polynomially evaluable' representation. In other words, when the learning algorithm is presented with a training sample for a target in C_n, then it outputs a representation ω of a hypothesis $h_\omega \in H_n$ such that one can determine in polynomial time whether or not a given example is a positive example of h_ω. We make no further reference to this, as all representations in this book have this propery.)

The hardness result proved in Section 5.5 has been generalised to wider families of boolean functions by Blum and Singh (1990). Fischer and Simon (1990) prove an analogous hardness result in the case when hypotheses are represented not in conjunctive normal form, but by 'ring-sum-expansions'.

EXERCISES

1. Why is it usually appropriate, in dealing with questions of efficiency, to take the size of an input which is a positive integer m to be $\lg m$?

2. The following is a fast algorithm for evaluating the mth power of a given value u. (The output is the final value of bot.)

```
bot:= 1; top:= u; q:= m;
while q > 0 do
   begin
   if q mod 2 = 1 then bot:= top*bot;
   top:= sqr(top);
   q:= q div 2
   end
```

Justify the assertion that the efficiency of the algorithm is $O(s)$, where s is the measure of the size of m as suggested in Exercise 1.

3. Devise an algorithm to determine the parity of a given n-bit string, and estimate its efficiency in terms of n.

4. Devise an algorithm to decide whether or not a given n-bit string is a palindrome, and estimate its efficiency in terms of n.

5. Let $G = (V, E)$ be the graph with vertex-set $V = \{1, 2, 3, 4, 5\}$ and edge-set $E = \{12, 13, 15, 23, 25, 34, 45\}$. Write down the corresponding training sample $\mathbf{s}(G)$ as indicated in Section 5.5. Find the least value of k for which there is a function in C_5^k consistent with $\mathbf{s}(G)$, and give an explicit formula for such a function.

6. Let $C_n = C_n^1$, that is, the space of boolean functions on $\{0, 1\}^n$ which can be represented by a single clause formula. Formulate a consistent learning algorithm for

C_n which is 'dual' to the standard algorithm for monomials, and justify the claim that its running time is polynomial in m and n.

7. The following problem is known to be NP-complete (Lovász 1973).

SET SPLITTING

Instance A pair $(U, \mathbf{S})$, where U is a finite set and $\mathbf{S}$ is a collection of sets with union U.

Question Do there exist $U_1, U_2 \subseteq U$ such that $U = U_1 \cup U_2$ and such that no set in $\mathbf{S}$ lies entirely within U_1 or U_2?

Reduce *SET SPLITTING* to $C^2-CONSISTENCY$, and deduce that the consistency problem for C^2 is NP-hard (Pitt and Valiant 1988).

Chapter 6: Efficient Learning – II

6.1 EFFICIENCY IN TERMS OF CONFIDENCE AND ACCURACY

The discussion in the previous chapter centred on the behaviour of the running time of a learning algorithm, considered only as a function of the size n of the examples. Clearly, there are other factors which determine the running time of learning algorithms, and we should like to have a notion of efficiency which takes account of these. To this end, we begin by discussing efficiency with respect to the levels of confidence and accuracy required. Then we shall discuss efficiency with respect to the size of the representation of the target concept. These considerations are relevant for any hypothesis space, and they can be combined with the ideas of Chapter 5 to give a quite general definition of what is meant by an *efficient* pac learning algorithm.

In the previous chapter, we regarded the confidence parameter δ and the accuracy parameter ϵ as fixed but arbitrary. It is clear that decreasing either of these quantities makes the learning task more difficult, and therefore the running time of an efficient pac learning algorithm should be constrained in some appropriate way as δ^{-1} and ϵ^{-1} increase. We could simply ask that the running time increases polynomially with δ^{-1} and ϵ^{-1}, but this dependence on δ^{-1} is not quite appropriate for the following reason. If the length of training sample input to an efficient learning algorithm is doubled, we might expect the probability that the output hypothesis is 'bad' to be approximately squared. In other words, the desired relationship between the sample complexity and δ^{-1} is logarithmic. Motivated by this, we shall say that a learning algorithm L is *efficient with respect to confidence* if its running time is polynomial in m and the sample complexity $m_L(H, \delta, \epsilon)$ depends polynomially on the quantity $\ln(\delta^{-1})$, which we shall denote by δ^*. In the case of the accuracy parameter, we shall say that L is *efficient with respect to accuracy* if its running time is polynomial in m and the sample complexity depends polynomially on ϵ^{-1}. If both these conditions hold, then the running time required to produce a pac output hypothesis is polynomial in δ^* and ϵ^{-1}.

For example, if H is any finite hypothesis space and L is a *consistent* learning algorithm for H, then the theory developed in Chapter 4 implies that an upper bound for the sample complexity is $m_0(H, \delta, \epsilon) = \lceil \epsilon^{-1} \ln(|H|/\delta) \rceil$. In this case m_0 is clearly bounded by a polynomial function of δ^* and ϵ^{-1}. If the running time of L is polynomial in m then L is a pac learning algorithm for H which runs in time polynomial in δ^* and ϵ^{-1}. The same argument works in the graded case. If $H = \bigcup H_n$ is a hypothesis space of boolean functions graded by example size, then an upper bound for the sample complexity is

$$m_0(H_n, \delta, \epsilon) = \left\lceil \frac{1}{\epsilon} \ln \left(\frac{|H_n|}{\delta} \right) \right\rceil .$$

In this case if the running time $R_L(m, n)$ is polynomial in m and n, and if $\ln |H_n|$ is polynomial in n, then L pac learns H_n with running time polynomial not only in n, but also in δ^* and ϵ^{-1}.

6.2 PAC LEARNING AND THE CONSISTENCY PROBLEM

The analysis given at the end of the previous section is motivated by the now familiar relationship between consistency and pac learning. Restricting our attention to the ungraded case, the result is simply that if there is a consistent learning algorithm L for a finite hypothesis space H which runs in time polynomial in the sample length m, then L pac learns H with running time polynomial in δ^* and ϵ^{-1}. Roughly speaking we may say that an efficient 'consistent-hypothesis-finder' is an efficient 'pac learner'. In this section we shall investigate to what extent the converse implication holds.

It turns out that efficient pac learning does imply efficient consistent-hypothesis-finding, provided we are prepared to accept a *randomised algorithm*. A full account of the meaning of this term may be found in the book of Cormen, Leiserson and Rivest (1990), but for our purposes the idea can be explained in a few paragraphs.

We suppose that there is available some form of *random number generator* which, given any integer $I \geq 2$, produces a stream of integers i in the range $1 \leq i \leq I$, each particular value being equally likely. This could be done electronically, or by tossing an I-sided die. A randomised algorithm A is allowed to use these random numbers as part of its input. The computation carried out by the algorithm is determined by its input, so that it depends on the particular sequence produced by the random number generator. It follows that we can speak of the probability that A has a given outcome, by which is meant the relative frequency of sequences which produce that outcome with respect to the total number of possible sequences.

We say that a randomised algorithm A 'solves' a search problem Π if it behaves in the following way. The algorithm always halts and produces an output. If A has failed to find a solution to Π then the output is simply *no*. But, with probability at least $\frac{1}{2}$ (in the sense explained above), A succeeds in finding a solution to Π and its output is this solution.

The practical usefulness of a randomised algorithm stems from the fact that repeating the algorithm several times dramatically increases the likelihood of success. If the algorithm fails at the first attempt, which happens with probability at most $\frac{1}{2}$, then we simply try again. The probability that it fails twice in succession is at most $\frac{1}{4}$. Similarly, the probability that it fails in k attempts is at most $(\frac{1}{2})^k$, which approaches zero very rapidly with increasing k. Thus in practice a randomised algorithm is almost as good as an ordinary one — provided of course that it has polynomial running time. We have the following theorem of Pitt and Valiant (1988) (see also Natarajan (1989) and Haussler *et al.* (1988)).

Theorem 6.2.1 Let H be a hypothesis space and suppose that there is a pac learning algorithm for H with running time polynomial in ϵ^{-1}. Then there is a randomised algorithm which solves the problem of finding a hypothesis in H consistent with a given training sample, and which has running time polynomial in m (the length of the training sample).

Proof Suppose that $\mathbf{s}^*$ is a training sample for a target hypothesis $t \in H$, and that $\mathbf{s}^*$ contains m^* distinct labelled examples. We shall show that it is possible to find a hypothesis consistent with $\mathbf{s}^*$ by running the given pac learning algorithm L on a related training sample.

Define a probability distribution μ on the example space X by
$$\mu(x) = \begin{cases} 1/m^*, & \text{if } x \text{ occurs in } \mathbf{s}^*; \\ 0, & \text{otherwise.} \end{cases}$$
We can use a random number generator with output values i in the range 1 to m^* to select an example from X according to this distribution: simply regard each random number as the label of one of the m^* equiprobable examples. Thus the selection of a training sample of length m for t, according to the probability distribution μ, can be simulated by generating a sequence of m random numbers in the required range.

Let L be a pac learning algorithm as postulated in the statement of the Theorem. Then, when the four usual objects δ, ϵ, μ, and t are given, we can find an integer $m_0(\delta, \epsilon)$ for which the probability (with respect to training samples $\mathbf{s} \in S(m_0, t)$) that the error of $L(\mathbf{s})$ is less than ϵ is greater than $1 - \delta$. Suppose we specify the confidence and accuracy parameters to be
$$\delta = \frac{1}{2}, \quad \epsilon = \frac{1}{m^*}.$$

Then if we run the given algorithm L on a training sample of length $m_0(1/2, 1/m^*)$, drawn randomly according to the distribution μ, the pac property of L ensures that the probability that the error of the output is less than $1/m^*$ is greater than $1 - \frac{1}{2} = \frac{1}{2}$. Since there are no examples with probability strictly between 0 and $1/m^*$, this implies that the probability that the output agrees exactly with the training sample is greater than $1/2$.

The procedure described in the previous paragraph is the basis for a randomised algorithm L^* for finding a hypothesis which agrees with the given training sample $\mathbf{s}^*$. In summary, L^* consists of the following steps.

- Evaluate $m_0 = m_0(1/2, 1/m^*)$.
- Using the random number generator, construct a training sample $\mathbf{s}$ of length m_0 according to the probability distribution μ.
- Run the given pac learning algorithm L on $\mathbf{s}$.
- Check the resulting hypothesis $L(\mathbf{s})$ explicitly to determine whether or not it agrees with $\mathbf{s}^*$.
- If the hypothesis does not agree with $\mathbf{s}^*$, output *no*. If the hypothesis does agree with $\mathbf{s}^*$, output the hypothesis.

As we noted, the pac property of L ensures that L^* succeeds with probability greater than $\frac{1}{2}$. Finally, it is clear that if the running time of L is polynomial in ϵ^{-1}, then the running time of L^* is polynomial in $m^* = \epsilon^{-1}$. □

Theorem 6.2.1 enables us to extend hardness results for the consistency problem, as proved in Section 5.5, to pac learning. Recall that both the decision problem for consistency and (consequently) the problem of finding a consistent hypothesis are NP-hard in some cases, such as when the hypothesis space is $C^k = \bigcup C_n^k$. The theorem tells us that if we could pac learn C_n^k with running time polynomial in ϵ^{-1} and n then we could find a consistent hypothesis, using a randomised algorithm with running time polynomial in m and n. In the language of Complexity Theory this would mean that the latter problem is in RP, the class of problems which can be solved in 'random polynomial time'. Now it is thought that RP does not contain any NP-hard problems — this is the 'RP $\neq$ NP' conjecture, which most people consider to be as reasonable as the 'P $\neq$ NP' conjecture. So if we accept the common view, it follows that there is no polynomial time pac learning algorithm for the graded space C^k when $k \geq 2$.

The above discussion shows that for $k \geq 2$, C^k is not pac learnable efficiently with respect to example size. However, for any n, C_n^k is contained in $D_{n,k}$, the space of disjunctions of monomials with at most k literals (Exercise 3). Valiant's learning algorithm for $D_k = \bigcup D_{n,k}$, described in Section 2.2, is a consistent algorithm with running time $R_L(m,n) = O(mn^k)$, polynomial in m and n (see Example 5.2.2). Therefore, for any training sample **s** for a hypothesis in C_n^k, this algorithm will produce, in polynomial time, a hypothesis of $D_{n,k}$ consistent with **s**. In the Further Remarks section of the previous chapter, we defined what is meant by a learning algorithm L for one graded space $\bigcup C_n$ by another graded space $\bigcup H_n$: given a training sample **s** for a hypothesis of C_n, L returns a hypothesis $L(\mathbf{s}) \in H_n$. Using this terminology, the standard learning algorithm for D_k is a pac learning algorithm for (C^k, D_k), efficient with respect to example size. Thus, in contrast to the negative result above, C^k *is* efficiently learnable by a *larger* space. There is no contradiction here. Roughly speaking, it is difficult to find a formula for a consistent hypothesis in C_n^k because this space is too 'limited'. Given the greater flexibility of working in the 'richer' space $D_{n,k}$, in which the algorithm can express its hypotheses in terms of $D_{n,k}$ formulae, fast learning can be achieved. The non-learnability result is therefore, in a sense, *representation-dependent*.

6.3 THE SIZE OF A REPRESENTATION

We have already mentioned in passing that the output of a realistic learning algorithm is not an abstract function, but rather a representation of that function by means of a formula or a state of a machine. Since a boolean function which can be represented by a short boolean formula is clearly 'simpler' than one which requires a longer formula, it may reasonably be expected that the latter is more difficult to learn than the former.

The framework needed for a careful discussion of such matters is provided by the notion of a representation $\Omega \to H$, as introduced in Section 2.5. The set Ω may be thought of as a set of formulae or a set of states of a machine, so that for each $\omega \in \Omega$ there is a corresponding hypothesis h_ω. In the next few sections, we shall investigate how the representation of hypotheses affects the running time of learning algorithms.

In order to do so, we first need to have some measure of the 'size' of a representation of a hypothesis. Of course there is no absolute measure, and so we must construct one which seems reasonable for the problem in hand. The boolean case is the most straightforward.

The standard method of representing boolean functions by means of formulae was described in Section 2.3. Formally, we use an alphabet of $4 + 2n$ symbols

$$(\quad) \quad \wedge \quad \vee \quad u_1 \; \bar{u}_1 \; u_2 \; \bar{u}_2 \quad \cdots \quad u_n \; \bar{u}_n$$

which are combined according to certain rules of formation. This alphabet can be encoded using $3 + \lceil \lg n \rceil$ bits for each symbol, as indicated in the following table. The idea is that the first three bits are used to code the nature of the symbol, and the remaining $\lceil \lg n \rceil$ bits are used to represent the subscripts on the literal symbols.

Symbol	Code
(	110 000...00
)	101 000...00
∨	100 000...00
∧	111 000...00
u_1	001 000...01
$\bar{u}_1$	000 000...01
u_2	001 000...10
and so on	

Let ω be a well-formed formula which can be obtained from the alphabet given above. If ω has s symbols, then it can be encoded by using $s(3 + \lceil \lg n \rceil)$ bits, and so the size of ω may be taken as

$$\|\omega\| = s(3 + \lceil \lg n \rceil).$$

For example, if $n = 3$ and $\omega = (u_1 \wedge u_2) \vee u_3$, then ω contains 7 symbols and $\|\omega\| = 7(3 + 2) = 35$.

As we remarked above, the output from a learning algorithm is not an abstract function or hypothesis, but rather a representation of a hypothesis by a formula or a state of a machine. In this light it is instructive to compare the size of such an output with the size of the input to the algorithm, which is simply a training sample of labelled examples.

Example 6.3.1 Suppose we supply a training sample of 20 labelled 30-bit vectors to the standard monomial learning algorithm. The total number of bits in the input is $20 \times (30 + 1) = 620$. The output is a monomial hypothesis, which can be represented by a formula with at most 30 literals and 29 conjunction symbols. Using the encoding scheme described above, the number of bits required to encode the output is at most

$$(30 + 29) \times (3 + \lceil \lg 30 \rceil) = 472.$$

Since this is rather less than the number of bits in the input, it is reasonable to claim that the output is, in some sense, a compressed form of the input. □

The preceeding example illustrates that, in favourable circumstances, we can expect the learning algorithm to output a representation ω of a hypothesis h_ω such that not only is h_ω an extension of the training sample, but ω is a compressed form of the input. That is, in a sense, ω contains as much information as is conveyed by the training sample, it defines an extended function, and it requires less bits than the training sample. In Section 6.5 we shall see that if a learning algorithm L outputs the representation of a hypothesis which, in a precise sense to be defined, is not too long, and is a significant compression of the input, then L has certain probably approximately correct properties.

6.4 FINDING THE SMALLEST CONSISTENT HYPOTHESIS

Suppose we are given a training sample for a monomial. The standard learning algorithm described in Section 2.2 produces, in polynomial time, a monomial consistent with the training sample. However, we might expect more, and ask for the smallest monomial consistent with the sample. In this context we can ignore the conjunction symbols in a monomial, and it suffices to use the approximation $\lceil k \log n \rceil$ for the size of a monomial formula with k literals, defined on $\{0,1\}^n$. Thus, in any given subset of M_n, the 'smallest' monomial is simply the one with the fewest literals. In this section we shall show that finding the smallest monomial consistent with a training sample is an NP-hard problem.

Our aim will be achieved by relating the problem to one which is known to be NP-complete. Suppose U is a finite set and $\mathbf{S}$ is a finite collection of sets with union U. We say that a subcollection $\mathbf{S}'$ of $\mathbf{S}$ is a *subcover* if the union of the sets in $\mathbf{S}'$ is also U. The following was one of the first problems shown to be NP-complete (Karp (1972); see also Cormen, Leiserson and Rivest (1990)).

> *SUBCOVER*
> **Instance** A pair $(U, \mathbf{S})$, as above, and a positive integer $k \leq |\mathbf{S}|$.
> **Question** Is there a subcover of $\mathbf{S}$ containing at most k sets?

Note that the size of the instance depends on both $|U| = u$ and $|\mathbf{S}| = n$. In fact we can describe $(U, \mathbf{S})$ by a matrix with u rows and n columns, which specifies whether or not each member of U is in each member of $\mathbf{S}$. The size un of this matrix may be regarded as the size of the instance $(U, \mathbf{S})$, and this is the parameter with respect to which we discuss the question of polynomiality.

The preceding problem is in 'decision' form. There is a related 'optimisation' problem which is more directly relevant to our aims.

> *MINIMUM COVER*
> **Instance** A pair $(U, \mathbf{S})$, as above.
> **Question** What is the minimum number of sets in a subcover of $(U, \mathbf{S})$?

Clearly, if we could answer the *MINIMUM COVER* problem with running time polynomial in un then we could answer the *SUBCOVER* problem also in polynomial time. Indeed, suppose that the pair $(U, \mathbf{S})$ and the positive integer k constitute an instance of *SUBCOVER*. If we solve *MINIMUM COVER* for the instance $(U, \mathbf{S})$, we find the least integer K such that $\mathbf{S}$ has a subcover with K sets. The answer to the instance of *SUBCOVER* is then immediate, being *yes* if and only if $k \geq K$. In fact a converse relationship also holds, although we do not need it here. (See Exercise 4.)

Let us now return to the problem of finding a monomial consistent with a given training sample $\mathbf{s}$ and containing the fewest possible literals.

SHORTEST MONOMIAL

Instance A training sample $\mathbf{s}$ of length m for a monomial in M_n.

Question What is the minimum number of literals appearing in a formula for a monomial consistent with $\mathbf{s}$?

We now show that *SHORTEST MONOMIAL* is NP-hard by reducing *MINIMUM COVER* to it. Our approach is based on that of Haussler (1988). Suppose we are given an instance of *MINIMUM COVER* with

$$\mathbf{S} = \{S_1, S_2, \ldots, S_n\}, \quad U = \{a_1, a_2, \ldots, a_u\}.$$

Then we form a corresponding instance $\mathbf{s}(\mathbf{S})$ of *SHORTEST MONOMIAL* as follows. The training sample $\mathbf{s}(\mathbf{S})$ has length $m = u + 1$ and consists of u negative examples and one positive example. For i in the range $1 \leq i \leq u$ the negative example z_i is the n-bit vector defined by

$$(z_i)_j = \begin{cases} 0, & \text{if } a_i \in S_j; \\ 1, & \text{otherwise.} \end{cases}$$

The positive example is the all-1 vector of length n.

Proposition 6.4.1 For each positive integer $k \leq n$, $\mathbf{S}$ has a subcover of size k if and only if there is a monomial with k literals which is consistent with $\mathbf{s}(\mathbf{S})$.

Proof Suppose that

$$\mathbf{S}' = \{S_{j_1}, S_{j_2}, \ldots, S_{j_k}\}$$

is a subcover of $\mathbf{S}$, and define h to be the monomial

$$h = \langle u_{j_1} u_{j_2} \ldots u_{j_k} \rangle.$$

The positive example in $\mathbf{s}(\mathbf{S})$ is correctly classified by h, because h contains no negated literals. Further, each a_i belongs to at least one set S_{j_i}, and therefore z_i has a 0 in the j_ith coordinate position and is a negative example of h. Thus h is consistent with $\mathbf{s}(\mathbf{S})$.

Conversely, suppose that h is a monomial consistent with $\mathbf{s}(\mathbf{S})$. Since the all-one vector is a positive example of h, h can contain no negated literals. Suppose then that

$$h = \langle u_{j_1} u_{j_2} \dots u_{j_k} \rangle.$$

We claim that

$$\{S_{j_1}, S_{j_2}, \dots, S_{j_k}\}$$

is a subcover of $\mathbf{S}$. If this were false, then there would be some $a_i \in U$ which belongs to none of the sets in $\mathbf{S}'$, and that would mean that $h(z_i) = 1$, contrary to the assumption that h is consistent with the training sample. The result follows. $\square$

It follows that if there is an algorithm for solving the *SHORTEST MONOMIAL* problem which runs in time polynomial in m and n, then this algorithm could be used to solve the *MINIMUM COVER* problem in time polynomial in un. (Recall that the training sample $\mathbf{s}(\mathbf{S})$ has length $m = u + 1$.) We have previously remarked that a polynomial time algorithm for *MINIMUM COVER* would imply one for *SUBCOVER*, and the latter is known to be NP-complete. Hence *SHORTEST MONOMIAL* is NP-hard.

In summary, we have shown that although the standard learning algorithm for monomials provides an efficient means of finding *some* monomial consistent with a given training sample, there is (if we accept that P $\neq$ NP) no algorithm L which finds a consistent monomial with fewest possible literals, and for which the running time $R_L(m, n)$ is polynomial in m and n.

6.5 OCCAM ALGORITHMS

Let $\Omega \rightarrow H$ be a representation of boolean functions, and let $\|\omega\|$ be a measure of size defined for each $\omega \in \Omega$. For each integer $r \geq 1$ define

$$\Omega_r = \{\omega \in \Omega \mid \|\omega\| = r\},$$

and let H_r denote the subset of H comprising those hypotheses h_ω whose minimal representation has size r. We shall say that such hypotheses have representation size r. Then H may be *graded by representation size* as $H = \bigcup H_r$. A learning algorithm L for H takes as input a training sample for some target function $t \in H$. Suppose t is in H_r; in other words, the smallest representation of t has size r. The output of L will be specified by a representation $\omega \in \Omega_q$, and we need to consider the relationship between q and r. By the result of the previous section, it may be difficult to find the smallest possible value of q, but we might ask, not that L finds the *shortest* possible representation, but merely a reasonably short one. This idea is made precise in the following definition, due to Blumer *et al.* (1987).

We say that a learning algorithm L for H is *Occam* with respect to the representation $\Omega \to H$ if

- L is consistent;
- given a training sample $\mathbf{s}$ of length m for a target function $t \in H_r$, the output hypothesis $L(\mathbf{s}) = h_\omega$ is such that $\|\omega\| \leq m^\alpha r^\beta$, where $0 < \alpha < 1$ and $\beta \geq 1$ are constants.

The bound for $\|\omega\|$ says that the output is compressed with respect to the length of the training sample and grows only polynomially as a function of the size of the minimal representation length of the target. The condition $\alpha < 1$ means that the output is truly a compressed form of the input; if we allowed $\alpha = 1$, then the output would be comparable in size with the training sample, whose bit-length is linear in m, and no significant compression of data would be achieved. The next theorem shows that outputting a short representation, in this sense, is sufficient for a form of pac learning.

In order to formulate the theorem we need to recall that our original definition of a learning algorithm allowed the concept space C and the hypothesis space H to be different. This distinction is useful here, because we are interested in learning hypotheses in a subset H_r by using the full resources of the space H.

Theorem 6.5.1 Let H be a space of boolean functions with representation $\Omega \to H$, and let $H = \bigcup H_r$ be graded, as above, by representation size. If L is an Occam learning algorithm with respect to the given representation then, for each r, L is a pac learning algorithm for (H_r, H), with sample complexity $m_L(H_r, \delta, \epsilon)$ polynomial in r, δ^* and ϵ^{-1}.

Proof Suppose that the usual objects δ, ϵ, μ, and t are given, and that $t \in H_r$. For a given m, let $L(m, t)$ denote the set of hypotheses $h \in H$ such that h is the output $L(\mathbf{s})$ of L, for some training sample $\mathbf{s}$ of length m for the target concept t. In other words, $L(m, t)$ is the 'effective' hypothesis space for t.

By the second Occam condition, the members of $L(m, t)$ are hypotheses h_ω for which ω has at most $M = \lfloor m^\alpha r^\beta \rfloor$ bits, and the total number of such ω is at most 2^{M+1}. Hence

$$|L(m, t)| \leq 2^{m^\alpha r^\beta + 1}.$$

Note that the bound depends only on r, not t itself; in other words it holds uniformly for all $t \in H_r$. We now repeat the argument given in Section 4.2. The probability that any one ϵ-bad hypothesis from H agrees with t on a training sample of length m is $(1 - \epsilon)^m$. Since L is consistent, its output hypotheses agree with the training sample, and thus the probability that the output hypothesis is ϵ-bad is at most

$$|L(m,t)|(1-\epsilon)^m \leq 2^{m^\alpha r^\beta + 1}(1-\epsilon)^m.$$

It remains to prove that this can be made less than δ by taking m sufficiently large, and that the value of m required is a polynomial function of r, δ^* and ϵ^{-1}. Using the inequality $(1-\epsilon)^m < \exp(-\epsilon m)$ and rearranging, we find that it suffices to have

$$\epsilon m \geq Am^\alpha + B,$$

where

$$A = r^\beta \ln 2, \quad B = \ln\left(\frac{2}{\delta}\right).$$

Since $\alpha < 1$, the condition holds if $m^{1-\alpha} \geq (A+B)/\epsilon$, that is,

$$m \geq m_0 = \left\lceil \left(\frac{A+B}{\epsilon}\right)^{1/(1-\alpha)} \right\rceil.$$

In other words, the expression m_0 is an upper bound for the sample complexity. Clearly m_0 is polynomial in r, because A is $O(r^\beta)$ and so m_0 is $O(r^{\beta/1-\alpha})$; furthermore m_0 is also polynomial in δ^* and ϵ^{-1}. The result follows.   □

We observe once again the importance of the condition $\alpha < 1$: it is clear that the condition $\epsilon m \geq Am^\alpha + B$ cannot be satisfied if $\alpha = 1$.

It is an immediate corollary of Theorem 6.5.1 that if the running time of an Occam algorithm is polynomial in the sample length m, then its running time as a pac learning algorithm is polynomial in r, δ^* and ϵ^{-1}. In other words an Occam algorithm L for H pac learns each H_r by H, and it does so efficiently with respect to the representation size and the confidence and accuracy parameters. Note that it does not necessarily follow that H itself is pac learnable, although this will be so if there is an upper bound on the representation size of hypotheses in H.

6.6 EXAMPLES OF OCCAM ALGORITHMS

Suppose we are given a collection $\mathbf{S} = \{S_1, S_2, \ldots, S_n\}$ of finite sets, with union U, and we wish to determine the smallest subcover of $(U, \mathbf{S})$; that is, the smallest subcollection of $\mathbf{S}$ whose union is also U. We have seen that this problem is NP-hard. That does not mean, however, that there is no efficient means of obtaining an approximate solution to the problem. Indeed, there is a simple intuitive method of finding an approximate solution, based on the 'greedy' method, which turns out to be very efficient. First, we choose a set S_{j_1} which contains the largest number of elements of U, and delete the members of S_{j_1}. Then we choose a set S_{j_2} which contains the largest number of remaining elements, and delete those elements. We continue in this manner, at each stage choosing the set which contains the largest number of remaining elements.

> set $X = U$;
> `while` $X \neq \emptyset$ `do`
> > `begin`
> > *choose* S_j *such that* $|S_j \cap X|$ *is maximal*;
> > *set* $X = X \setminus S_j$
> > `end`

Since **S** covers U, the process must terminate with a subcover $\mathbf{S}' = \{S_{j_1}, S_{j_2}, \ldots, S_{j_k}\}$. We call this the *greedy algorithm* for *MINIMUM COVER*. Of course, the size k of the resulting subcover will not in general be the minimum possible size of a subcover, but it has been shown (Nigmatullin (1969) and Johnson (1974)) that k is related to the size l of a minimum subcover as follows:

$$k \leq l(\ln |U| + 1).$$

This yields a good upper bound for the *performance ratio* k/l and, in this sense, the greedy algorithm is a good approximation algorithm for the problem.

The running time depends on both $u = |U|$ and $n = |\mathbf{S}|$. The number k of selection steps is at most n, since we cannot select more sets than there are in **S**; it is also at most u, since we cannot need more sets than there are elements to be covered. In other words, $k \leq \min(u, n)$. (Note that the result on the performance ratio yields $k \leq n(\ln u + 1)$.) Each selection step involves finding the maximum of at most n integers and deleting at most u elements from each of at most n sets. The number of operations required for each selection is thus $O(un)$. The overall running time may therefore be expressed as

$$O(un \min(u, n)),$$

which can be further simplified according to the context.

The greedy method can be used to derive learning algorithms for certain classes of boolean formulae. In this context, the result on the performance ratio turns out to be just what is needed for an Occam algorithm. Following Haussler (1988), we shall illustrate the technique by showing how the greedy algorithm for the covering problem can be transferred to the space M_n of monomials, and we shall prove that the resulting learning algorithm is Occam.

The initial hypothesis is the monomial formula with no literals, in other words the identically-1 function. At each stage, one literal is added to the current conjunction of literals according to a rule based on the greedy algorithm for the covering problem. Let us say that a literal λ *eliminates* a negative example x if $\langle\lambda\rangle(x) = 0$. We take the elements to be covered to be the set of negative examples in the given training sample, and the covering sets as the sets of negative examples eliminated by literals of a certain kind. At each stage we select the literal which eliminates the largest number of negative examples in the sample, add this literal to the formula, and delete the examples which it eliminates. We continue in this manner, until all negative examples in the sample have been eliminated.

In order to explain why this method works, we need some rather more detailed arguments. Let s be a training sample for a monomial, and let E be the set of examples occurring in s, so that E is partitioned into positive and negative examples, $E = E^+ \cup E^-$. For any literal λ let S_λ be the set of negative examples eliminated by λ, that is

$$S_\lambda = \{x \in E^- \mid \langle\lambda\rangle(x) = 0\}.$$

Finally, let

$$\Lambda = \{\lambda \mid \langle\lambda\rangle(x) = 1 \text{ for all } x \in E^+\}.$$

Lemma 6.6.1 The collection of sets $\mathbf{S} = \{S_\lambda \mid \lambda \in \Lambda\}$ covers E^-.

Proof Since s is a training sample for a monomial, we know that there is a monomial $t = \langle\lambda_1 \wedge \ldots \wedge \lambda_l\rangle$ such that, for $x \in E$, $t(x)$ is 1 or 0 according as x is in E^+ or E^-. This implies, first, that $\lambda_1, \ldots, \lambda_l$ all belong to Λ. Secondly, it implies that for any $x \in E^-$ at least one of the literals λ_j occurring in t is such that $\langle\lambda_j\rangle(x) = 0$. In other words, $x \in S_{\lambda_j} \in \mathbf{S}$. □

Lemma 6.6.2 If

$$\mathbf{S}' = \{S_{\lambda_1}, \ldots, S_{\lambda_k}\}$$

is any subcover of $(E^-, \mathbf{S})$, then the monomial $h = \langle\lambda_1 \wedge \ldots \wedge \lambda_k\rangle$ is consistent with s.

Proof Suppose $x \in E^+$. Since $\lambda_1, \ldots, \lambda_k$ are members of Λ, they all evaluate to 1 on x, and so $h(x) = 1$. Suppose $x \in E^-$. Since $\mathbf{S}'$ is a subcover, there is some j $(1 \leq j \leq k)$ such that $x \in S_{\lambda_j}$. Thus $\langle\lambda_j\rangle(x) = 0$ and consequently $h(x) = 0$. □

These lemmas show that the greedy algorithm for the covering problem can be transformed into an algorithm for finding a monomial consistent with a given training sample. To see that it is indeed an Occam algorithm, consider its behaviour on a training sample for a monomial t whose smallest representation is by a formula containing l literals. The minimum representation size of t is thus $r = \lceil l \lg n \rceil$. The result on the performance ratio of the greedy algorithm for the covering problem implies that the number k of literals in the output formula is such that $k \leq l(\ln |E^-| + 1)$. Therefore the size of the output formula ω satisfies

$$\|\omega\| = \lceil k \lg n \rceil \leq \lceil l(\ln |E^-| + 1) \lg n \rceil \leq r(\ln |E^-| + 1).$$

The number $|E^-|$ of negative examples in the training sample is bounded by m, the length of the training sample. Hence $\|\omega\| \leq (\ln m + 1)r$, which trivially implies the Occam compression condition $\|\omega\| \leq m^{\alpha} r^{\beta}$ with $\alpha = 1/2$ and $\beta = 1$ (for example).

The greedy algorithm differs in a number of important aspects from the standard learning algorithm for M_n described in Section 2.2. Instead of starting with the identically-0 function (the conjunction of all $2n$ literals) and then deleting literals using the positive examples, the new algorithm starts with the identically-1 function (the empty conjunction of literals) and then adds literals using the negative examples. Also, while the standard algorithm is a memoryless on-line algorithm, the greedy algorithm certainly is not. However, as an Occam algorithm, the greedy algorithm has the important advantage that it outputs consistent hypotheses which are relatively simple.

Rivest (1987) has observed that the greedy method can also be used to develop an Occam algorithm for the space $DL(M_{n,k})$ of decision lists formed from monomials of length at most k (for a fixed k). We shall say that the pair (g, c), with $g \in M_{n,k}$ and $c \in \{0, 1\}$, *explains* a subset T of the m examples in a training sample for t if $g(x) = 1$ implies $t(x) = c$ for all $x \in T$. The greedy learning algorithm for decision lists is again based on the greedy algorithm for *MINIMUM COVER*. We can think of the set to be covered as the set of examples in the sample, and the covering sets as the set of examples explained by the pairs (g, c) as above. The algorithm builds up a decision list from the empty decision list, at each stage adding the term (g, c) which explains the largest number of examples in the sample which have not been explained by earlier terms in the list. As above, we can show that the length of the resulting decision list is at most a factor $(\ln m + 1)$ larger than the length of the shortest decision list consistent with the sample. An analysis similar to that for monomials shows that the greedy learning algorithm for decision lists is an Occam algorithm (see Exercise 7).

6.7 EPAC LEARNING

We have seen that there are several natural parameters of a learning problem which affect its difficulty. Clearly, as greater confidence and accuracy are demanded, the learning task becomes harder. However, if a given learning algorithm L is to be practicable, the learning task should not become 'hugely' more difficult as these parameters are varied. We formalised this notion by insisting that the sample complexity

$m_L(H, \delta, \epsilon)$ should depend polynomially on δ^* and ϵ^{-1}. We have also discussed the effect of representation size on the difficulty of a learning problem. Again, to ensure efficiency, we insisted that the sample complexity depends polynomially on the representation size. Yet again, back in Chapter 5, we discussed learning algorithms for graded hypothesis spaces, and this provided a framework for studying the efficiency of such algorithms with respect to the size of the examples.

All these aspects can be combined in an attempt to capture the full meaning of efficiency in the context of learning algorithms. Suppose that $H = \bigcup H_n$ is a hypothesis space graded by example size, and that $\Omega \to H$ is a representation for H. Then, we may grade each H_n by representation size as $H_n = \bigcup H_{n,r}$, where $H_{n,r}$ consists of those hypotheses of H_n which have minimal representation size r. In this situation we shall say that

$$H = \bigcup_n \bigcup_r H_{n,r}$$

is *doubly-graded*. Usually we shall use a single union sign for a doubly-graded space when this causes no confusion.

Let L be a learning algorithm for H, in the usual sense that $L(\mathbf{s})$ is in H_n whenever $\mathbf{s}$ is a training sample for a hypothesis in H_n. We say that L is *efficiently pac* or (following Valiant (1991)) *epac* if

- the running time $R_L(m, n)$ is polynomial in m and n;
- the sample complexity $m_L(H_{n,r}, \delta, \epsilon)$ is polynomial in n, r, δ^*, and ϵ^{-1}.

Thus an epac learning algorithm is guaranteed to produce a probably approximately correct output, with running time polynomial in n, r, δ^* and ϵ^{-1}.

One way of ensuring that the second property holds is to impose a version of the Occam conditions. In the present context we say that L is *Occam* if the conditions stated in Section 6.5 hold for each H_n, with the constants α and β independent of n. Then we have the following result.

Theorem 6.7.1 Suppose that the hypothesis space is $H = \bigcup H_{n,r}$, as above, and that L is an Occam algorithm for learning $H_{n,r}$ by H_n, with polynomial running time $R_L(m, n)$. Then L is epac.

Proof From the proof of Theorem 6.5.1, we have the upper bound

$$m_0(H_r, \delta, \epsilon) = \left\lceil \left(\frac{A + B}{\epsilon} \right)^{1/(1-\alpha)} \right\rceil$$

for the sample complexity of L on $H_{n,r}$, where $A = r^\beta \ln 2$ and $B = \ln(2/\delta)$. As we noted, this is polynomial in r, δ^* and ϵ^{-1}. Since α and β are independent of n, so too is $m_0\left(H_r, \delta, \epsilon\right)$. The result follows on observing that an upper bound on the running time of L in pac learning $H_{n,r}$ is

$$R_L\left(m_0\left(H_{n,r}, \delta, \epsilon\right), n\right),$$

which is polynomial in n, r, δ^* and ϵ^{-1}.

□

Example 6.7.2 The graded hypothesis space $M = \bigcup M_n$ of monomials can be doubly graded as $M = \bigcup M_{n,r}$, where $M_{n,r}$ consists of those monomials on n variables which have representation size r. (Note that the notation $M_{n,k}$ used in previous chapters has a slightly different meaning.) In Section 6.6 we described an algorithm for learning $M_{n,r}$ by M_n, based on the greedy method, and we showed that it has the Occam property, with $\alpha = 1/2$ and $\beta = 1$. The running time $R_L(m,n)$ is $O(mn \min(m,n))$, which is certainly polynomial in m and n. Thus we can conclude that the greedy algorithm for M is efficiently pac.

□

In the same way, one can show that, for a fixed k, the greedy algorithm for decision lists gives rise to an epac algorithm for the space $\bigcup_n DL(M_{n,k})$, graded by example size n.

These examples raise a few interesting points. Any monomial in M_n has at most n literals and so has representation size at most $\lceil n \log n \rceil$. That is, in the doubly-graded space $M = \bigcup M_{n,r}$, if $r > \lceil n \log n \rceil$ then $M_{n,r}$ is empty. Thus r is bounded polynomially by n. Similarly, for the space of decision lists based on $M_{n,k}$, the representation size is polynomial in n.

More generally, let $H = \bigcup H_n$ be a graded space with representation $\Omega \to H$. Suppose that there is some polynomial $p(n)$ such that, when H is doubly graded as $H = \bigcup H_{n,r}$, then

$$r > p(n) \implies H_{n,r} = \emptyset;$$

that is, as in the two examples above, r is bounded polynomially in n. In this case, we say that H has *polynomial representation size*. Suppose that L is an epac learning algorithm for such a space H. Then the sample complexity $m_L\left(H_{n,r}, \delta, \epsilon\right)$ is polynomial in r and n, and hence is polynomial in n. In addition, L runs in polynomial time. Therefore any epac learning algorithm for H, considered as a pac learning algorithm for the graded space $H = \bigcup H_n$, is efficient with respect to example size, confidence and accuracy. Thus, for hypothesis spaces with polynomial representation size, the definition of epac learning is a restriction, or a narrowing, of the definition of pac learning: not only must there be a pac learning algorithm for H efficient with respect to example size, confidence and accuracy, but there must be one which is, in addition, efficient with respect to representation size.

On the other hand, consider the following important example.

Example 6.7.2 Let us denote by DNF_n the space of all 2^{2^n} boolean functions defined on $\{0,1\}^n$. We use the notation DNF_n because every boolean function can be expressed in disjunctive normal form, and because we consider the representation by DNF formulae. The representation size of $h \in DNF_n$ is the least size (as defined in Section 3.3) of a DNF formula representing h. The space $DNF = \bigcup DNF_n$ of *all* boolean functions can then be doubly-graded as $DNF = \bigcup DNF_{n,r}$. Unlike the previous examples, the graded space $DNF = \bigcup DNF_n$ does not have polynomial representation size (see Exercise 8). □

We shall see in Chapter 9 that there can be no pac learning algorithm for DNF which is efficient with respect to example size (essentially because DNF_n is 'too large'). However, it is still possible that there is an epac learning algorithm for DNF. (Such an algorithm need not have running time polynomial in n since its running time can depend polynomially on the representation size r, which is not bounded by any polynomial in n.) This example serves to illustrate that there are some hypothesis spaces for which the definition of epac learning can be regarded as a generalisation, or a widening, of the definition of pac learning. Epac learning admits a natural limited form of 'non-uniformity' into the learning process.

We remark that whether there is an epac learning algorithm for DNF is a major open problem in Computational Learning Theory, first raised by Valiant (1984).

FURTHER REMARKS
As mentioned above, the fact that C^k is not learnable efficiently with respect to example size is a representation-dependent result. If the output hypotheses can be represented in ways other than as conjunctions of at most k clauses, then generation of probably approximately correct hypotheses is easy. It could be argued, therefore, that such negative results are not very strong. Kearns and Valiant (1989) (see also Kearns (1990)) have obtained very strong hardness results based on cryptographic hardness assumptions. In order to describe their results, recall that a graded concept space $C = \bigcup C_n$ is *efficiently predictable* if there is some graded hypothesis space $H = \bigcup H_n$ and some pac learning algorithm for (C, H) efficient with respect to n. Kearns and Valiant show that for a number of boolean concept spaces $C = \bigcup C_n$, efficiently predicting C is as hard as some of the problems traditionally thought of as intractable in cryptography, and upon which many cipher systems are based.

These hardness assumptions are weaker than the RP$\neq$NP assumption, but the results obtained are significantly stronger. For example, for p a fixed polynomial function, let BF_n^p be the space of boolean functions on $\{0,1\}^n$ which can be represented by some boolean formula of size at most $p(n)$, and let BF^p be the graded space $BF^p = \bigcup BF_n^p$. Then their results show that there is a polynomial p such that BF^p is not pac learnable efficiently with respect to example size, no matter how the output hypotheses are represented.

Clearly, it is possible to introduce representation size into the definition of efficient prediction. We may say that a doubly graded space $C = \bigcup C_{n,r}$ is *epac predictable* if there is some hypothesis space $H = \bigcup H_n$ and some polynomial time learning algorithm L for (C, H) such that L has sample complexity $m_L(C_{n,r}, \delta, \epsilon)$ polynomial in $n, r, \delta^*, \epsilon^{-1}$. We mentioned that the epac learnability of DNF is an open problem. It is also unknown whether DNF is epac predictable.

In our definition of efficiency with respect to confidence, we required the sample complexity and running time of the learning algorithm to be polynomial in the quantity δ^*, and we gave some informal motivation for this. In fact, Haussler *et al.* (1988) have shown that any pac learning algorithm which has running time polynomial in δ^{-1} can be used to construct one which has running time polynomial in δ^*. Thus if a hypothesis space is pac learnable by an algorithm which has running time polynomial in δ^{-1} and ϵ^{-1}, then it is learnable by an algorithm efficient with respect to confidence and accuracy in our sense.

If we fix $\delta = 1/2$ in the definition of epac learning, we obtain a different model of learning, in which arbitrarily high confidence is not required. Although this seems significantly less strong than epac learning, Haussler *et al.* (1988) have shown that if there is an efficient learning algorithm for a hypothesis space in this model, then this algorithm can be used (by repetition) to construct a full epac learning algorithm for H. Thus, the two models are essentially the same: it is computationally just as feasible to learn with arbitrarily high confidence as it is to learn with fixed confidence $\delta = 1/2$.

Another variant of epac learning has been defined by Kearns and Valiant (1989). A doubly-graded space $C = \bigcup C_{n,r}$ is said to be (efficiently) *weakly learnable* if there is some hypothesis space H, a learning algorithm L for (C, H), a polynomial $p(n, r)$ and a function $m_0(C_{n,r}, \delta)$ such that the following hold:
- $R_L(m, n)$ is polynomial in m and n,
- $m_0(C_{n,r}, \delta)$ is polynomial in n, r and δ^{-1}, and

- for $m \geq m_0(C_{n,r}, \delta)$,

$$\mu^m \left\{ \mathbf{s} \in S(m,t) \,\middle|\, \mathrm{er}_\mu \left(L(\mathbf{s}) \right) < \frac{1}{2} - \frac{1}{p(n,r)} \right\} > 1 - \delta,$$

for any $t \in C_{n,r}$ and for any probability distribution μ on $\{0,1\}^n$.

Thus, the main difference between weak learning and epac prediction is that the learning algorithm does not have to achieve arbitrarily high accuracy; it simply has to perform better than random guessing by an amount which decreases as the parameters n and r, characterising the difficulty of the problem, increase. This therefore looks an easier definition to satisfy than the definition of epac prediction. But Schapire (1990) has shown that a hypothesis space is efficiently weakly learnable if and only if it is epac predictable (see also Freund (1990)). Note that, in view of this and the comments above, one could equally well have demanded poynomiality in δ^* in the definition of weak learnability.

The preceeding few paragraphs illustrate that the models of epac learning and epac prediction are robust: seemingly different variants of the models make no further spaces efficiently learnable.

EXERCISES

1. In Section 6.2 we said that a randomised algorithm solves a search problem if it outputs the 'correct answer' with probability at least $\frac{1}{2}$. Explain why the value $\frac{1}{2}$ can be replaced by any fixed value $\theta > 0$.

2. Let F_2 denote the set of all arithmetical expressions in two variables with integer coefficients, such as

$$f(x_1, x_2) = (x_1 - x_2)^2 - x_1^2 - x_2^2 + 2x_1 x_2.$$

Devise a randomised algorithm for deciding whether a given $f \in F_2$ is identically zero. [Hint: If f is not identically zero, the probability that it will always evaluate to zero when r different pairs of values are substituted decreases rapidly as r increases. See Welsh (1988, pp.151-2).]

3. Show that $C_n^k \subseteq D_{n,k}$ for all k and n, and that the inclusion is strict for some values of k and n. Discuss fully the implications of this result for learning C^k, as sketched at the end of Section 6.2.

4. Given a decision problem of the following form:

  • Is there an object in a given set with integral 'cost' at most k?

there is a corresponding optimisation problem:

  • Find the least value of k for which there is an object in the given set with cost exactly k.

Show that if there is a suitable upper bound for the cost in terms of the size of an instance and the decision problem can be solved in polynomial time, then the optimisation problem can also be solved in polynomial time. Deduce that if the *SUBCOVER* problem could be solved in polynomial time, then so could the *MINIMUM COVER* problem.

5. Formulate the set-covering problem which corresponds (as in Section 6.6) to finding the shortest monomial consistent with the following examples.

$$E^+ = \{1110011, 1111011, 1011001, 1011011, 1110001\};$$

$$E^- = \{1010100, 0111011, 0001111, 1001010, 0101111, 1100000\}.$$

Solve the set-covering problem 'by inspection', and hence write down the shortest monomial.

6. Use the greedy algorithm as described in Section 6.6 to construct a 'short' monomial consistent with the training sample given in Exercise 5.

7. Formulate carefully a greedy algorithm for finding an element of $DL(M_{n,k})$ consistent with a given training sample, and verify that it has the Occam property.

8. Prove that if the graded boolean space $H = \bigcup H_n$ (with representation $\Omega \to H$) has polynomial representation size then $\ln |H_n|$ is polynomial in n. Deduce that DNF (where the hypotheses are represented by boolean formulae in disjunctive normal form) does not have polynomial representation size.

Chapter 7: The VC Dimension

7.1 MOTIVATION

Suppose that, as in the framework of previous chapters, we have a hypothesis space H defined on an example space X. In Chapter 4 we proved that if H is finite, then it is potentially learnable. The proof depends critically on the finiteness of H and cannot be extended to provide results for infinite H. However, there are many situations where the hypothesis space is infinite, and it is desirable to extend the theory to cover this case. A pertinent comment is that most hypothesis spaces which occur 'naturally' have a high degree of structure, and even if the space is infinite it may contain functions only of a special type. This is true, almost by definition, for any hypothesis space H which is constructed by means of a representation $\Omega \to H$.

The key to extending results on potential learnability to infinite spaces is the observation that what matters is not the cardinality of H, but rather what may be described as its 'expressive power'. In this chapter we shall formalise this notion in terms of the *Vapnik-Chervonenkis dimension* of H, a notion originally defined by Vapnik and Chervonenkis (1971), and introduced into learnability theory by Blumer *et al.* (1986, 1989). The development of this notion is probably the most significant contribution that mathematics has made to Computational Learning Theory.

In order to illustrate some of the ideas, we consider the *real perceptron*. This is a machine which operates in the same manner as the linear threshold machine of Section 2.5, but with real-valued inputs. Thus, as shown in Figure 7.1, there are n inputs and a single active node. The arcs carrying the inputs have real-valued weights $\alpha_1, \alpha_2, \ldots, \alpha_n$ and there is a real threshold value θ at the active node. As with the linear threshold machine, the weighted sum of the inputs is applied to the active node and this node outputs 1 if and only if the weighted sum is at least the threshold value θ.

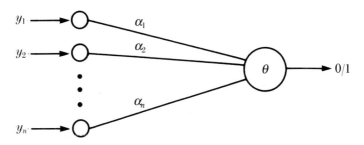

Figure 7.1: The real perceptron P_n

More precisely, the real perceptron P_n on n inputs is defined by means of a representation $\Omega \to H$, where the set of states Ω is $\mathbf{R}^{n+1}$. For a state $w = (\alpha_1, \alpha_2, \ldots, \alpha_n, \theta)$, the function $h_w \in H$, from $X = \mathbf{R}^n$ to $\{0, 1\}$, is given by

$$h_w(y) = \begin{cases} 1, & \text{if } \sum_{i=1}^n \alpha_i y_i \geq \theta; \\ 0, & \text{otherwise.} \end{cases}$$

It should be noted that $w \mapsto h_w$ is not an injection: for any $\lambda > 0$ the state λw defines the same function as w.

Example 7.1.1 As an example, consider P_2, the real perceptron with two inputs. In state $w = (\alpha_1, \alpha_2, \theta)$, P_2 computes the boolean-valued function h_w for which

$$h_w(y_1, y_2) = 1 \iff \alpha_1 y_1 + \alpha_2 y_2 \geq \theta.$$

It is useful to describe this geometrically (Figure 7.2). The example $y = (y_1, y_2)$, considered as a point in the plane $\mathbf{R}^2$, is a positive example of h_w if and only if y lies on the straight line l_w with equation $\alpha_1 y_1 + \alpha_2 y_2 = \theta$ or on the side of l_w consisting of points with $\alpha_1 y_1 + \alpha_2 y_2 > \theta$.

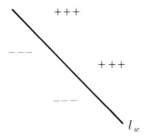

Figure 7.2: Geometrical interpretation of a hypothesis in P_2

Given a sample of m points in $\mathbf{R}^2$, the machine P_2 can only achieve certain classifications of the sample into positive and negative examples: precisely those for which, as above, the positive examples are separated from the negative examples by a line in the plane. When a classification of the sample can be realised in this way, we shall say that it is *linearly separable*. The fact that relatively few classifications are linearly separable is an indication of the restricted 'expressive power' of P_2. □

7.2 THE GROWTH FUNCTION

Suppose that H is a hypothesis space defined on the example space X, and let $\mathbf{x} = (x_1, x_2, \dots, x_m)$ be a sample of length m of examples from X. We define $\Pi_H(\mathbf{x})$, the *number of classifications of* $\mathbf{x}$ *by* H, to be the number of distinct vectors of the form

$$(h(x_1), h(x_2), \dots, h(x_m)),$$

as h runs through all hypotheses of H. Although H may be infinite, we observe that $H|E_{\mathbf{x}}$, the hypothesis space obtained by restricting the hypotheses of H to domain $E_{\mathbf{x}} = \{x_1, x_2, \dots, x_m\}$, is finite and is of cardinality $\Pi_H(\mathbf{x})$. Note that for any sample $\mathbf{x}$ of length m, $\Pi_H(\mathbf{x}) \leq 2^m$. An important quantity, and one which shall turn out to be crucial in applications to potential learnability, is the maximum possible number of classifications by H of a sample of a given length. We define the *growth function* Π_H by

$$\Pi_H(m) = \max\{\Pi_H(\mathbf{x}) : \mathbf{x} \in X^m\}.$$

We have used the notation Π_H for both the number of classifications and the growth function, but this should cause no confusion.

Example 7.2.1 Let $X = \mathbf{R}$ be the real line and let H be the set of rays, as defined in Chapter 2. Suppose that m is a positive integer and that $\mathbf{x} = (x_1, x_2, \dots, x_m)$ is a sample of length m, in which the examples are arranged in strictly increasing order:

$$x_1 < x_2 < \dots < x_m.$$

Given $\theta \in \mathbf{R}$, $r_\theta(x_i) = 1$ if and only if $x_i \geq \theta$. Therefore, for any $h = r_\theta$ and any k between 1 and $m-1$, $h(x_k) = 1$ implies $h(x_{k+1}) = 1$. Thus the set of 'classification vectors' (vectors of the form $(h(x_1), h(x_2), \dots, h(x_m))$ for some $h \in H$) consists only of the $m+1$ vectors

$$(111\dots11),\ (011\dots11),\ (001\dots11),\ \dots,\ (000\dots00).$$

Now any sample in which the examples are distinct can be obtained from one in which the examples are in strictly increasing order by a permutation, and this permutation of the sample will simply give another set of $m+1$ classification vectors. If not all the examples are distinct, there will clearly be fewer possible classifications. Thus $\Pi_H(m)$, the maximum number of classifications, is $m + 1$. $\square$

In general, it is difficult to find an exact formula for the growth function of a hypothesis space. In the next section we shall define a numerical parameter of a hypothesis space which is easier to estimate than the growth function, and which can be used to provide upper bounds for the growth function.

7.3 THE VC DIMENSION

We noted above that the number of possible classifications by H of a sample of length m is at most 2^m, this being the number of binary vectors of length m. We say that a sample $\mathbf{x}$ of length m is *shattered* by H, or that H *shatters* $\mathbf{x}$, if this maximum possible value is attained; that is, if H gives all possible classifications of $\mathbf{x}$. Note that if the examples in $\mathbf{x}$ are not distinct then $\mathbf{x}$ cannot be shattered by any H. When the examples are distinct, $\mathbf{x}$ is shattered by H if and only if for any subset S of $E_{\mathbf{x}}$, there is some hypothesis h in H such that for $1 \le i \le m$,

$$h(x_i) = 1 \iff x_i \in S.$$

S is then the subset of $E_{\mathbf{x}}$ comprising the positive examples of h.

Based on the intuitive notion that a hypothesis space H has high expressive power if it can achieve all possible classifications of a large set of examples, we use as a measure of this power the *Vapnik-Chervonenkis dimension*, or *VC dimension*, of H, defined as follows. The VC dimension of H is the maximum length of a sample shattered by H; if there is no such maximum, we say that the VC dimension of H is infinite. Using the notation introduced in the previous section, we can say that the VC dimension of H, denoted VCdim(H), is given by

$$\mathrm{VCdim}(H) = \max\{m : \Pi_H(m) = 2^m\},$$

where we take the maximum to be infinite if the set is unbounded.

Example 7.3.1 Consider again the case in which X is the real line and H is the space of rays. Given a sample (y, y') of length 2, we may suppose without loss that $y < y'$. Then there is no ray $h = r_\theta$ such that $h(y) = 1$ and $h(y') = 0$, because if such a ray were to exist, we should have $y' < \theta \le y$. Therefore H shatters no sample of length 2. Clearly H shatters any sample consisting of just one example, and therefore VCdim(H) $= 1$. $\square$

Example 7.3.2 Let X be the plane $\mathbf{R}^2$, and H the hypothesis space of P_2. Suppose that $\mathbf{x} = (x_1, x_2, x_3)$ is any sample consisting of three distinct non-collinear points.

We observed earlier that H can achieve precisely those classifications of a sample into positive and negative examples which are linearly separable. Thus, $\mathbf{x}$ is shattered by H if and only if for any subset S of $E_{\mathbf{x}} = \{x_1, x_2, x_3\}$, S and $E_{\mathbf{x}} \setminus S$ are linearly separable. This is easily seen to be true in this case (Figure 7.3), and hence VCdim(H) ≥ 3.

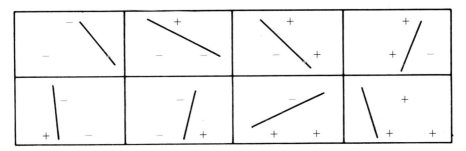

Figure 7.3: P_2 shatters three non-collinear points

In order to prove that VCdim(H) $= 3$, we have to show that *no* sample of length 4 is shattered by H. Suppose, by way of contradiction, that the sample $\mathbf{x} = (x_1, x_2, x_3, x_4)$ of length 4 is shattered by H. Then for every $S \subseteq E_{\mathbf{x}}$, S and $E_{\mathbf{x}} \setminus S$ are linearly separable and so, in particular, no three of x_1, x_2, x_3, x_4 can be collinear. There are two cases to consider: either all four points are boundary points of the smallest closed polygonal region containing $E_{\mathbf{x}}$, or one of the points (without loss, x_4) lies in the interior of this region. Typical examples of these cases are illustrated in Figure 7.4.

In the first case, $\{x_1, x_3\}$ and $\{x_2, x_4\}$ (for example) are not linearly separable, while in the second case $\{x_4\}$ and $\{x_1, x_2, x_3\}$ are not linearly separable. Therefore H shatters no sample of length 4 and, consequently, as claimed, VCdim(H) $= 3$.   □

Figure 7.4: The two cases for a sample of four points

When the hypothesis space H is the set of functions defined by some representation $\Omega \to H$, we shall take the VC dimension of the representation to be the VC dimension of H. Thus, we have shown that the VC dimension of P_2 is 3.

The following simple result on *finite* hypothesis spaces is often useful.

Proposition 7.3.3 If H is a finite hypothesis space, then

$$\mathrm{VCdim}(H) \le \lg |H|.$$

Proof The VC dimension of H is the greatest integer d for which $\Pi_H(d) = 2^d$. But the number of classifications by a finite hypothesis space H of a sample of any length is certainly at most the number of distinct hypotheses in H. Hence, for any positive integer m, $\Pi_H(m) \le |H|$. In particular,

$$2^d = \Pi_H(d) \le |H|.$$

Taking logarithms gives the result.   □

Example 7.3.4 Using the foregoing Proposition, we can obtain an upper bound on the VC dimension of M_n, the hypothesis space of monomial concepts defined on $\{0,1\}^n$. Recall that $|M_n| = 3^n$ and therefore, by the Proposition, the VC dimension of M_n is at most $\lg 3^n$. That is

$$\mathrm{VCdim}(M_n) \le (\lg 3)\, n.$$

In order to get a lower bound, we claim that M_n shatters the sample $(e_1, e_2, \ldots, e_n)$ where, for i between 1 and n, e_i is the point in $\{0,1\}^n$ with 1 as entry in position i and with all other entries 0. It will follow immediately from this that the VC dimension of M_n is at least n. To prove our claim, suppose that

$$q = (q_1, q_2, \ldots, q_n) \in \{0,1\}^n.$$

We have to show that there is h in M_n such that

$$h(e_1) = q_1,\ h(e_2) = q_2, \ldots, h(e_n) = q_n.$$

If q is the all-1 vector, we take h to be the empty monomial in which no literal appears; otherwise we take h to be the conjunction of those literals $\bar{u}_j$ for which $q_j = 0$. Summarising, we have

$$n \le \mathrm{VCdim}(M_n) \le (\lg 3)\, n$$

for any n.   □

7.4 THE VC DIMENSION OF THE REAL PERCEPTRON

We have seen that the VC dimension of P_2 is 3. Furthermore, if one interprets P_1 in the obvious way (Exercise 2), then it is easy to verify that P_1 has VC dimension 2. We shall prove in this section that, more generally, for any positive integer n, the VC dimension of P_n is precisely $n+1$. In order to do so, we need some geometrical ideas.

Consider the perceptron P_n with n inputs. In state

$$\omega = (\alpha_1, \alpha_2, \ldots, \alpha_n, \theta),$$

the function h_ω computed by the perceptron is the $\{0,1\}$-function such that

$$h_\omega(y) = 1 \iff \alpha_1 y_1 + \alpha_2 y_2 + \ldots + \alpha_n y_n \geq \theta.$$

Thus the set of positive examples of h_ω is the *closed half-space*

$$l_\omega^+ = \left\{ y \in \mathbf{R}^n \; \Big| \; \sum_{i=1}^n \alpha_i y_i \geq \theta \right\},$$

bounded by the *hyperplane*

$$l_\omega = \left\{ y \in \mathbf{R}^n \; \Big| \; \sum_{i=1}^n \alpha_i y_i = \theta \right\}.$$

The set of negative examples of h_ω is then the *open half-space*

$$l_\omega^- = \left\{ y \in \mathbf{R}^n \; \Big| \; \sum_{i=1}^n \alpha_i y_i < \theta \right\}.$$

Roughly speaking, l_ω divides $\mathbf{R}^n$ into the set of positive examples of h_ω and the set of negative examples of h_ω

A subset C of $\mathbf{R}^n$ is *convex* if, given any two points x, y of S, the line segment between x and y lies entirely in C. More formally, C is convex if given any x, y in C and any real number λ with $0 \leq \lambda \leq 1$, the point $\lambda x + (1 - \lambda)y$ belongs to C. (The notation here is the standard one for the real vector space $\mathbf{R}^n$.) It is clear that the intersection of any number of convex sets is again convex and therefore for any non-empty set S of points of $\mathbf{R}^n$, there is a smallest convex set containing S. This set, denoted by conv(S), is called the *convex hull* of S; conv(S) is the intersection of all convex sets containing S. For example, suppose that S is any finite set of points in the plane $\mathbf{R}^2$. Then conv(S) is the smallest closed region which is bounded by a polygon and which contains S.

We shall find the following result, known as *Radon's Theorem*, extremely useful. Let n be any positive integer, and let E be any set of $n + 2$ points in $\mathbf{R}^n$. Then there is a non-empty subset S of E such that

$$\operatorname{conv}(S) \cap \operatorname{conv}(E \setminus S) \neq \emptyset.$$

A proof is given by Grunbaum (1967).

Theorem 7.4.1 For any positive integer n, let P_n be the real perceptron with n inputs. Then

$$\operatorname{VCdim}(P_n) = n + 1.$$

Proof Let $\mathbf{x} = (x_1, x_2, \ldots, x_{n+2})$ be any sample of length $n + 2$. As we have noted, if two of the examples are equal then $\mathbf{x}$ cannot be shattered. Suppose then that the set $E_{\mathbf{x}}$ of examples in $\mathbf{x}$ consists of $n + 2$ distinct points in $\mathbf{R}^n$. By Radon's Theorem, there is a non-empty subset S of $E_{\mathbf{x}}$ such that

$$\operatorname{conv}(S) \cap \operatorname{conv}(E_{\mathbf{x}} \setminus S) \neq \emptyset.$$

Suppose that there is a hypothesis h_ω in P_n such that S is the set of positive examples of h_ω in $E_{\mathbf{x}}$. Then we have

$$S \subseteq l_\omega^+, \quad E_{\mathbf{x}} \setminus S \subseteq l_\omega^-.$$

Since open and closed half-spaces are convex subsets of $\mathbf{R}^n$, we also have

$$\operatorname{conv}(S) \subseteq l_\omega^+, \quad \operatorname{conv}(E_{\mathbf{x}} \setminus S) \subseteq l_\omega^-.$$

Therefore

$$\operatorname{conv}(S) \cap \operatorname{conv}(E_{\mathbf{x}} \setminus S) \subseteq l_\omega^+ \cap l_\omega^- = \emptyset.$$

We deduce that no such h_ω exists and therefore that $\mathbf{x}$ is not shattered by P_n. Thus *no* sample of length $n + 2$ is shattered by P_n and $\operatorname{VCdim}(P_n) \leq n + 1$.

It remains to prove the reverse inequality. Let o denote the origin of $\mathbf{R}^n$ and, for $1 \leq i \leq n$, let e_i be the point with a 1 in the ith coordinate and all other coordinates 0. We shall show that P_n shatters the sample

$$\mathbf{x} = (o, e_1, e_2, \ldots, e_n)$$

of length $n + 1$.

Suppose that S is a subset of $E_{\mathbf{x}} = \{o, e_1, \ldots, e_n\}$. For $i = 1, 2, \ldots, n$, let

$$\alpha_i = \begin{cases} 1, & \text{if } e_i \in S; \\ -1, & \text{if } e_i \notin S; \end{cases}$$

and let

$$\theta = \begin{cases} -1/2, & \text{if } o \in S; \\ 1/2, & \text{if } o \notin S. \end{cases}$$

Then it is straightforward to verify that if ω is the state

$$\omega = (\alpha_1, \alpha_2, \ldots, \alpha_n, \theta)$$

of P_n then the set of positive examples of h_ω in $E_{\mathbf{x}}$ is precisely S. Therefore $\mathbf{x}$ is shattered by P_n and, consequently, $\text{VCdim}(P_n) \geq n + 1$. Combining these two results, we have the stated equality. □

7.5 SAUER'S LEMMA

In this section we assume that H has finite VC dimension. The growth function $\Pi_H(m)$ is a measure of how many different classifications of an m-sample into positive and negative examples can be achieved by the hypotheses of H, while the VC dimension of H is the maximum value of m for which $\Pi_H(m) = 2^m$. Clearly these two quantities are related, because the VC dimension is defined in terms of the growth function. But there is another, less obvious, relationship: the growth function $\Pi_H(m)$ can be bounded by a polynomial function of m, and the degree of the polynomial is the VC dimension d of H. Explicitly, we have the following theorem, due to Sauer (1972) and Shelah (1972) independently (see Assouad (1983)). In combinatorial circles it is usually known as *Sauer's Lemma*.

Theorem 7.5.1 (Sauer's Lemma) Let $d \geq 0$ and $m \geq 1$ be given integers and let H be a hypothesis space with $\text{VCdim}(H) = d$. Then

$$\Pi_H(m) \leq 1 + \binom{m}{1} + \binom{m}{2} + \ldots + \binom{m}{d},$$

where the binomial numbers are defined by

$$\binom{m}{i} = \frac{m(m-1)\ldots(m-i+1)}{1.2\ldots m}.$$

□

Before we give the proof, it may be helpful to interpret the result. First, it should be noted that the explicit definition of the binomial numbers means that $\binom{a}{b}$ is zero whenever $b > a \geq 1$. Thus for values of m not exceeding d the result asserts only that

$$\Pi_H(m) \leq 1 + \binom{m}{1} + \ldots + \binom{m}{m} + 0 + 0 + \ldots + 0 = 2^m,$$

which is trivial; we already know that Π_H takes these values in this range. However, when m is greater than d, the sum

$$\Phi(d, m) = 1 + \binom{m}{1} + \binom{m}{2} + \ldots + \binom{m}{d}$$

is strictly less than 2^m: indeed, it follows from the explicit formula for the binomial numbers that it is a polynomial function of m with degree d.

For convenience, we let $\Phi(d, m)$ denote this sum of binomial numbers for *any* $d \geq 0$ and $m \geq 1$. We have:

$$\Phi(0, m) = 1 \ (m \geq 1); \quad \Phi(d, 1) = 2 \ (d \geq 1).$$

The binomial numbers satisfy the identity

$$\binom{a}{b} = \binom{a-1}{b} + \binom{a-1}{b-1},$$

which can be verified explicitly using the formula. From this we can immediately derive the identity

$$\Phi(d, m) = \Phi(d, m-1) + \Phi(d-1, m-1),$$

which is valid for all $d \geq 1$ and $m \geq 2$ (Exercise 5).

Proof of Sauer's Lemma If H is a hypothesis space with $d = \text{VCdim}(H) = 0$ then, for any example x, $h(x)$ is the same (either 0 or 1) for all hypotheses $h \in H$. It follows that $\Pi_H(\mathbf{x}) = 1$ for any sample $\mathbf{x}$ of any length m. Thus $\Pi_H(m) = 1 = \Phi(0, m)$, and the theorem is true in the case $d = 0$.

If $m = 1$ and $d \geq 1$, then for any H we have $\Pi_H(1) \leq 2 = \Phi(d, 1)$, so the theorem is true in this case also.

Using these 'boundary conditions' we can prove the theorem by induction on $d + m$. The case $d + m = 2$ is covered explicitly by the boundary conditions. Suppose the result holds for all cases with $d + m \leq k$, where $k \geq 2$, and let H be a hypothesis space of VC dimension d and $\mathbf{x}$ a sample of length m, where $d + m = k + 1$. The cases $(d, m) = (0, k+1)$ and $(d, m) = (k, 1)$ are covered by the boundary conditions, so we may assume that $d \geq 1, m \geq 2$.

If the given sample $\mathbf{x} = (x_1, x_2, \ldots, x_m)$ contains repeated examples, then we can remove the repetitions and obtain a shorter sample. The result then follows by the induction hypothesis. So we may suppose that $\mathbf{x}$ contains m distinct examples. Let E be the set of examples in $\mathbf{x}$ and let $H_E = H|E$ be the hypothesis space on E obtained by restricting the hypotheses of H to the domain E. Then, as remarked earlier, H_E is finite and $\Pi_H(\mathbf{x}) = |H_E|$. We shall show that $|H_E| \leq \Phi(d, m)$.

Let $F = E \setminus \{x_m\}$ and consider the hypothesis space $H_F = H|F$. Two distinct hypotheses h, g of H_E give, on restriction to F, the same hypothesis of H_F precisely when h and g agree on F and disagree on x_m. Denote by H_* the set of hypotheses of H_F which arise in this manner from two distinct hypotheses of H_E. Thus, if $h_* \in H_*$ then both possible extensions of h_* to a $\{0,1\}$-function on E are hypotheses of H_E. It follows that

$$|H_E| = |H_F| + |H_*|.$$

We now bound $|H_F|$ and $|H_*|$.

Let $\mathbf{x}' = (x_1, x_2, \ldots, x_{m-1})$ be the sample consisting of the first $m-1$ examples of $\mathbf{x}$. Then H_F is a hypothesis space on F and therefore

$$|H_F| = \Pi_H(\mathbf{x}') \leq \Pi_H(m - 1).$$

Using the induction hypothesis we can conclude that

$$|H_F| \leq \Pi_H(m - 1) \leq \Phi(d, m - 1),$$

since $d + (m - 1) \leq k$.

We claim that $\mathrm{VCdim}\,(H_*)$ is at most $d - 1$. Indeed, suppose that H_* shatters some sample $\mathbf{z} = (z_1, z_2, \ldots, z_d)$ of length d of examples from F. For each $h_* \in H_*$, there are $h_1, h_2 \in H_E$ such that h_1 and h_2 agree with h_* on F, and $h_1(x_m) = 0, h_2(x_m) = 1$. It follows that H_E, and hence H, shatters the sample $(z_1, \ldots, z_d, x_m)$ of length $d + 1$, an impossibility since $\mathrm{VCdim}(H) \leq d$. Hence $\mathrm{VCdim}\,(H_*) \leq d - 1$. Using the induction hypothesis again we have

$$|H_*| = \Pi_{H_*}(\mathbf{x}') \leq \Pi_{H_*}(m - 1) \leq \Phi(d - 1, m - 1),$$

since $(d - 1) + (m - 1) \leq k$.

Combining the results obtained, we have

$$\Pi_H(\mathbf{x}) = |H_E| = |H_F| + |H_*| \leq \Phi(d, m - 1) + \Phi(d - 1, m - 1) = \Phi(d, m),$$

as required. $\square$

Example 7.5.2 Let H be the hypothesis space of the real perceptron P_n. Then H has VC dimension $n+1$ and therefore, for any positive integer m, $\Pi_H(m) \leq \Phi(n+1, m)$. For example, when $n = 2$

$$\Pi_H(4) \leq \Phi(3, 4) = 1 + 4 + 6 + 4 = 15.$$

This corresponds to the fact, illustrated in Figure 7.4, that not all the 2^4 classifications of a 4-sample can be realised by P_2. In fact, careful analysis of the cases shows that $\Pi_H(4) = 14$ (Exercise 3).   □

We shall now elaborate on the fact that $\Phi(d, m)$ is bounded by a polynomial function of m, of degree d. A simple form of this result, $\Phi(d, m) \leq m^d$ for $m \geq d > 1$, is fairly easy to prove (Exercise 6). But there is some advantage in having a better bound, as given by the following result of Blumer *et al.* (1989).

Proposition 7.5.3 For all $m \geq d \geq 1$,

$$\Phi(d, m) < \left(\frac{em}{d}\right)^d,$$

where e is the base of natural logarithms.

Proof The proof is in two stages. First, we claim that for all positive integers d,

$$\Phi(d, m) \leq \frac{2m^d}{d!}$$

for all $m \geq d$. This can be proved by an inductive argument, as follows. If $d = 1$ then $\Phi(d, m) = m + 1 \leq 2m$. If $m = d > 1$ then $\Phi(d, m) = \Phi(d, d) = 2^d$. Now, for $d \geq 1$, we have

$$\left(1 + \frac{1}{d}\right)^d \geq 1 + d\frac{1}{d} = 2.$$

This justifies the induction step in the following argument:

$$2^{d+1} \leq \left(\frac{d+1}{d}\right)^d 2^d \leq 2 \left(\frac{d+1}{d}\right)^d \frac{d^d}{d!} = 2\frac{(d+1)^{d+1}}{(d+1)!},$$

and verifies the claim for $m = d > 1$.

Suppose that $m > d \geq 1$. Since

$$\Phi(d+1, m+1) = \Phi(d+1, m) + \Phi(d, m),$$

it suffices to prove that

$$2\frac{m^d}{d!} + 2\frac{m^{d+1}}{(d+1)!} \leq 2\frac{(m+1)^{d+1}}{(d+1)!}.$$

It is straightforward to verify that this is true if and only if

$$1 + \left(\frac{d+1}{m}\right) \leq \left(1 + \frac{1}{m}\right)^{d+1},$$

which follows from the binomial theorem. Thus, for all $m \geq d$, $\Phi(d,m) \leq 2m^d/d!$.

It remains to show that, for all $m \geq d \geq 1$,

$$2\left(\frac{d}{e}\right)^d < d!.$$

The result clearly holds when $d = 1$. Suppose it holds for a given value of $d \geq 1$: then

$$(d+1)! = (d+1)\,d! > (d+1)\,2\left(\frac{d}{e}\right)^d.$$

Thus it suffices to prove that

$$(d+1)\,2\left(\frac{d}{e}\right)^d > 2\left(\frac{d+1}{e}\right)^{d+1};$$

that is,

$$\left(1 + \frac{1}{d}\right)^d \leq e,$$

which is indeed true for any $d \geq 1$. The result follows. $\square$

In conjunction with Sauer's Lemma, this last result implies that when $\mathrm{VCdim}(H) = d$, we have

$$\Pi_H(m) < \left(\frac{em}{d}\right)^d$$

for $m \geq d$. We shall see in the next chapter that this result is very significant, because it gives an explicit polynomial bound for Π_H as a function of m.

The following consequence of the results in this section will be of use to us later.

Proposition 7.5.4 Let H be any hypothesis space consisting of at least two hypotheses and defined on a finite example space X. Then

$$\mathrm{VCdim}(H) > \frac{\ln|H|}{1 + \ln|X|}.$$

Proof Observe that two hypotheses of H are distinct precisely when they give different classifications of the whole example space X into positive and negative examples. Since there are $\Pi_H(|X|)$ such classifications, we have $|H| = \Pi_H(|X|)$. It follows from Sauer's Lemma and Proposition 7.5.3 that

$$|H| = \Pi_H(|X|) < \left(\frac{e|X|}{d}\right)^d,$$

where $d \geq 1$ is the VC dimension of H. Now,

$$|H| < \left(\frac{e|X|}{d}\right)^d \implies d\,(1 + \ln|X|) - d\ln d > \ln|H|$$

$$\implies d > \frac{\ln|H|}{1 + \ln|X|},$$

as required.   □

We remark that if $\mathrm{VCdim}(H) \geq 2$, then this result can be improved to

$$\mathrm{VCdim}(H) \geq \frac{\ln|H|}{\ln|X|},$$

using the result $\Phi(d, m) \leq m^d$ for $m \geq d > 1$.

FURTHER REMARKS

For any positive integer n, let G_n be the subset of the hypothesis space of P_n consisting of the hypotheses for which the zero vector (the origin) is a negative example. Thus, G_n is the set of characteristic functions of all those closed half-spaces of $\mathbf{R}^n$ which do not contain the origin. Then one can show that $G = G_n$ has VC dimension n (Exercise 10) and that for any m, $\Pi_G(m) = \Phi(n, m)$ (see Vapnik and Chervonenkis (1971)). Thus the major result of this chapter, $\Pi_H(m) \leq \Phi(d, m)$ is the best possible result of its kind.

EXERCISES

1. Show that if $X = \mathbf{R}$ and H is the set of all closed intervals, then

$$\Pi_H(m) = 1 + m + \frac{1}{2}m(m - 1).$$

2. Describe explicitly the hypothesis space of P_1 and show that the VC dimension of P_1 is 2.

3. Show that when H is the hypothesis space of the real perceptron P_2, $\Pi_H(4) = 14$.

4. Let H be a hypothesis space of finite VC dimension. For $h \in H$, define the $\{0, 1\}$-valued function $\bar{h}$ by

$$\bar{h}(x) = 1 \iff h(x) = 0,$$

and let the *complement* of H be the space $\left\{ \bar{h} \mid h \in H \right\}$. Prove that this space has the same VC dimension as H.

5. Prove that $\Phi(d, m) = \Phi(d, m - 1) + \Phi(d - 1, m - 1)$ for $d \geq 1$ and $m \geq 2$.

6. Prove that $\Phi(d, m) \leq m^d$, for all $m \geq d > 1$.

7. A monomial is *monotone* if it contains no negated literals. Prove that the space of monotone monomials defined on $\{0, 1\}^n$ has VC dimension precisely n.

8. A hypothesis space H is *linearly ordered* if it has at least two hypotheses and if for any $h, g \in H$, either
$$h(x) = 1 \implies g(x) = 1$$
or
$$g(x) = 1 \implies h(x) = 1.$$
Prove that if H is linearly ordered then $\mathrm{VCdim}(H) = 1$. (This is a result of Wenocur and Dudley (1981).) Deduce that the space of rays has VC dimension 1.

9. Suppose that H contains the identically-0 function and the identically-1 function, and that $\mathrm{VCdim}(H) = 1$. Prove that H is linearly ordered. (This is a result of Wenocur and Dudley (1981).)

10. Let G_n be the set of hypotheses of P_n for which the zero vector o is a negative example. Suppose that the sample $\mathbf{x} = (x_1, x_2, \ldots, x_m)$ is shattered by G_n. Why can none of the x_i be o? Prove that the sample $(x_1, \ldots, x_m, o)$ is shattered by P_n. Using this, prove that $\mathrm{VCdim}(G_n) = n$.

11. Use the result on G_n stated in the Further Remarks to prove that for $m \geq 2$,
$\Pi_{P_n}(m) = 2\Phi(n, m - 1)$.
[Hint: Let $\mathbf{x}$ be a sample of length m for which $\Pi_{P_n}(\mathbf{x}) = \Pi_{P_n}(m)$. Without loss of generality, we may assume that the origin o is one of the examples in $\mathbf{x}$, since clearly the number of classifications by P_n of a vector is unchanged if the vector is translated. Thus, $\mathbf{x} = (x_1, \ldots, x_{m-1}, o)$. How are $\Pi_{P_n}(\mathbf{x})$ and $\Pi_{G_n}((x_1, \ldots, x_{m-1}))$ related?]

Chapter 8: Learning and the VC Dimension

8.1 INTRODUCTION

In the previous chapter we discussed the theory of VC dimension, with the promise that this theory would prove useful in the study of learning. The results to be proved in this chapter fulfil that promise. We show that, for any hypothesis space H, the condition that H has finite VC dimension is both necessary and sufficient for potential learnability. Thus we have a complete characterisation of potentially learnable hypothesis spaces: they are precisely those of finite VC dimension.

The details of this characterisation provide a general upper bound for the sample complexity of a consistent learning algorithm, when the hypothesis space is potentially learnable. We shall also give two general lower bounds for the sample complexity of pac learning algorithms, one in terms of the VC dimension and accuracy, the other in terms of confidence and accuracy.

8.2 VC DIMENSION AND POTENTIAL LEARNABILITY

We shall find it useful to introduce some slight elaborations of our standard notation. We use the notation $\mathbf{s} = (\mathbf{x}, \mathbf{b})$ for the training sample

$$\mathbf{s} = ((x_1, b_1), (x_2, b_2), \dots, (x_m, b_m))$$

in $(X \times \{0, 1\})^m$. If t is a target concept and $\mathbf{s}$ is a training sample for t (that is, $b_i = t(x_i)$ for each i), then we denote $\mathbf{s}$ by $(\mathbf{x}, t(\mathbf{x}))$. This notation emphasises the fact that, when $\mathbf{s}$ belongs to the set $S(m, t)$ of training samples of length m for t, only the values of t on the elements of the sample $\mathbf{x}$ are given. However, for the sake of compactness, we shall denote the subset of H which agrees with $\mathbf{s}$ by $H[\mathbf{x}, t]$, rather than $H[(\mathbf{x}, t(\mathbf{x}))]$.

Given $\mathbf{s} = (\mathbf{x}, \mathbf{b})$, the *observed error* of a hypothesis $h \in H$ on $\mathbf{s}$ is defined to be

$$\mathrm{er}_\mathbf{s}(h) = \frac{1}{m} |\{i : h(x_i) \neq b_i\}|.$$

Note that $H[\mathbf{s}]$ is the set of hypotheses having observed error zero on $\mathbf{s}$. If $\mathbf{s} = (\mathbf{x}, t(\mathbf{x}))$

then $\mathrm{er}_{\mathbf{s}}(h)$ is called the observed error of h on $\mathbf{x}$ with respect to t, and is denoted by $\mathrm{er}_{\mathbf{x}}(h,t)$, or $\mathrm{er}_{\mathbf{x}}(h)$ when t is clear.

Our first result is that finite VC dimension is necessary for potential learnability.

Theorem 8.2.1 If a hypothesis space has infinite VC dimension then it is not potentially learnable.

Proof Suppose that H has infinite VC dimension, so that for any positive integer m there is a sample $\mathbf{z}$ of length $2m$ which is shattered by H. Let $E = E_{\mathbf{z}}$ be the set of examples in this sample and define a probability distribution μ on X by

$$\mu(x) = \begin{cases} 1/2m, & \text{if } x \in E; \\ 0, & \text{otherwise.} \end{cases}$$

In other words, μ is uniform on E and zero elsewhere. Informally, with respect to μ, each example in E is equally likely to be presented, and all other examples have zero probability of being presented. We observe that μ^m is uniform on E^m and zero elsewhere. Thus, with probability one, a randomly chosen sample $\mathbf{x}$ of length m is a sample of examples from E.

Let $\mathbf{s} = (\mathbf{x}, t(\mathbf{x})) \in S(m,t)$ be a training sample of length m for a target concept $t \in H$. With probability 1 (with respect to μ^m), we have $x_i \in E$ for $1 \le i \le m$. Since $\mathbf{z}$ is shattered by H, there is a hypothesis $h \in H$ such that $h(x_i) = t(x_i)$ for each x_i ($1 \le i \le m$), and $h(x) \ne t(x)$ for all other x in E. It follows that h is in $H[\mathbf{s}]$, whereas h has error at least $\frac{1}{2}$ with respect to t. We have shown that for any positive integer m, and any target concept t, there is a probability distribution μ on X such that the event $H[\mathbf{s}] \cap B_{\frac{1}{2}} = \emptyset$ has probability zero. Thus there is no positive integer $m_0 = m_0(\frac{1}{2}, \frac{1}{2})$ for which we can assert that, whenever $m \ge m_0$,

$$\mu^m \left\{ \mathbf{s} \in S(m,t) \mid H[\mathbf{s}] \cap B_{\frac{1}{2}} = \emptyset \right\} > \frac{1}{2}.$$

That is, H is not potentially learnable. □

In passing, it is worth noting that the preceding proof actually shows that there is no suitable value of m_0 for any particular target concept t, so that there certainly is no such value for all $t \in H$. An application requiring the full strength of the result may be found in Exercise 1.

Example 8.2.2 A simple example of a space H with infinite VC dimension may be constructed as follows. For each subset $A \subseteq \mathbf{R}$, define the *characteristic function* χ_A by

$$\chi_A(y) = \begin{cases} 1, & \text{if } y \in A; \\ 0, & \text{otherwise.} \end{cases}$$

Let U denote the collection of all subsets of $\mathbf{R}$ which can be expressed as a finite union of closed intervals, and let $J = \{\chi_A \mid A \in U\}$, the *interval union space*.

In order to show that $\mathrm{VCdim}(J)$ is infinite, let $\mathbf{x} = (x_1, x_2, \ldots, x_m)$ be any sample of distinct points in $\mathbf{R}$, and let $E_{\mathbf{x}}$ denote the corresponding set of examples. Given any $S \subseteq E_{\mathbf{x}}$ we can construct a set $A \in U$ such that $S \subseteq A$ and $(E_{\mathbf{x}} \setminus S) \cap A = \emptyset$, as follows. For each $x_i \in S$ let A_i be a closed interval which contains x_i but no other element of $E_{\mathbf{x}}$, and let A be the union of all such A_i. The set A is a finite union of closed intervals, and χ_A is 1 on S and 0 on $E_{\mathbf{x}} \setminus S$. In other words, J shatters $\mathbf{x}$. Since this argument works for any finite sample, of whatever length, we conclude that $\mathrm{VCdim}(J)$ is infinite. □

Note that the space H constructed in this example is contained in the space of (characteristic functions of) closed sets in $\mathbf{R}$. Thus the latter space also has infinite VC dimension. It follows from Theorem 8.2.1 that neither space is potentially learnable.

The converse of the preceding theorem is also true: finite VC dimension is sufficient for potential learnability. This result can be traced back to the statistical researches of Vapnik and Chervonenkis (1971) (see also Vapnik (1982)). The work of Blumer *et al.* (1986, 1989), showed that it is one of the key results in Computational Learning Theory. The proof is rather involved, and the details will be given in the next section. For the moment, we shall describe only the underlying ideas.

Suppose that the hypothesis space H is defined on the example space X, and let t be any target concept in H, μ any probability distribution on X and ϵ any real number with $0 < \epsilon < 1$. The objects t, μ, ϵ are to be thought of as fixed, but arbitrary, in what follows. Define

$$Q_m^\epsilon = \{\mathbf{x} \in X^m \mid H[\mathbf{x}, t] \cap B_\epsilon \neq \emptyset\}.$$

The probability of choosing a training sample for which there is a consistent, but ϵ-bad, hypothesis is

$$\mu^m \{\mathbf{s} \in S(m, t) \mid H[\mathbf{s}] \cap B_\epsilon \neq \emptyset\},$$

which is, by definition (Section 3.2), $\mu^m(Q_m^\epsilon)$. Thus, in order to show that H is potentially learnable, it suffices to find an upper bound $f(m, \epsilon)$ for $\mu^m(Q_m^\epsilon)$ which is independent of both t and μ and which tends to 0 as m tends to infinity. For if there is such a bound then, given any δ between 0 and 1, we can use the fact that $f(m, \epsilon)$ tends to 0 to find m_0 such that for all $m \geq m_0$, $f(m, \epsilon) < \delta$. The value of m_0 depends on δ and ϵ but is independent of t and μ. So we have the $m_0(\delta, \epsilon)$ required in the definition of potential learnability.

Note that the m_0 thus obtained is also an upper bound for the sample complexity of any consistent learning algorithm for H. The hard part of the proof is to find the upper bound $f(m, \epsilon)$. In the next section we shall prove the following result, which, in this specific form, is due to Blumer *et al.* (1986, 1989), and generalises a result of Haussler and Welzl (1987).

Proposition 8.2.3 Suppose that H is a hypothesis space defined on an example space X, and that t, μ, and ϵ are arbitrary, but fixed. Then

$$\mu^m \{\mathbf{s} \in S(m, t) \,|\, H[\mathbf{s}] \cap B_\epsilon \neq \emptyset\} < 2\,\Pi_H(2m)\,2^{-\epsilon m/2}$$

for all positive integers $m \geq 8/\epsilon$.   □

The right-hand side is the bound $f(m, \epsilon)$ for $\mu^m(Q_m^\epsilon)$, as postulated above. We have to show that it tends to zero as $m \to \infty$. If H has finite VC dimension then, by Sauer's Lemma, $\Pi_H(2m)$ is bounded by a polynomial function of m, and therefore $f(m, \epsilon)$ is eventually dominated by the negative exponential term. Thus the right-hand side tends to 0 as m tends to infinity and, by the above discussion, this establishes potential learnability for spaces of finite VC dimension.

8.3 PROOF OF THE FUNDAMENTAL THEOREM

In this section, we present a proof of the key result that finite VC dimension implies potential learnability. The proof is rather involved, and it is worth giving first a very informal explanation of the method.

We aim to bound the probability that a given sample of length m is 'bad', in the sense that there is some hypothesis which is consistent with the target concept on the sample but which has actual error greater than ϵ. We transform this problem into a slightly more manageable one involving samples of length $2m$. For such a sample, the sub-sample $\mathbf{x}$ comprising the first half of the sample may be thought of as a randomly drawn sample of length m, while the second half may be thought of as a 'testing' sample on which to evaluate the performance of a hypothesis consistent with the target concept on $\mathbf{x}$. We obtain a bound on the probability that some hypothesis consistent with the target on the first half of the sample is 'bad', in the sense that it has observed error greater than $\epsilon/2$ on the second half of the sample. A given example is just as likely to occur in the first half as in the second half. A group action based on this idea enables us to find the required bound by solving a simple counting problem.

We shall assume some measure-theoretic properties of the hypothesis spaces without explicit comment. These were mentioned in the Further Remarks of Chapter 3, and the details are discussed fully by Pollard (1984) and Blumer *et al.* (1989).

Theorem 8.3.1 If a hypothesis space has finite VC dimension, then it is potentially learnable.

Proof We use the notation introduced at the end of the previous section. There are four stages.

- Bound $\mu^m(Q_m^\epsilon)$ by the probability (with respect to μ^{2m}) of a certain subset R_m^ϵ of X^{2m}.
- Using a group action, bound the probability of R_m^ϵ in finite terms.
- Express this bound in terms of Π_H by combinatorial arguments.
- Apply the argument given in the last paragraph of Section 8.2 to conclude that $\mu^m(Q_m^\epsilon)$ tends to zero as m tends to infinity.

Stage 1 Given samples $\mathbf{x}, \mathbf{y} \in X^m$, let $\mathbf{xy} \in X^{2m}$ denote the sample of length $2m$ obtained by concatenating $\mathbf{x}$ and $\mathbf{y}$. With this notation, define

$$R_m^\epsilon = \left\{ \mathbf{xy} \in X^{2m} \mid \exists h \in B_\epsilon \text{ for which } \mathrm{er}_\mathbf{x}(h) = 0 \text{ and } \mathrm{er}_\mathbf{y}(h) > \frac{\epsilon}{2} \right\}.$$

Lemma 8.3.2 For all $m \geq 8/\epsilon$,

$$\mu^m(Q_m^\epsilon) \leq 2\mu^{2m}(R_m^\epsilon).$$

Proof Let χ_Q be the characteristic function of Q_m^ϵ; that is, $\chi_Q(\mathbf{x}) = 1$ if $\mathbf{x} \in Q_m^\epsilon$ and $\chi_Q(\mathbf{x}) = 0$ otherwise. If we define the characteristic function χ_R similarly, then

$$\chi_R(\mathbf{xy}) = \chi_Q(\mathbf{x})\psi_\mathbf{x}(\mathbf{y}),$$

where

$$\psi_\mathbf{x}(\mathbf{y}) = \begin{cases} 1, & \text{if } \exists h \in H[\mathbf{x}] \cap B_\epsilon \text{ with } \mathrm{er}_\mathbf{y}(h) > \epsilon/2; \\ 0, & \text{otherwise.} \end{cases}$$

Now we have

$$\mu^{2m}(R_m^\epsilon) = \int \chi_R(\mathbf{xy}) = \int \left(\chi_Q(\mathbf{x}) \int \psi_\mathbf{x}(\mathbf{y}) \right),$$

where the integrals are taken over the whole of the relevant spaces, with respect to the product measures. The inner integral is the probability that, given $\mathbf{x}$, there is some $h \in B_\epsilon$ which is consistent with $\mathbf{x}$ and satisfies $\mathrm{er}_\mathbf{y}(h) > \epsilon/2$. This is certainly not less than the probability that a particular $h \in B_\epsilon$ which is consistent with $\mathbf{x}$ satisfies $\mathrm{er}_\mathbf{y}(h) > \epsilon/2$.

Thus it suffices to show that the above-mentioned quantity is at least $\frac{1}{2}$, for then we have

$$\mu^{2m}(R_m^\epsilon) \geq \int \frac{1}{2}\chi_Q(\mathbf{x}) = \frac{1}{2}\mu^m(Q_m^\epsilon).$$

In order to prove this, we use the following bound on the 'tail' of the binomial distribution. Let $0 \le p \le 1$ and let $LE(p, m, s)$ denote the probability of at most s successes in m independent trials each of which has a probability p of success. Then

$$LE\left(p, m, (1 - \beta)mp\right) \le e^{-\beta^2 mp/2},$$

for any $0 \le \beta \le 1$. This is often known as a Chernoff bound, since it follows from a special case of a result of Chernoff (1952). (See also Angluin and Valiant (1979) and, for a generalisation of this result, McDiarmid (1989).)

Let $h \in B_\epsilon$, so that $\mathrm{er}_\mu(h) = \epsilon_h > \epsilon$. For $\mathbf{y} \in X^m$, $m\,\mathrm{er}_\mathbf{y}(h)$ is the number of components of $\mathbf{y}$ on which h and t disagree, and so it is a binomially distributed random variable. Now, applying the above Chernoff bound, we have

$$\mu^m\left\{\mathbf{y} \;\middle|\; \mathrm{er}_\mathbf{y}(h) \le \frac{\epsilon}{2}\right\} = \mu^m\left\{\mathbf{y} \;\middle|\; m\,\mathrm{er}_\mathbf{y}(h) \le \frac{\epsilon}{2}m\right\}$$

$$\le \mu^m\left\{\mathbf{y} \;\middle|\; m\,\mathrm{er}_\mathbf{y}(h) \le \frac{\epsilon_h}{2}m\right\}$$

$$= LE\left(\epsilon_h, m, \left(1 - \frac{1}{2}\right)m\epsilon_h\right)$$

$$\le \exp\left(-\frac{\epsilon_h m}{8}\right)$$

$$< \exp\left(-\frac{\epsilon m}{8}\right).$$

For $m \ge 8/\epsilon$, this is at most $1/e$. It follows that for any $h \in B_\epsilon$,

$$\mu^m\left\{\mathbf{y} \;\middle|\; \mathrm{er}_\mathbf{y}(h) > \frac{\epsilon}{2}\right\} > 1 - \frac{1}{e} > \frac{1}{2}.$$

This completes the proof of Stage 1. $\qquad\square$

Stage 2 The next stage is to bound the probability of R_m^ϵ by using a group action on X^{2m}. Following Pollard (1984), we use the 'swapping group' to convert the problem into an easy counting problem.

For $i \in \{1, \ldots, m\}$ let τ_i be the permutation of $\{1, \ldots, 2m\}$ which switches i and $m + i$. There is an induced transformation of X^{2m} defined by letting τ_i act on the coordinates, and we use τ_i to denote this transformation also. Thus, for example, if $m = 4$,

$$\tau_2(z_1, z_2, z_3, z_4, z_5, z_6, z_7, z_8) = (z_1, z_6, z_3, z_4, z_5, z_2, z_7, z_8).$$

Let G_m be the group generated by the permutations τ_i $(1 \le i \le m)$. As an abstract group G_m is just the direct product of m copies of the group of order 2, so $|G_m| = 2^m$.

Lemma 8.3.3 Given $\mathbf{z} \in X^{2m}$, let $\Gamma(\mathbf{z})$ denote the number of $\sigma \in G_m$ for which $\sigma\mathbf{z}$ is in R_m^ϵ. Then

$$|G_m|\, \mu^{2m}(R_m^\epsilon) \leq \max \Gamma(\mathbf{z}),$$

where this maximum is taken over all $\mathbf{z} \in X^{2m}$.

Proof The proof is quite general, applying to any finite group G of transformations of a space X^n induced by coordinate-permutations, and any subset S of X^n. Let χ_S be the characteristic function of S. Since G is finite we can interchange summation and integration as follows (where the integral sign represents integration over the entire space with respect to the product measure derived from μ):

$$\sum_{\sigma \in G} \int \chi_S(\sigma\mathbf{z}) = \int \sum_{\sigma \in G} \chi_S(\sigma\mathbf{z}).$$

The left-hand side is the sum over σ of the measure of $\sigma^{-1}(S)$, which is the same as the measure of S, since coordinate-permutations preserve the product measure. Hence the left-hand side is just $|G|\, \mu^n(S)$. The integrand on the right-hand side is just the number of σ in G for which $\sigma\mathbf{z} \in S$. Since the total weight of a probability measure is 1, the integral is bounded by the maximum of this quantity, taken over $\mathbf{z}$. Putting $n = 2m$, $G = G_m$, and $S = R_m^\epsilon$, the result follows.   □

Stage 3 Given any $h \in B_\epsilon$, let

$$R_m^\epsilon(h) = \left\{ \mathbf{xy} \in X^{2m} \;\middle|\; \mathrm{er}_\mathbf{x}(h) = 0 \text{ and } \mathrm{er}_\mathbf{y}(h) > \frac{\epsilon}{2} \right\}.$$

Also, for $\mathbf{z} \in X^{2m}$, let $\Gamma(h, \mathbf{z})$ denote the number of $\sigma \in G_m$ which transform $\mathbf{z}$ to a vector in $R_m^\epsilon(h)$.

Lemma 8.3.4 Suppose that m is any positive integer and that $h \in B_\epsilon$. Then

$$\Gamma(h, \mathbf{z}) < 2^{m(1 - \epsilon/2)},$$

for all $\mathbf{z} \in X^{2m}$.

Proof Suppose that $\Gamma(h, \mathbf{z}) \neq 0$. If $\mathbf{z} \notin R_m^\epsilon(h)$, then for some $\tau \in G_m$, $\tau\mathbf{z} \in R_m^\epsilon(h)$. But the number of σ such that $\sigma\mathbf{z} \in R_m^\epsilon(h)$ is precisely the number of σ for which $\sigma\tau\mathbf{z} \in R_m^\epsilon(h)$ (since G_m is a group). Hence, we may, without loss of generality, suppose that $\mathbf{z} \in R_m^\epsilon(h)$.

Now, $\mathbf{z} = \mathbf{xy}$ where $\mathrm{er}_\mathbf{x}(h) = 0$ and $\mathrm{er}_\mathbf{y}(h) > \epsilon/2$. To simplify notation, let us suppose that the $r > m\epsilon/2$ entries of $\mathbf{z}$ on which h and the target concept t disagree are

$$z_{m+1}, z_{m+2}, \ldots, z_{m+r}.$$

Recall that a transformation $\sigma \in G_m$ interchanges some pairs (z_j, z_{m+j}). If $\sigma \mathbf{z}$ is in $R_m^\epsilon(h)$ then σ does not interchange (z_j, z_{m+j}) for $1 \leq j \leq r$. Conversely, any σ which satisfies this condition is in $R_m^\epsilon(h)$. Since σ is uniquely determined by the set of j for which $\sigma(z_j) = z_{m+j}$, the number of such σ is just the number of subsets of $\{r+1, r+2, \ldots, m\}$; that is, $\Gamma(h, \mathbf{z}) = 2^{m-r}$. Since $r > \epsilon m/2$, we have

$$\Gamma(h, \mathbf{z}) < 2^{m - \epsilon m/2},$$

as required. □

Lemma 8.3.5 For any positive integer m,

$$\mu^{2m}(R_m^\epsilon) < \Pi_H(2m) \, 2^{-\epsilon m/2}.$$

Proof Let $\mathbf{z} \in X^{2m}$ be fixed but arbitrary, and let $s = \Pi_{B_\epsilon}(\mathbf{z})$. Then there are hypotheses $h_1, \ldots, h_s$ in B_ϵ which give s different classifications of $\mathbf{z}$ and, further, any classification of $\mathbf{z}$ by a hypothesis in B_ϵ is one of these s classifications. We have

$$s = \Pi_{B_\epsilon}(\mathbf{z}) \leq \Pi_H(\mathbf{z}) \leq \Pi_H(2m).$$

Suppose $\sigma \mathbf{z} = \mathbf{ab}$ is in R_m^ϵ. This means that there is some $h \in H$ such that $\mathrm{er}_\mathbf{a}(h) = 0$ and $\mathrm{er}_\mathbf{b}(h) > \epsilon/2$. Since all classifications of $\mathbf{z}$, and hence of its rearrangement $\sigma \mathbf{z} = \mathbf{ab}$, are realised by some h_i $(1 \leq i \leq s)$, it follows that $\sigma \mathbf{z}$ is in one of the sets $R_m^\epsilon(h_i)$. Thus the set of σ for which $\sigma \mathbf{z}$ is in R_m^ϵ is the union of the sets of those σ for which $\sigma \mathbf{z}$ is in $R_m^\epsilon(h_i)$. In terms of the notation previously introduced, we therefore have

$$\Gamma(\mathbf{z}) \leq \sum_{i=1}^s \Gamma(h_i, \mathbf{z}).$$

The last expression is the sum of $s \leq \Pi_H(2m)$ terms and, by Lemma 8.3.4, each of them is bounded above by $2^{m(1-\epsilon/2)}$. Thus, from Lemma 8.3.3, we have

$$\mu^{2m}(R_m^\epsilon) \leq |G_m|^{-1} \max_\mathbf{z} \Gamma(\mathbf{z}) \leq 2^{-m} \Pi_H(2m) \, 2^{m(1-\epsilon/2)} = \Pi_H(2m) \, 2^{-m\epsilon/2},$$

as claimed. □

Stage 4 The bound

$$\mu^m(Q_m^\epsilon) < 2 \, \Pi_H(2m) \, 2^{-m\epsilon/2}$$

follows by combining Lemmas 8.3.2 and 8.3.5. If H has finite VC dimension then, by Sauer's Lemma, $\Pi_H(2m)$ is bounded by a polynomial function of m. The right-hand side is eventually dominated by the negative exponential term, and tends to 0 as m tends to infinity; so it can be made less than any given $\delta > 0$ by choosing $m \geq m_0(\delta, \epsilon)$, a quantity depending only on δ and ϵ. Thus H is potentially learnable. □

In the above proof, the 'testing' sample was taken to be the same length as the original sample. It is possible to perform a similar, though rather more complicated analysis, in which, instead of samples of length $2m$, one considers samples of length $m + k$, for a general k. Judicious choice of k then yields better bounds on $\mu^m(Q_m^\epsilon)$; see Anthony, Biggs and Shawe-Taylor (1990) and Anthony (1991) for details.

8.4 SAMPLE COMPLEXITY OF CONSISTENT ALGORITHMS

We have seen that if a hypothesis space H has finite VC dimension, then H is potentially learnable. In other words, given a confidence parameter δ and an accuracy parameter ϵ $(0 < \delta, \epsilon < 1)$, there is a sample length $m_0 = m_0(H, \delta, \epsilon)$ such that

$$m \geq m_0 \implies \mu^m \left\{ \mathbf{s} \in S(m, t) \mid H[\mathbf{s}] \cap B_\epsilon = \emptyset \right\} > 1 - \delta,$$

for any probability distribution μ on X and any target concept $t \in H$. It follows that any consistent learning algorithm L for H is pac and, further, that any $m_0(H, \delta, \epsilon)$ for which the above condition holds is an upper bound on the sample complexity $m_L(H, \delta, \epsilon)$. In this section, we use Proposition 8.2.3 to obtain an explicit expression for m_0, and thus an upper bound for the sample complexity of any consistent learning algorithm L for H.

Recall that in Chapter 4 we showed that if H is a finite hypothesis space and L is a consistent learning algorithm for H, then L is pac and

$$m_L(H, \delta, \epsilon) \leq \left\lceil \frac{1}{\epsilon} \ln \left(\frac{|H|}{\delta} \right) \right\rceil.$$

The upper bound for $m_L(H, \delta, \epsilon)$ which will be derived in this section depends on the VC dimension of H, rather than the cardinality of H.

Theorem 8.4.1 Suppose that H is a hypothesis space of finite VC dimension $d \geq 1$ and that $0 < \delta, \epsilon < 1$. Let

$$m_0 = m_0(H, \delta, \epsilon) = \left\lceil \frac{4}{\epsilon} \left(d \lg \left(\frac{12}{\epsilon} \right) + \lg \left(\frac{2}{\delta} \right) \right) \right\rceil.$$

Then for any $m \geq m_0$,

$$\mu^m \left\{ \mathbf{s} \in S(m, t) \mid H[\mathbf{s}] \cap B_\epsilon \neq \emptyset \right\} < \delta.$$

Proof Let $t \in H$ be any target concept and let μ be any probability distribution on X. The given value of m_0 exceeds $8/\epsilon$, and so it follows from Proposition 8.2.3 that, for all $m \geq m_0$,

$$\mu^m \left\{ \mathbf{s} \in S(m, t) \mid H[\mathbf{s}] \cap B_\epsilon \neq \emptyset \right\} < 2 \, \Pi_H(2m) \, 2^{-\epsilon m/2}.$$

Also $m_0 > d$ and so, by Sauer's Lemma, $\Pi_H(2m) < (2em/d)^d$ whenever $m \geq m_0$. Therefore, it suffices to show that for all $m \geq m_0$,

$$2 \left(\frac{2em}{d} \right)^d 2^{-\epsilon m/2} \leq \delta.$$

Now,

$$2 \left(\frac{2em}{d} \right)^d 2^{-\epsilon m/2} \leq \delta$$

$$\Longleftrightarrow d \ln \left(\frac{2e}{d} \right) + d \ln m - \frac{\epsilon m}{2} \ln 2 \leq \ln \left(\frac{\delta}{2} \right)$$

$$\Longleftrightarrow \frac{\epsilon m}{2} \ln 2 - d \ln m \geq d \ln \left(\frac{2e}{d} \right) + \ln \left(\frac{2}{\delta} \right).$$

It can be verified easily by some elementary differential calculus (see Exercise 2) that, for any $x > 0$ and any $c > 0$,

$$\ln x \leq \left(\ln \left(\frac{1}{c} \right) - 1 \right) + cx.$$

Thus, choosing $c = \epsilon \ln 2/4d$ and $x = m$, we have

$$d \ln m \leq d \left(\ln \left(\frac{4d}{\epsilon \ln 2} \right) - 1 \right) + \frac{\epsilon \ln 2}{4} m.$$

Therefore, it will suffice to have

$$\frac{\epsilon m}{4} \ln 2 \geq d \ln \left(\frac{2e}{d} \right) + \ln \left(\frac{2}{\delta} \right) + d \ln \left(\frac{4d}{\epsilon \ln 2} \right) - d,$$

which, observing that $8/\ln 2 < 12$, is true if

$$m \geq \frac{4}{\epsilon} \left(d \lg \left(\frac{12}{\epsilon} \right) + \lg \left(\frac{2}{\delta} \right) \right).$$

The result follows. $\qquad\qquad\qquad\qquad\qquad\qquad\qquad\qquad\qquad\qquad\qquad$ □

Corollary 8.4.2 Suppose that hypothesis space H has VC dimension $d \geq 1$. Then any consistent learning algorithm L for H is pac, with sample complexity

$$m_L(H, \delta, \epsilon) \leq \left\lceil \frac{4}{\epsilon} \left(d \lg \left(\frac{12}{\epsilon} \right) + \lg \left(\frac{2}{\delta} \right) \right) \right\rceil.$$

$\qquad\qquad\qquad\qquad\qquad\qquad\qquad\qquad\qquad\qquad\qquad\qquad\qquad\qquad$ □

This corollary is the promised extension of the bound for finite spaces, mentioned at the beginning of the section, to spaces with finite VC dimension.

Example 8.4.3 Let H be the space of rays, as in Section 2.5. Then VCdim$(H) = 1$, and so if L is any consistent learning algorithm for the space of rays, we have

$$m_L(H, \delta, \epsilon) \leq \left\lceil \frac{4}{\epsilon} \left(\lg \left(\frac{12}{\epsilon} \right) + \lg \left(\frac{2}{\delta} \right) \right) \right\rceil.$$

In particular, this is an upper bound on the sample complexity of the learning algorithm described in Chapter 3. We proved directly there that this algorithm had sample complexity at most

$$m_0 = \left\lceil \frac{1}{\epsilon} \ln \left(\frac{1}{\delta} \right) \right\rceil.$$

In this case, the bound obtained directly is better than that given by the VC dimension. However, direct arguments are often difficult, and it is clear that if δ and ϵ are of the same order, then these bounds differ only by a constant factor. □

Example 8.4.4 The real perceptron P_n has VC dimension $n + 1$. Suppose that for any training sample for a hypothesis of P_n, we can find a state ω of the perceptron such that h_ω is consistent with the sample. Then if we use a training sample of length

$$\left\lceil \frac{4}{\epsilon} \left((n + 1) \lg \left(\frac{12}{\epsilon} \right) + \lg \left(\frac{2}{\delta} \right) \right) \right\rceil,$$

we are guaranteed a probably approximately correct output hypothesis, regardless of both the target hypothesis and the probability distribution on the examples. □

8.5 LOWER BOUNDS ON SAMPLE COMPLEXITY
At the beginning of the chapter, we proved that if H has infinite VC dimension, then it is not potentially learnable. We can refine the argument given there to provide the following simple result.

Theorem 8.5.1 Suppose that the hypothesis space H has VC dimension $d \geq 1$. Then there is a consistent pac learning algorithm L for H such that, for any δ and ϵ, the sample complexity satisfies

$$m_L(H, \delta, \epsilon) \geq d(1 - \epsilon).$$

Proof There is a sample $\mathbf{z}$ of length d which is shattered by H. Let $E = E_{\mathbf{z}}$ be the set of examples in $\mathbf{z}$ and let μ be the probability distribution that is uniform on E and zero elsewhere. Let t be any hypothesis in H and $\mathbf{s} = (\mathbf{x}, t(\mathbf{x})) \in S(m, t)$ any training sample for t. With probability 1, $\mathbf{x} \in E^m$. Since $\mathbf{z}$ is shattered by H, there is some $h \in H[\mathbf{s}]$ with $h(z_i) \neq t(z_i)$ for $z_i \in E \setminus E_{\mathbf{x}}$. Thus

$$\text{er}_\mu(h, t) = \frac{d - m}{d} > \epsilon,$$

provided $m < d(1 - \epsilon)$. Therefore, given any training sample $\mathbf{s}$ for t of length $m < d(1 - \epsilon)$, there is a hypothesis $h \in H[\mathbf{s}] \cap B_{\epsilon}$. We may define L so that $L(\mathbf{s}) = h$: then L is a consistent learning algorithm such that

$$\mu^m \left\{ \mathbf{s} \in S(m,t) \mid \mathrm{er}_{\mu} \left(L(\mathbf{s}) \right) > \epsilon \right\} = 1.$$

Thus

$$m_L(H, \delta, \epsilon) \geq d(1 - \epsilon),$$

as claimed.   □

The above result, although attractively simple, applies specifically to consistent learning algorithms. Furthermore, it does not provide a universal lower bound on the sample complexity of a consistent learning algorithm; rather, it deals only with a 'worst possible' consistent learning algorithm. We shall now present a more powerful result of Ehrenfeucht *et al.* (1989) which provides a lower bound on the sample complexity of *any* pac learning algorithm for a hypothesis space of finite VC dimension.

In order to prove this result we make use of another Chernoff bound (see Angluin and Valiant (1979) and McDiarmid (1989)). For $0 \leq p \leq 1$, let $GE(p, m, s)$ denote the probability of at least s successes in m independent trials each of which has a probability p of success. Then for any $0 \leq \beta \leq 1$,

$$GE\left(p, m, (1 + \beta)mp\right) \leq e^{-\beta^2 mp/3}.$$

Theorem 8.5.2 For any hypothesis space H of VC dimension $d \geq 1$, and for any pac learning algorithm L for H,

$$m_L(H, \delta, \epsilon) > \frac{d - 1}{32\epsilon},$$

for $\delta \leq 1/100$ and $\epsilon \leq 1/8$.

Proof We shall prove that there is some probability distribution μ and some hypothesis $t \in H$ such that for any $\epsilon \leq 1/8$ and for any positive integer $m \leq (d - 1)/32\epsilon$,

$$\mu^m \left\{ \mathbf{s} \in S(m,t) \mid \mathrm{er}_{\mu} \left(L\left(\mathbf{s} \right) \right) \geq \epsilon \right\} \geq \frac{1}{100}.$$

Since H has VC dimension d, there is a sample $\mathbf{z}$ of length d shattered by H. Let $E_{\mathbf{z}} = E$ be $\{z_0, z_1, z_2, \ldots, z_r\}$, where $r = d - 1$. Define a probability distribution μ on X by

$$\mu(z_0) = 1 - 8\epsilon, \qquad \mu(z_i) = \frac{8\epsilon}{r} \ (1 \leq i \leq r).$$

Then a randomly chosen sample $\mathbf{x}$ is, with probability one, a sample of examples from E. We therefore need consider only samples drawn from E, and we can regard the hypothesis space H to be simply the (finite) space of all $\{0,1\}$-valued functions defined on domain E: we make this assumption throughout the rest of this proof.

Suppose that L is a pac learning algorithm for H. For convenience, given a sample $\mathbf{x}$ and $h \in H$, we shall denote $L\left((\mathbf{x}, h(\mathbf{x}))\right)$ by $L(\mathbf{x}, h)$. Let H_0 be the set of hypotheses $h \in H$ for which $h(z_0) = 0$ and let F be the set $\{z_1, z_2, \ldots, z_r\}$.

Fix a particular sample $\mathbf{y} \in E^m$, and let l be the number of distinct elements of F appearing as examples in $\mathbf{y}$. Let $h \in H_0$ and let x be any one of the $(r - l)$ examples in F not appearing in $\mathbf{y}$. Now, H_0 shatters F, since H shatters $E = F \cup \{z_0\}$. Hence precisely half of the hypotheses h' in H_0 satisfy $h'(x) = 1$ (and half of them satisfy $h'(x) = 0$).

For $x \in F$, let us define $\Delta_x(\mathbf{y}, h)$ to be 1 if $L(\mathbf{y}, h)$ and h disagree on x and 0 otherwise. Then $D(\mathbf{y}, h) = \sum_{x \in F} \Delta_x(\mathbf{y}, h)$ is the number of x in F for which $L(\mathbf{y}, h)$ and h disagree. By the above remarks,

$$\sum_{h \in H_0} D(\mathbf{y}, h) = \sum_{h \in H_0} \sum_{x \in F} \Delta_x(\mathbf{y}, h) = \sum_{x \in F} \sum_{h \in H_0} \Delta_x(\mathbf{y}, h) \geq \sum_{x \in F \setminus E_\mathbf{y}} \frac{1}{2}|H_0| = \frac{1}{2}(r - l)|H_0|.$$

If $l < r/2$ then $(r - l) > r/2$. Hence, noting that $\mathbf{y}$ is arbitrary in the above analysis, if S is the set of samples which contain fewer than $r/2$ distinct elements of F, then we have

$$D = \sum_{\mathbf{x} \in S} \sum_{h \in H_0} D(\mathbf{x}, h) > \frac{r}{4}|H_0||S|.$$

We can interchange the order of summation to obtain

$$D = \sum_{h \in H_0} \sum_{\mathbf{x} \in S} D(\mathbf{x}, h) > \frac{r}{4}|S||H_0|,$$

from which it follows that for some $t \in H_0$,

$$\sum_{\mathbf{x} \in S} D(\mathbf{x}, t) > \frac{r}{4}|S|.$$

For any $\mathbf{x} \in S$, $D(\mathbf{x}, t) \leq r$, and so if N is the number of samples $\mathbf{x}$ in S such that $D(\mathbf{x}, t) > r/8$, then

$$\frac{r}{4}|S| < \sum_{\mathbf{x} \in S} D(\mathbf{x}, t) \leq Nr + (|S| - N)\frac{r}{8},$$

yielding $N \geq |S|/7$. Now, if $D(\mathbf{x}, t) \geq r/8$ then $L(\mathbf{x}, t)$ has error at least

$$\frac{8\epsilon}{r}\frac{r}{8} = \epsilon.$$

Hence (observing that each element of S has equal probability according to μ^m),

$$\mu^m \left\{ \mathbf{s} \in S(m, t) \;\middle|\; \mathrm{er}_\mu \left(L(\mathbf{s}) \right) \geq \epsilon \right\} \geq \frac{N}{|S|} \mu^m(S) \geq \frac{1}{7} \mu^m(S).$$

We can now apply the result on $GE(p, m, s)$. The probability that a point chosen according to the distribution μ lies in $F = \{z_1, z_2, \ldots, z_r\}$ is 8ϵ. The probability that a sample of length m has at least $d/2$ entries from F is therefore $GE(8\epsilon, m, r/2)$. If $m \leq r/32\epsilon$, this quantity is bounded as follows:

$$GE(8\epsilon, m, r/2) \leq GE\left(8\epsilon, \frac{r}{32\epsilon}, \frac{r}{2}\right) \leq e^{-r/12} \leq e^{-1/12} < \frac{93}{100}.$$

Therefore we have

$$m \leq \frac{r}{32\epsilon} = \frac{d-1}{32\epsilon} \implies \mu^m \left\{ \mathbf{s} \in S(m, t) \;\middle|\; \mathrm{er}_\mu \left(L(\mathbf{s}) \right) \geq \epsilon \right\} \geq \frac{1}{7} \frac{7}{100} = \frac{1}{100},$$

as required.   □

A trivial modification of the proof establishes that the sample complexity exceeds $(d_0 - 1)/32\epsilon$, where d_0 is any positive integer satisfying $\mathrm{VCdim}(H) \geq d_0$. So we have the following important consequence, which extends Theorem 8.2.1.

Corollary 8.5.3 If a hypothesis space H has infinite VC dimension then there is no pac learning algorithm for H.   □

These results, in particular Theorem 8.5.2, support the claim that the VC dimension is a good measure of the 'expressive power' of a hypothesis space H: the greater the VC dimension of H, the greater must be the sample complexity for pac learning H. In fact, the results can be generalised to cover the case when C is any concept space with VC dimension at least $d_0 \geq 1$ and H is any hypothesis space (not necessarily equal to C). If L is a learning algorithm for (C, H), the input to L must be a training sample of length greater than $(d_0 - 1)/32\epsilon$ in order to guarantee accuracy $\epsilon \leq 1/8$ with probability $1 - \delta > 99/100$. In particular, if C has infinite VC dimension then there can be no learning algorithm for (C, H) which is pac, for any hypothesis space H.

Example 8.5.4 If J is the interval union space of Example 8.2.2, then, because J has infinite VC dimension, there is *no* pac learning algorithm for (J, H) for *any* hypothesis space H. The above result is very strong. It shows not merely that there is no consistent or efficient pac learning algorithm, but also that, given unbounded computational resources, no algorithm can pac learn J, no matter how it represents its output hypotheses. Of course, these conclusions hold for any space of infinite VC dimension, such as the space of closed sets, or the space of characteristic functions of all polygonal regions in $\mathbf{R}^2$ (Exercise 3).   □

Another useful result concerning lower bounds is the following, due to Blumer *et al.* (1989). This bound involves ϵ and δ, but is independent of the VC dimension of the hypothesis space. It applies to *non-trivial* hypothesis spaces. By this we simply mean hypothesis spaces which consist of more than two hypotheses.

Theorem 8.5.5 Suppose that L is any pac learning algorithm for the non-trivial hypothesis space H. Then

$$m_L(H, \delta, \epsilon) > \frac{(1 - \epsilon)}{\epsilon} \ln\left(\frac{1}{\delta}\right),$$

for any $0 < \delta, \epsilon < 1$.

Proof Since H is non-trivial, it contains a hypothesis h_1 and another hypothesis h_2 which is not the 'complement' of h_1. It follows that we can find $a, b \in X$ such that $h_1(a) = h_2(a)$ and $h_1(b) = 1, h_2(b) = 0$. We give the proof for $h_1(a) = h_2(a) = 1$; the other case is analogous.

Let $0 < \delta, \epsilon < 1$ and let μ be the probability distribution for which $\mu(a) = 1 - \epsilon$ and $\mu(b) = \epsilon$ (and μ is zero elsewhere on X). The probability that a sample of length m has all its entries equal to a is $(1 - \epsilon)^m$. Now,

$$(1 - \epsilon)^m \geq \delta \iff m \ln(1 - \epsilon) \geq \ln \delta \iff m \leq \frac{1}{-\ln(1 - \epsilon)} \ln\left(\frac{1}{\delta}\right).$$

Further,

$$-\ln(1 - \epsilon) = \ln\left(1 + \frac{\epsilon}{1 - \epsilon}\right) \leq \frac{\epsilon}{1 - \epsilon}.$$

It follows that if

$$m \leq \frac{(1 - \epsilon)}{\epsilon} \ln\left(\frac{1}{\delta}\right)$$

then, with probability greater than δ, a sample $\mathbf{x}$ of length m has all its entries equal to a. Let $\mathbf{a}^1$ denote the training sample

$$\mathbf{a}^1 = ((a, 1), \ldots, (a, 1))$$

of length m. Then $\mathbf{a}^1$ is a training sample for both h_1 and h_2. Suppose that L is a pac learning algorithm for H. If b is a positive example of $L(\mathbf{a}^1)$ then $L(\mathbf{a}^1)$ has error at least ϵ (the probability of b) with respect to h_1, while if b is a negative example of $L(\mathbf{a}^1)$ then this hypothesis has error at least ϵ with respect to h_2. It follows that there is $t \in H$, which is either h_1 or h_2 as above, such that

$$m \leq \frac{(1-\epsilon)}{\epsilon} \ln\left(\frac{1}{\delta}\right) \implies \mu^m\left\{\mathbf{s} \in S(m,t) \mid \mathrm{er}_\mu\left(L(\mathbf{s})\right) > \epsilon\right\} > \delta.$$

The result follows.   □

8.6 COMPARISON OF SAMPLE COMPLEXITY BOUNDS

We have already mentioned in passing that many of the results in preceding sections can be generalised to deal with the case in which the concept space and the hypothesis space are different. In all cases the proof is easily supplied by making minor alterations to the proof as given above. In this section we shall compare the bounds for sample complexity, in this more general context.

First, it is clear that the following generalisation of Corollary 8.4.2 holds.

Theorem 8.6.1 Let C be a concept space and H a hypothesis space, and suppose that H has finite VC dimension at least 1. If L is any consistent learning algorithm for (C, H), then L is pac and the sample complexity of L satisfies

$$m_L(C, \delta, \epsilon) \leq \left\lceil \frac{4}{\epsilon}\left(\mathrm{VCdim}(H)\lg\left(\frac{12}{\epsilon}\right) + \lg\left(\frac{2}{\delta}\right)\right)\right\rceil,$$

for any δ and ϵ.   □

Secondly, generalising and combining Theorems 8.5.2 and 8.5.5, we obtain the following result.

Theorem 8.6.2 Let C be a concept space and H a hypothesis space, such that C has VC dimension at least 1. Suppose that L is any pac learning algorithm for (C, H). Then the sample complexity of L satisfies

$$m_L(C, \delta, \epsilon) > \max\left(\frac{\mathrm{VCdim}(C) - 1}{32\epsilon}, \frac{1}{\epsilon}\ln\left(\frac{1}{\delta}\right)\right),$$

for all $\epsilon \leq 1/8$ and $\delta \leq 1/100$.   □

The significant factors in the bounds are the VC dimensions of the concept and the hypothesis spaces, and the parameters ϵ and δ. To simplify matters, and to suppress the less important constant factors in these expressions, we can use the O-notation and the Ω-notation. We have already met the O-notation in our discussion of running time in Chapter 5. We can extend its use to positive real-valued functions as follows: we write $f = O(g)$ when there is some constant C such that for all relevant values of x (which may be a vector of real values) $f(x) \leq Cg(x)$. Similarly, we write $f = \Omega(g)$ when there is some positive constant K such that $f(x) \geq Kg(x)$.

Using these notations we can re-state the sample complexity bounds, remembering that the functions involved depend on the VC dimension of C or H and the accuracy and confidence parameters.

- If L is pac then C must have finite VC dimension, and

$$m_L(C, \delta, \epsilon) = \Omega \left(\frac{\text{VCdim}(C)}{\epsilon} + \frac{1}{\epsilon} \ln \left(\frac{1}{\delta} \right) \right).$$

- If H has finite VC dimension and L is consistent then L is pac, and

$$m_L(C, \delta, \epsilon) = O \left(\frac{\text{VCdim}(H)}{\epsilon} \ln \left(\frac{1}{\epsilon} \right) + \frac{1}{\epsilon} \ln \left(\frac{1}{\delta} \right) \right).$$

- If H is finite and L is consistent then L is pac and

$$m_L(C, \delta, \epsilon) = O \left(\frac{1}{\epsilon} \ln |H| + \frac{1}{\epsilon} \ln \left(\frac{1}{\delta} \right) \right).$$

In the case when $C = H$, the VC dimension d is finite, and L is consistent, we have the 'lower' and 'upper' bounds

$$m_L(H, \delta, \epsilon) = \Omega \left(\frac{d}{\epsilon} + \frac{1}{\epsilon} \ln \left(\frac{1}{\delta} \right) \right);$$

$$m_L(H, \delta, \epsilon) = O \left(\frac{d}{\epsilon} \ln \left(\frac{1}{\epsilon} \right) + \frac{1}{\epsilon} \ln \left(\frac{1}{\delta} \right) \right).$$

In general, the factor $\ln(1/\epsilon)$ which distinguishes the upper bound from the lower bound is unavoidable. Results of Haussler, Littlestone and Warmuth (1988) show that, for every $d \geq 1$ there is a hypothesis space H_d and a consistent learning algorithm L for H_d with sample complexity meeting the upper bound. On the other hand, it is an open problem to decide whether for every d and for every concept space C of VC dimension d, there is *some* hypothesis space H and *some* (C, H) learning algorithm L for which the sample complexity meets the lower bound.

In the next chapter we shall see that for many interesting hypothesis spaces there are pac learning algorithms which are optimal, in the sense that the sample complexity meets the lower bound.

FURTHER REMARKS

The condition of potential learnability implies that a consistent learning algorithm is pac. However, we should like to give performance guarantees for learning algorithms which output hypotheses not necessarily consistent with the training sample, but rather only consistent on at least a definite fraction of the sample. The theory developed in Section 8.3 can be modified to cover this case; see Vapnik (1982), Pollard (1984), Anthony (1991) for details. It follows from this theory that, for hypothesis spaces of finite VC dimension, the following holds (as for finite spaces). For any fixed constant $\alpha < 1$, there is a function $m_0(\alpha, \delta, \epsilon)$ such that if a hypothesis h disagrees with at most a fraction $\alpha\epsilon$ of a training sample of length m_0, then, with probability at least $1 - \delta$, h has actual error less than ϵ. Thus, for spaces of finite VC dimension, one can, by taking long enough training samples, infer from small observed error that a hypothesis has small actual error.

EXERCISES

1. Let H be a hypothesis space with the property that for any $t \in H$ and any $0 < \delta, \epsilon < 1$, there is $m_0(t, \delta, \epsilon)$ such that

$$m \geq m_0(t, \delta, \epsilon) \implies \mu^m \left\{ \mathbf{s} \in S(m, t) \mid H[\mathbf{s}] \cap B_\epsilon = \emptyset \right\} > 1 - \delta$$

for any probability distribution μ on the input space. Thus, m_0 can depend on the target concept. Following the proof of Theorem 8.2.1, show that H must have finite VC dimension and is therefore potentially learnable. (See Ben-David *et al.* (1989) for similar results.)

2. Prove that for any $c > 0$,

$$\ln x \leq \left(\ln \left(\frac{1}{c} \right) - 1 \right) + cx,$$

for all $x > 0$. (This result is useful in proving Theorem 8.4.1.)

3. Show that the space of characteristic functions of closed and bounded polygonal regions of the plane $\mathbf{R}^2$ is not pac learnable.

4. Suppose that H is *any* hypothesis space of finite VC dimension $d \geq 1$ and that L is *any* consistent learning algorithm for H. Given that there is *some* fixed probability distribution on the example space, how large a random training sample would you present in order to obtain, with at least a 90% chance, a hypothesis which has error less than 5%?

5. A boolean function f is said to be *symmetric* if $f(x)$ depends only on the number of entries of x which are equal to 1. For example, for any n, the parity concept

defined on $\{0,1\}^n$ is symmetric. Let n be a positive integer, and let S_n denote the set of all symmetric functions defined on $\{0,1\}^n$. What is the VC dimension of S_n? Give upper and lower bounds on the sample complexity of any consistent pac learning algorithm for S_n. Note that any hypothesis h of S_n can be represented by a vector $(h_0, h_1, \ldots, h_n) \in \{0,1\}^n$, where h_i is the value of h on examples having precisely i ones. Devise a consistent learning algorithm for S_n which represents the space in this way.

6. Let H, G be hypothesis spaces defined on the same example space X. For hypotheses $h \in H, g \in G$, define $h \vee g$ by

$$h \vee g = \begin{cases} 1, & \text{if } h(x) = 1 \text{ or } g(x) = 1; \\ 0, & \text{otherwise}, \end{cases}$$

and let

$$H \vee G = \{h \vee g \mid h \in H, g \in G\}.$$

Prove that

$$\Pi_{H \vee G}(m) \leq \Pi_H(m)\, \Pi_G(m)$$

for all m. Defining $H \wedge G$ in the obvious (dual) manner, prove the analogous result for this space. Deduce that if H and G are potentially learnable, then so too are $H \vee G$ and $H \wedge G$.

7. Let H be a hypothesis space of finite VC dimension $d \geq 1$ and, for $s \geq 1$, define $H(s)$ inductively by setting $H(1) = H$ and

$$H(k) = H \vee H(k-1) \quad (k \geq 2).$$

Using Exercise 6 and Sauer's Lemma, prove that for $m > d$,

$$\Pi_{H(s)} \leq \left(\frac{em}{d}\right)^{sd}.$$

Hence show that the VC dimension of $H(s)$ is at most $2sd \lg(3s)$. (This is a result of Blumer *et al.* (1989).)
[Hint: Use the fact that if D is the VC dimension of $H(s)$ then $\Pi_{H(s)}(D) = 2^D$. To obtain the bound on the VC dimension, it may be helpful to use the result of Exercise 2.]

8. Suppose that $H_1, H_2, \ldots, H_s$ are hypothesis spaces on the same example space, and that each is linearly ordered (see Exercise 8 of Chapter 7). Prove that the hypothesis space $H = H_1 \vee H_2 \vee \ldots \vee H_s$ has VC dimension at most s. (This is a result of Wenocur and Dudley (1981).)
[Hint: Let $\mathbf{x}$ be a sample of length $s + 1$. How many vectors with only one entry equal to 1 can be realised as classification vectors of $\mathbf{x}$ by H?]

Chapter 9: VC Dimension and Efficient Learning

9.1 GRADED REAL HYPOTHESIS SPACES

In Chapters 5 and 6 we made a careful study of the efficiency of learning algorithms for graded boolean hypothesis spaces. In this chapter, we shall consider the corresponding notions for real hypothesis spaces, obtaining a comprehensive theory of efficiency of learning algorithms, for both real and boolean spaces.

Recall that a graded boolean hypothesis space is defined to be a disjoint union $H = \bigcup H_n$ of spaces of boolean functions, where H_n consists of hypotheses defined on $\{0,1\}^n$. Similarly, we define a *graded real hypothesis space* to be a disjoint union $H = \bigcup H_n$, where H_n is a real hypothesis space defined on (possibly some subset of) n-dimensional Euclidean space $\mathbf{R}^n$. Thus, the *example size* of a vector with real entries is taken to be precisely the length of the vector, or the dimension of the space containing the vector. This corresponds to the definition of example size in the boolean case, since a boolean example is a vector with coordinates 0 and 1, and its size is simply the length of this vector.

Example 9.1.1 A simple example of a graded real space is the *perceptron space* $P = \bigcup P_n$, where P_n is the hypothesis space of the real perceptron on n inputs (as defined in Section 7.1). Here, following the usual convention, we use the same notation for the machine and its hypothesis space. Recall that P_n has a geometric interpretation; it is the set of characteristic functions of closed half-spaces in n-dimensional Euclidean space $\mathbf{R}^n$. □

Example 9.1.2 The *non-negative quadrant* $\mathbf{R}_+^2$ in two dimensions is the set of points (y_1, y_2) with $y_1 \geq 0, y_2 \geq 0$. The translate of $\mathbf{R}_+^2$ by any vector $v = (v_1, v_2)$ is also known as a *quadrant*:

$$\mathbf{R}_+^2 + v = \{(y_1, y_2) \mid y_1 \geq v_1, y_2 \geq v_2\} = [v_1, \infty) \times [v_2, \infty).$$

In general, for a positive integer n, the *non-negative quadrant* $\mathbf{R}_+^n$ is the set of vectors in $\mathbf{R}^n$ with every entry non-negative, and the translate of $\mathbf{R}_+^n$ by the real n-vector

$v = (v_1, v_2, \ldots, v_n)$ is the quadrant

$$\mathbf{R}_+^n + v = [v_1, \infty) \times \ldots \times [v_n, \infty).$$

We denote by Q_n the space of characteristic functions of such sets, together with the *empty quadrant* — the identically-0 function. We call Q_n the *n-dimensional quadrant space*. The hypotheses of Q_n are the identically-0 function and the functions q_v, for $v \in \mathbf{R}^n$, where

$$q_v(y_1 y_2 \ldots y_n) = \begin{cases} 1, & \text{if } y_i \geq v_i \ (1 \leq i \leq n); \\ 0, & \text{otherwise.} \end{cases}$$

Note that the space Q_1 is precisely the space of rays, introduced in Chapter 3. We call the graded space $Q = \bigcup Q_n$ the *quadrant space*.   □

Example 9.1.3 In Exercise 6 of Chapter 3, we defined the space of *intervals*. This is the space of characteristic functions of all closed and bounded intervals $[\alpha, \beta]$ in $\mathbf{R}$. Here we shall denote this space by B_1. An obvious generalisation is obtained by considering the subsets of $\mathbf{R}^2$ of the form $[\alpha_1, \beta_1] \times [\alpha_2, \beta_2]$, which consists of all (y_1, y_2) with $\alpha_1 \leq y_1 \leq \beta_1$ and $\alpha_2 \leq y_2 \leq \beta_2$. We shall call this set, the cartesian product of two closed and bounded intervals, a *box*, and we define B_2, the space of boxes in $\mathbf{R}^2$, to be the space of characteristic functions of all such sets. It is clear that we may generalise further; B_n is the space of characteristic functions of subsets of $\mathbf{R}^n$ which are n-fold cartesian products of closed and bounded intervals. In addition, each B_n shall contain the identically-0 function, which in this context is called the *empty box*. We shall call the graded space $B = \bigcup B_n$ the space of *boxes*.   □

We may define a learning algorithm for a graded real space as for graded boolean spaces. Thus, a learning algorithm for $H = \bigcup H_n$ is a function L, from the set of training samples for hypotheses in H, to H, such that when $\mathbf{s}$ is a training sample for a hypothesis in H_n, we have $L(\mathbf{s}) \in H_n$.

Example 9.1.4 There is a simple learning algorithm for the quadrant space $Q = \bigcup Q_n$. Given a training sample $\mathbf{s}$ for a hypothesis of Q_n, if $\mathbf{s}$ contains positive examples, we take $L(\mathbf{s})$ to be (the characteristic function of) the 'least' translate of the non-negative quadrant that contains all the positive examples in the sample. That is, if there are positive examples in $\mathbf{s}$, we have $L(\mathbf{s}) = q_v$ where, for each $1 \leq j \leq n$,

$$v_j = \min_{1 \leq i \leq m} \{(x_i)_j \mid b_i = 1\}.$$

The actual calculation of the minima may be done by the same technique as used for the space Q_1 of rays (Section 3.1). Indeed, the algorithm for Q_n may be thought of as n learning algorithms for Q_1 running in parallel. If $\mathbf{s}$ contains only negative examples, we let $L(\mathbf{s})$ be the empty quadrant. In either case, it is clear that $L(\mathbf{s})$ is consistent with $\mathbf{s}$.   □

Example 9.1.5 There is also a consistent learning algorithm for the space of boxes. To help motivate this algorithm, consider first the space B_1. Suppose the target concept t is the characteristic function of $[\alpha^*, \beta^*]$, and that we are given a training sample $\mathbf{s}$ for t. Let us suppose that $\mathbf{s}$ contains at least one positive example; for any such example x, we know $\alpha^* < x \leq \beta^*$. Let α denote the minimal positive example in the sample, and β the maximal one. Then the characteristic function of $[\alpha, \beta]$ correctly classifies all examples in $\mathbf{s}$; furthermore, it is, in a sense, the 'smallest' hypothesis of B_1 consistent with $\mathbf{s}$. Therefore if $\mathbf{s}$ contains positive examples, we take $L(\mathbf{s})$ to be this hypothesis. On the other hand, if $\mathbf{s}$ consists only of negative examples, then we take $L(\mathbf{s})$ to be the empty interval, which is again consistent with $\mathbf{s}$. The action of L on B_n is defined similarly: given a training sample which contains some positive examples, L finds the smallest box consistent with the sample, and returns the corresponding hypothesis. If the training sample contains no positive examples, then L outputs the empty box. It is easy to see that L is a consistent learning algorithm. Explicitly, the algorithm may be described as follows.

```
empty:= true;
for i:= 1 to m do
    if bᵢ = 1 then
        if empty then
            begin
            for j:= 1 to n do
                set αⱼ = (xᵢ)ⱼ and βⱼ = (xᵢ)ⱼ;
            empty:= false
            end
                    else
            for j:= 1 to n do
                begin
                if (xᵢ)ⱼ > βⱼ then set βⱼ = (xᵢ)ⱼ;
                if (xᵢ)ⱼ < αⱼ then set αⱼ = (xᵢ)ⱼ
                end
    if empty then set L(s) = empty box
        else set L(s) = [α₁, β₁] × [α₂, β₂] × ... [αₙ, βₙ]
```

□

The measure of example size and the definition of learning algorithms for graded real hypothesis spaces are, as we have seen, generalisations of those for graded boolean spaces. Therefore we shall often use the term *graded hypothesis space* to refer to either a graded boolean hypothesis space or a graded real hypothesis space.

9.2 EFFICIENT LEARNING OF GRADED SPACES

In an attempt to discuss efficiency of learning algorithms for graded spaces, we may take an initial approach similar to that of Section 5.3. Let $H = \bigcup H_n$ be a graded hypothesis space, and suppose that L is a learning algorithm for H. Then we have

$$\text{VCdim}(H_n) \text{ finite} \implies H_n \text{ potentially learnable};$$

$$H_n \text{ potentially learnable} \quad \text{and} \quad L \text{ consistent for } H_n \implies L \text{ pac learns } H_n.$$

The first of these implications is the main result of the previous chapter (Theorem 8.3.1), while the second comes from Chapter 4.

A learning algorithm L for the graded space $H = \bigcup H_n$ is *efficient with respect to example size* if, for fixed confidence and accuracy parameters, L can pac learn H_n in time bounded polynomially in n. In addition, we say that L is *efficient with respect to confidence and accuracy* if, for a fixed n, L can pac learn H_n to accuracy ϵ with confidence $1 - \delta$ in time polynomial in $\delta^* = \ln(\delta^{-1})$ and ϵ^{-1}. An immediate problem is to formulate conditions which ensure that, in these terms, L pac learns $H = \bigcup H_n$ efficiently.

We now describe some important general results which extend those of Chapters 5 and 6 for boolean spaces. As we shall see in the next section, these results provide more complete answers to some of the issues raised in previous chapters. It will be convenient to discuss simultaneously efficiency with respect to example size and efficiency with respect to confidence and accuracy. The following straightforward result, analogous to Theorem 5.3.1, provides *sufficient* conditions for a consistent learning algorithm to be efficient with respect to example size.

Theorem 9.2.1 Let $H = \bigcup H_n$ be a graded hypothesis space and suppose that L is a consistent learning algorithm for H with running time $R_L(m, n)$. If
- $R_L(m, n)$ is polynomial in m and n, and
- $\text{VCdim}(H_n)$ is polynomial in n,

then L is a pac learning algorithm for H, efficient with respect to example size, confidence, and accuracy.

Proof By Corollary 8.4.2, L, as a consistent learning algorithm for H_n, is pac and its sample complexity satisfies

$$m_L(H_n, \delta, \epsilon) \leq m_0(H_n, \delta, \epsilon) = \left\lceil \frac{4}{\epsilon} \left(\text{VCdim}(H_n) \lg \left(\frac{12}{\epsilon} \right) + \lg \left(\frac{2}{\delta} \right) \right) \right\rceil.$$

An upper bound on the running time of L to pac learn H_n is $R_L(m_0(H_n, \delta, \epsilon), n)$. Since VCdim($H_n$) is polynomial in n, m_0 is polynomial in n, δ^* and ϵ^{-1}. Further, since $R_L(m, n)$ is polynomial in m and n, it follows that the running time is also polynomial in n, δ^* and ϵ^{-1}. □

In this theorem, the quantity VCdim(H_n) replaces the $\ln|H_n|$ of Theorem 5.3.1. When H_n is finite for each n, we have the relationship VCdim(H_n) $\leq \lg|H_n|$. Therefore if $\ln|H_n|$ is polynomial in n, so too is VCdim(H_n). Hence this result subsumes Theorem 5.3.1. (Of course, a corresponding result holds for ungraded spaces: if H is a hypothesis space of finite VC dimension and L is any consistent learning algorithm for H which runs in time polynomial in m, then L is a pac learning algorithm, efficient with respect to confidence and accuracy.)

Example 9.2.2 The learning algorithm L for the quadrant space $Q = \bigcup Q_n$ is consistent, and has running time $R_L(m, n) = O(mn)$ since, for each of the positive examples in the sample, the algorithm makes n comparisons.

We shall show that VCdim(Q_n) $= n$. (In fact, only the result VCdim(Q_n) $\leq n$ is needed for the present application, but we obtain the exact result for the sake of completeness.) Let $\mathbf{x} = (x_1, x_2, \ldots, x_{n+1})$ be a sample of length $n + 1$, where each example is a real n-vector. For each coordinate position j, let j^* be such that the example x_{j^*} has the least jth coordinate of the examples in $\mathbf{x}$; if there are several examples with this property, choose any one of them. Since there are n values of j and $n + 1$ examples, there is an example which is not in the set $\{x_{j^*} \mid 1 \leq j \leq n\}$. We may suppose the notation is chosen so that x_1 is such an example. Then

$$(x_1)_j \geq (x_{j^*})_j \quad (1 \leq j \leq n).$$

Now, there can be no hypothesis $q_v \in Q_n$ for which

$$q_v(x_1) = 0, \quad q_v(x_2) = \ldots = q_v(x_{n+1}) = 1.$$

For if all conditions except the first hold we must have $v_j \leq (x_i)_j$ for all (i, j) in the ranges $(2 \leq i \leq n + 1, 1 \leq j \leq n)$. The choice of x_1 ensures that $v_j \leq (x_{j^*})_j \leq (x_1)_j$ for j between 1 and n, so that we must have $q_v(x_1) = 1$ also. This shows that not all classifications of an $(n + 1)$-sample can be realised, whence VCdim(Q_n) $\leq n$.

In order to show that VCdim(Q_n) $= n$ we construct an n-sample $\mathbf{z} = (z_1, z_2, \ldots, z_n)$ which is shattered by Q_n. Let z_i $(1 \leq i \leq n)$ be the vector with 1 in all coordinates except the ith, which is 0. Let T be any subset of $\{z_1, z_2, \ldots, z_n\}$. If $T = \emptyset$ take v to be the all-1 vector. If $T \neq \emptyset$ define $v = (v_1, \ldots, v_n)$ as follows:

$$v_j = \begin{cases} 1, & \text{if } (z_i)_j = 1 \text{ for all } z_i \in T; \\ 0, & \text{otherwise.} \end{cases}$$

Clearly, $q_v(z_i) = 1$ for all $z_i \in T$. On the other hand, if $z_i \notin T$ then every member of T has ith coordinate equal to 1. Then, by definition, $v_i = 1$, and since $(z_i)_i = 0$ it follows that $q_v(z_i) = 0$. Hence $\mathbf{z}$ is shattered by Q_n, as claimed.

It follows from Theorem 9.2.1 that L is a pac learning algorithm for $Q = \bigcup Q_n$ which is efficient with respect to example size, confidence and accuracy.   □

Example 9.2.3 The consistent learning algorithm for the space $B = \bigcup B_n$ of boxes, described in Example 9.1.5, has running time $O(mn)$. Furthermore, it can be shown that B_n has VC dimension $2n$ (Exercise 5). It follows that B is pac learnable efficiently with respect to example size, confidence, and accuracy. We may follow the argument given in the proof of Theorem 9.2.1 to obtain an explicit bound on the running time of L as a pac learning algorithm. Since $\mathrm{VCdim}(B_n) = 2n$, the sample complexity of L on H_n satisfies

$$m_L(H_n, \delta, \epsilon) \le m_0(H_n, \delta, \epsilon) = O\left(\frac{n}{\epsilon}\ln\left(\frac{1}{\epsilon}\right) + \frac{1}{\epsilon}\ln\left(\frac{1}{\delta}\right)\right) = O\left(\frac{n}{\epsilon}\ln\left(\frac{1}{\epsilon\delta}\right)\right).$$

It follows that L pac learns H_n in running time

$$R_L(m_0(H_n, \delta, \epsilon), n) = O\left(\frac{n^2}{\epsilon}\ln\left(\frac{1}{\epsilon\delta}\right)\right),$$

polynomial in n, δ^* and ϵ^{-1}.   □

The following key result from the paper of Blumer *et al.* (1989) (see also Pitt and Valiant (1988) and Haussler *et al.* (1988)) provides *necessary* conditions for a graded hypothesis space to be pac learnable efficiently with respect to example size.

Theorem 9.2.4 Let $H = \bigcup H_n$ be a graded hypothesis space and suppose there is a learning algorithm for H which pac learns H_n in time polynomial in ϵ^{-1} and n. Then
- $\mathrm{VCdim}(H_n)$ is polynomial in n, and
- there is a randomised algorithm L which solves the problem of finding a hypothesis in H_n consistent with a given training sample, and which has running time $R_L(m, n)$ polynomial in m and n.

Proof To obtain the first condition we use the lower bound result, Theorem 8.5.2. Suppose that L is a pac learning algorithm for $H = \bigcup H_n$ which has running time polynomial in n. By Theorem 8.5.2, the sample complexity of L satisfies

$$m_L\left(H_n, \frac{1}{2}, \frac{1}{2}\right) = \Omega\left(\mathrm{VCdim}(H_n)\right).$$

Since L must be presented with at least this many examples in order to produce a probably approximately correct hypothesis, the running time of L is $\Omega\left(\mathrm{VCdim}(H_n)\right)$.

Therefore, if the running time is polynomial in n, then we certainly must have VCdim(H_n) polynomial in n.

Theorem 6.2.1, which provides a link between pac learning boolean spaces efficiently with respect to accuracy and the existence of randomised consistent-hypothesis-finders, is equally valid for real hypothesis spaces, as can be seen from inspection of its proof. Thus, if there is a learning algorithm L for H_n which has running time polynomial in c^{-1}, then there is a polynomial time randomised consistent-hypothesis-finder for H_n. If L runs in time polynomial in n, then so too does this latter algorithm. This gives us the second of the necessary conditions.   □

Thus, allowing randomised learning algorithms, H is pac learnable efficiently with respect to example size, confidence and accuracy *if and only if* the VC dimension of H_n is bounded by some polynomial in n *and* there is an efficient consistent-hypothesis-finder for H.

9.3 VC DIMENSION AND BOOLEAN SPACES

In this section, we return again to learning algorithms for graded *boolean* hypothesis spaces. We have remarked that the results in the previous section apply to such spaces, and that they generalise corresponding results from Chapters 5 and 6. However, as we shall see, these results have other significant implications for learning boolean spaces.

Suppose that $H = \bigcup H_n$ is a graded boolean space. In Theorem 5.3.1 we showed that if L is a consistent learning algorithm for H with running time $R_L(m, n)$ polynomial in m and n, and if $\ln |H_n|$ is polynomial in n, then L is a pac learning algorithm for H which is efficient with respect to example size (and also with respect to confidence and accuracy). This was a one-way implication, and at that stage we could not claim the converse: that if such an algorithm exists, then $\ln |H_n|$ must be polynomial in n. However, one can use the results of the previous section to prove a strong version of the converse, which applies to any pac learning algorithm, consistent or not.

We require a simple but important lemma which provides a connection between VC dimension and cardinality for boolean spaces.

Lemma 9.3.1 Suppose that $H = \bigcup H_n$ is a boolean hypothesis space. Then $\ln |H_n|$ is polynomial in n if and only if VCdim(H_n) is polynomial in n.

Proof If $\ln |H_n|$ is polynomial in n then certainly so is $\lg |H_n|$. The 'only if' implication then follows directly from the fact that VCdim(H_n) $\leq \lg |H_n|$.

Conversely, suppose $\text{VCdim}(H_n) \leq p(n)$ for some polynomial p. H_n is defined on the finite example space $\{0,1\}^n$, of cardinality 2^n. Hence, by Proposition 7.5.4,

$$p(n) \geq \text{VCdim}(H_n) > \frac{\ln|H_n|}{1 + n \ln 2}.$$

Therefore

$$\ln|H_n| \leq p(n)\,(1 + n \ln 2),$$

which is polynomial in n. $\square$

The following result is due to Natarajan (1989) and Blumer *et al.* (1989). In view of the previous lemma, the result is a consequence of Theorem 9.2.4.

Theorem 9.3.2 Suppose that $H = \bigcup H_n$ is a graded boolean space and that there is a pac learning algorithm for H which has running time polynomial in n. Then $\ln|H_n|$ is polynomial in n. $\square$

It is worth remarking that a stronger result is true. Suppose that $C = \bigcup C_n$ is any graded boolean concept space, and that $H = \bigcup H_n$ is *any* graded boolean hypothesis space. Using the more general lower bound result, Theorem 8.6.2, the proof of the above theorem can be adapted to show that if $\ln|C_n|$ is not polynomial in n, there can be no pac learning algorithm for (C, H) which is efficient with respect to example size.

Example 9.3.3 Consider the graded space $DNF = \bigcup DNF_n$ of all boolean functions (represented in disjunctive normal form). We have $|DNF_n| = 2^{2^n}$, so that $\ln|DNF_n| = 2^n \ln 2$. This is exponential in n and so there is no pac learning algorithm for DNF which has running time polynomial in n. Note, however, that as explained in Section 6.7, this result does not preclude the existence of an epac learning algorithm for DNF, with respect to the disjunctive normal form representation. $\square$

Combining Lemma 9.3.1 with Theorem 9.2.4, we have

Theorem 9.3.4 Let $H = \bigcup H_n$ be a graded boolean hypothesis space and suppose there is a learning algorithm for H which pac learns H_n in time polynomial in ϵ^{-1} and n. Then

- $\ln|H_n|$ is polynomial in n, and
- there is a randomised algorithm which solves the problem of finding a hypothesis in H_n consistent with a given training sample, and which has running time $R_L(m, n)$ polynomial in m and n. $\square$

Hence, allowing randomised algorithms, a boolean space is pac learnable efficiently with respect to example size, confidence and accuracy *if and only if* $\ln |H_n|$ is polynomial in n *and* there is an efficient consistent-hypothesis-finder for H.

9.4 OPTIMAL SAMPLE COMPLEXITY FOR BOOLEAN SPACES

We say that a pac learning algorithm L for a graded space $H = \bigcup H_n$ has *optimal sample complexity* if, for any pac learning algorithm L' for H,

$$m_L(H_n, \delta, \epsilon) = O\left(m_{L'}(H_n, \delta, \epsilon)\right).$$

Informally, L has optimal sample complexity if any other pac learning algorithm for H requires at least (of the order of) as many examples as does L in order to produce a probably approximately correct hypothesis.

Section 8.6 provides explicit upper bounds on the sample complexity of consistent pac learning algorithms, and lower bounds on the sample complexity of (not necessarily consistent) pac learning algorithms, in terms of the VC dimension of the spaces involved. Using these bounds, we obtain the following result, due to Ehrenfeucht *et al.* (1988).

Theorem 9.4.1 Let $H = \bigcup H_n$ be a graded boolean hypothesis space. If

$$\ln |H_n| = O\left(\text{VCdim}(H_n)\right),$$

then any consistent learning algorithm for H has optimal sample complexity.

Proof Suppose that

$$\ln |H_n| = O\left(\text{VCdim}(H_n)\right),$$

and that L is a consistent learning algorithm for H. Since H_n is finite, we have

$$m_L(H_n, \delta, \epsilon) = O\left(\frac{1}{\epsilon}\ln |H_n| + \frac{1}{\epsilon}\ln\left(\frac{1}{\delta}\right)\right) = O\left(\frac{\text{VCdim}(H_n)}{\epsilon} + \frac{1}{\epsilon}\ln\left(\frac{1}{\delta}\right)\right).$$

Now, as in Section 8.6, if L' is *any* pac learning algorithm for H, then

$$m_{L'}(H_n, \delta, \epsilon) = \Omega\left(\frac{\text{VCdim}(H_n)}{\epsilon} + \frac{1}{\epsilon}\ln\left(\frac{1}{\delta}\right)\right).$$

Comparing these two results,

$$m_L(H_n, \delta, \epsilon) = O\left(m_{L'}(H_n, \delta, \epsilon)\right)$$

and hence L has optimal sample complexity.   □

Note that the 'reverse' condition $\mathrm{VCdim}(H_n) = O\left(\ln|H_n|\right)$ always holds because

$$\mathrm{VCdim}(H_n) \leq \lg|H_n| = \frac{\ln|H_n|}{\ln 2}.$$

However, there are boolean spaces for which the condition $\ln|H_n| = O(\mathrm{VCdim}(H_n))$ fails; one such space BP_n will be defined in the next chapter. But from Proposition 7.5.4 we have

$$\ln|H_n| < (1 + n\ln 2)\,\mathrm{VCdim}(H_n),$$

(assuming H_n consists of more than one hypothesis) and hence for any boolean hypothesis space, $\ln|H_n| = O\left(n\,\mathrm{VCdim}(H_n)\right).$

Example 9.4.2 Consider the space $M = \bigcup M_n$ of monomials. Recall (Example 7.3.4) that $n \leq \mathrm{VCdim}(M_n) \leq n\ln 3$ and $\ln|M_n| = n\ln 3$. Therefore

$$\ln|M_n| = O\left(\mathrm{VCdim}(M_n)\right) = O(n).$$

It follows that the standard learning algorithm for monomials has optimal sample complexity, since it is consistent. $\qquad\square$

Example 9.4.3 We described, in Chapter 2, a consistent learning algorithm L for the space $D_k = \bigcup D_{n,k}$ of disjunctions of small monomials. Ehrenfeucht *et al.* (1988), showed, as follows, that $\mathrm{VCdim}(D_{n,k}) = \Omega(n^k)$. Consider the set S of examples in $\{0,1\}^n$ which have precisely k entries equal to 1. Then S can be shattered by $D_{n,k}$. Indeed, suppose T is any subset of S. For each $x = (x_1, x_2, \ldots, x_n) \in T$, form the monomial which is the conjunction of those literals u_i such that $x_i = 1$. Since $x \in S$, this monomial has k literals; further, x is the only positive example in S of this monomial. The disjunction of these monomials, one for each member of T, is therefore a hypothesis in $D_{n,k}$ whose positive examples in S are precisely the members of T. But T was any subset of S and hence S is shattered by $D_{n,k}$. Now,

$$|S| = \binom{n}{k} = \frac{n(n-1)\ldots(n-k+1)}{k(k-1)\ldots 1},$$

which, for a fixed k, is $\Omega(n^k)$. Further, for $n \geq k > 1$, $|D_{n,k}| \leq 2^{(2n)^k}$ (see Chapter 2, Exercise 7), and so

$$\ln|D_{n,k}| \leq (2n)^k \ln 2 = O(n^k).$$

It follows that

$$\ln|D_{n,k}| = O\left(\mathrm{VCdim}(D_{n,k})\right) = O(n^k),$$

and the learning algorithm L has optimal sample complexity. $\qquad\square$

9.5 EFFICIENCY WITH RESPECT TO REPRESENTATIONS

Recall that the space B_1 of intervals is the space of characteristic functions of all closed intervals $[\alpha, \beta]$ on the real line (together with the identically-0 function). For any $r \geq 1$, let B_1^r be the space of (characteristic functions of) subsets of $\mathbf{R}$ which can be realised as the union of r disjoint closed intervals. For example, for each $\omega = (\alpha_1, \beta_1, \alpha_2, \beta_2)$ with $\alpha_1 \leq \beta_1 \leq \alpha_2 \leq \beta_2$, we have the hypothesis $h_\omega \in B_1^2$ defined by

$$h_\omega(y) = \begin{cases} 1, & \text{if } \alpha_1 \leq y \leq \beta_1 \text{ or } \alpha_2 \leq y \leq \beta_2; \\ 0, & \text{otherwise.} \end{cases}$$

That is, h_ω is the characteristic function of the set $[\alpha_2, \beta_2] \cup [\alpha_2, \beta_2]$. There is a representation $\mathbf{R}^{2r} \to B_1^r$ for each r; a hypothesis in B_1^r is represented by the real numbers $\alpha_1, \beta_1, \alpha_2, \beta_2, \dots, \alpha_r, \beta_r$, the end-points of the r intervals forming the union. The representation size of a hypothesis in B_1^r may be taken as $2r$, the number of real numbers needed to describe it. Note that this takes no account of the need to approximate a real number by a finite decimal expansion; such an approach is characteristic of what is known as the *unit cost* model for computations with real numbers.

Example 9.5.1 Let $I_n = \bigcup B_n^r$ be the hypothesis space of (characteristic functions of) finite unions of n-dimensional boxes. We call I_n the *n-dimensional box union space*. So I_1 is the interval union space J (Example 8.2.2). For completeness, we shall assume the *empty box*, the identically-0 function, belongs to each I_n. Clearly, an n-dimensional box can be represented by $2n$ real numbers; for example, the box $[\alpha_1, \beta_1] \times [\alpha_2, \beta_2]$ in $\mathbf{R}^2$ is represented by $(\alpha_1, \beta_1, \alpha_2, \beta_2)$. In general, $2nr$ real numbers are needed to represent a hypothesis in B_n^r: $2n$ real numbers for each of the r boxes. We therefore take the representation size of a hypothesis in B_n^r to be $2nr$.   □

As for boolean hypothesis spaces, we may grade a real space by representation size. For example, the interval union space J can be graded as $J = \bigcup J_r$, where $J_r = B_1^r$ comprises unions of r intervals. (Note that the hypotheses of J_r have representation size $2r$, not r; this causes no difficulty.) We may discuss the learnability of such spaces in the usual way. Suppose that $H = \bigcup H_r$ is a hypothesis space graded by representation size. We say that a learning algorithm L for H is *efficient with respect to representation size* if for each r, L is a pac learning algorithm for (H_r, H), with running time polynomial in r.

Example 9.5.2 We shall describe a consistent algorithm for learning the space J_r of r-fold interval unions by J. Suppose the training sample

$$\mathbf{s} = ((x_1, b_1), (x_2, b_2), \dots, (x_m, b_m))$$

for a hypothesis in J_r is given. The first step is to arrange the examples in increasing order, which requires $O(m \ln m)$ comparisons. Assuming this has been done, we choose the notation so that

$$x_1 \leq x_2 \leq \ldots \leq x_m.$$

The main part of the algorithm is as follows.

```
if b₁ = 1 then begin k:=1;  set α₁ = x₁  end
            else k:=0;
for i:= 2 to m do
   begin
   if bᵢ = 1 and bᵢ₋₁ = 0 then
      begin
      k:=k+1;
      set αₖ = xᵢ
      end;
   if bᵢ = 0 and bᵢ₋₁ = 1 and k>0 then
      set βₖ = xᵢ₋₁
   end
if k=0 then   set L(s) = empty interval
         else   set L(s) = [α₁, β₁] ∪ ... ∪ [αₖ, βₖ]
```

Observe that the algorithm produces a hypothesis which is formed from the union of k intervals, where k cannot exceed, but may equal, r. It can be shown that J_r has VC dimension $2r$ (Exercise 7), and hence it follows from Corollary 8.4.2 that L is a pac learning algorithm for J_r with sample complexity

$$m_L(J_r, \delta, \epsilon) = O\left(\frac{r}{\epsilon} \ln\left(\frac{1}{\epsilon}\right) + \frac{1}{\epsilon} \ln\left(\frac{1}{\delta}\right)\right) = O\left(\frac{r}{\epsilon} \ln\left(\frac{1}{\epsilon\delta}\right)\right).$$

The running time of the main part of the algorithm is $O(m)$, and hence the whole procedure runs in polynomial time. The bound for the sample complexity is polynomial in r, and L is therefore a pac learning algorithm for J which is efficient with respect to the representation size.   □

As in our discussion in Section 6.7, efficiency with respect to representation size can be regarded in two different ways. That discussion was in the context of doubly-graded boolean spaces. However, similar points can be made for hypothesis spaces graded only by representation size.

Suppose first that L is a pac learning algorithm for a space H which can be graded by representation size as $H = \bigcup H_r$. In this situation, demanding that L be efficient with respect to representation size is an additional restriction on the performance of L: not only must it be pac, but it must also learn the 'simpler' hypotheses 'more quickly', and the rate of increase for more complex hypotheses must be polynomial. Here, efficiency with respect to representation size can be thought of as a stronger form of pac learning.

On the other hand, consider again the interval union space J. This space has infinite VC dimension and therefore is not pac learnable (see Example 8.5.4). However, if we grade the space as $J = \bigcup J_r$, then there is a pac learning algorithm L (as described above) for each J_r. Furthermore, this algorithm operates in the same manner for each J_r. Quite explicitly, L is not a pac learning algorithm for the ungraded space J, because the running time it *requires* to learn a hypothesis in J_r to prescribed degrees of accuracy and confidence, is (by the lower bound result Theorem 8.5.2) proportional to r, and r may be arbitrarily large. However, it is clear that if we know that the target concept has representation size r (or if we know an upper bound for this value), then we can use L to produce a probably approximately correct approximation to the target. What is more, the running time of L varies only polynomially with r. Thus, even though a space may not be pac learnable, it may be learnable efficiently when graded by representation size. Hence, in some cases, the idea of efficiency with respect to representation size allows useful widening of the definition of pac learning.

9.6 DIMENSION-BASED OCCAM ALGORITHMS

Suppose that $H = \bigcup H_r$ is a hypothesis space (real or boolean) graded by representation size, according to a representation $\Omega \to H$. We have seen (Section 6.4) that, for a boolean space, it may be NP-hard to find the simplest hypothesis consistent with a training sample. The same is true of real hypothesis spaces graded by representation size. A result of Masek (from an unpublished manuscript of 1978) shows that the following problem is NP-hard: given a training sample for a hypothesis in some B_2^r, find a hypothesis $h \in B_2^r$ consistent with the sample. In other words, it is hard to find a hypothesis consistent with a training sample for some target concept in I_2 such that the hypothesis is as *simple* as possible, involving the union of *fewest* possible boxes. However, as with boolean spaces, it will sometimes be sufficient to find a consistent hypothesis which is 'simple enough', rather than the simplest possible.

In our discussion of Occam algorithms in Chapter 6, the output of a learning algorithm L for $H = \bigcup H_r$ was deemed to be 'simple enough' if, given a training sample $\mathbf{s}$ of length m for a hypothesis in H_r, $L(\mathbf{s})$ has representation size at most $m^\alpha r^\beta$, for fixed constants $0 < \alpha < 1$ and $\beta \geq 1$. In this case, the set of hypotheses used by L to approximate hypotheses in H_r is a subset of

$$\bigcup_{i=1}^{m^\alpha r^\beta} H_i.$$

Learnability then follows from the fact that this space is finite; efficiency with respect to r from the fact that it is 'small enough'.

This discussion suggests that, for any hypothesis space $H = \bigcup H_r$ and for any learning algorithm L for H, we should define the *effective hypothesis space* $L(m, H_r)$ to be the set of all hypotheses $L(\mathbf{s})$ obtained as $\mathbf{s}$ ranges through all training samples of length m for hypotheses in H_r,

$$L(m, H_r) = \bigcup_{t \in H_r} \{L(\mathbf{s}) \mid \mathbf{s} \in S(m, t)\}.$$

Thus the Occam algorithms for boolean spaces are consistent learning algorithms which have effective hypothesis spaces with 'small enough' cardinalities. The appropriate generalisation to general (and, in particular, real) hypothesis spaces, is to define an Occam algorithm to be a consistent learning algorithm for which the effective hypothesis spaces have 'small enough' VC dimension. Following Blumer *et al.* (1989), we make the following definition.

We say that a learning algorithm L for H is *Occam* with respect to the representation $\Omega \to H$ if

- L is consistent;
- VCdim $(L(m, H_r)) \leq m^\alpha r^\beta$, where $0 < \alpha < 1$ and $\beta \geq 1$ are constants.

As for boolean spaces, we have the following result.

Theorem 9.6.1 Let H be a space of real or boolean hypotheses having representation $\Omega \to H$. If L is an Occam learning algorithm (with respect to the representation) then, for each r, L is a pac learning algorithm for (H_r, H), with sample complexity $m_L(H_r, \delta, \epsilon)$ polynomial in r, δ^* and ϵ^{-1}.

Proof Let $t \in H_r$ be a given target concept, μ any distribution on X, and δ and ϵ given confidence and accuracy parameters. Consider these quantities as fixed but arbitrary in what follows. For convenience, denote $L(m, H_r)$ by H^*. By definition of the effective hypothesis space, L is a learning algorithm for (H_r, H^*). It is easy to see that Proposition 8.2.3 can be modified to yield

$$\mu^m \{\mathbf{s} \in S(m, t) \mid H^*[\mathbf{s}] \cap B_\epsilon \neq \emptyset\} < 2 \, \Pi_{H^*}(2m) \, 2^{-\epsilon m/2}.$$

We are given that H^* has VC dimension at most $D = m^\alpha r^\beta$. If $m > D$ then, by Sauer's Lemma, the quantity on the right-hand side of the inequality is less than

$$2 \left(\frac{2em}{D}\right)^D 2^{-\epsilon m/2}.$$

We need to show that this can be bounded by δ for a value of m which is polynomial in r, δ^* and ϵ^{-1}. Now,

$$2 \left(\frac{2em}{D}\right)^D 2^{-\epsilon m/2} \le \delta \iff m^\alpha r^\beta \ln \left(\frac{2e}{r^\beta}\right) + m^\alpha r^\beta \ln \left(m^{1-\alpha}\right) - \frac{\epsilon m}{2} \ln 2 \le \ln \left(\frac{\delta}{2}\right).$$

Now (see Chapter 8, Exercise 2), for any $x > 0$ and any $c > 0$,

$$\ln x \le \left(\ln \left(\frac{1}{c}\right) - 1\right) + cx.$$

Taking $c = \epsilon \ln 2 / 4 r^\beta$ and $x = m^{1-\alpha}$, we see that it suffices to have

$$\frac{\epsilon m}{4} \ln 2 - m^\alpha r^\beta \left(\ln \left(\frac{6 r^\beta}{\epsilon}\right) - 1\right) \ge m^\alpha r^\beta \ln \left(\frac{2e}{r^\beta}\right) + \ln \left(\frac{2}{\delta}\right).$$

Since $\alpha < 1$, this holds if

$$m \ge m_0 = \left\lceil \left(\frac{A+B}{\epsilon}\right)^{1/(1-\alpha)} \right\rceil,$$

where

$$A = \frac{4 r^\beta}{\epsilon} \lg \left(\frac{12}{\epsilon}\right), \quad B = \frac{4}{\epsilon} \lg \left(\frac{2}{\delta}\right).$$

This is an upper bound on the sample complexity $m_L(H_r, \delta, \epsilon)$, and it is polynomial in r, δ^* and $1/\epsilon$. The result follows. □

We remark that if the running time of L is polynomial in m then the running time of L as a pac learning algorithm for H_r is polynomial in r, δ^* and ϵ^{-1}. That is, an efficient Occam algorithm is a pac learning algorithm for $H = \bigcup H_r$, efficient with respect to representation size, confidence and accuracy. It is worth noting that a more careful analysis yields an upper bound on sample complexity better than the value m_0 given above; see Blumer *et al.* (1989).

Suppose H is a boolean hypothesis space, graded by representation size as $H = \bigcup H_r$, and that L is an Occam learning algorithm for H, as defined in Section 6.5. Then there are constants $\alpha < 1$ and $\beta \ge 1$ such that if $\mathbf{s}$ is a training sample for a hypothesis of H_r then $L(\mathbf{s})$ has representation size at most $m^\alpha r^\beta$. The proof of Theorem 6.5.1 then shows that

$$\lg |L(m, H_r)| \le m^\alpha r^\beta + 1.$$

By Proposition 7.3.3, we therefore have

$$\text{VCdim}\,(L(m, H_r)) \le \lg |L(m, H_r)| \le m^\alpha r^\beta + 1 \le m^\alpha r^{\beta+1}.$$

It follows that any Occam algorithm for a boolean space, as defined in Chapter 5, is an Occam algorithm as defined above. Hence Theorem 9.6.1 subsumes Theorem 6.5.1.

The algorithm for learning the space $J = I_1$ of unions of intervals on the real line cannot be extended or generalised to I_n, $n \geq 2$. Indeed, in view of the NP-hardness result of Masek mentioned above, (under the assumption P $\neq$ NP) there can be no polynomial time learning algorithm for general I_n which produces a consistent hypothesis in B_n^r whenever the target concept is in B_n^r. However, there is an Occam algorithm for the space I_n. This is based on the greedy method for *MINIMUM COVER*, and it has running time polynomial in m. Therefore the space I_n of finite unions of n-dimensional boxes is pac learnable efficiently with respect to representation size. The learning algorithm is due to Blumer *et al.* (1989), and we refer the reader to their paper for the details.

9.7 EPAC LEARNING AGAIN

Suppose that $H = \bigcup H_n$ is a graded (real or boolean) hypothesis space, and that each H_n can be graded by representation size as $H_n = \bigcup H_{n,r}$. As usual, $H = \bigcup \bigcup H_{n,r}$ is said to be *doubly-graded*, and we conventionally omit one of the union signs.

A learning algorithm for a doubly-graded space $H = \bigcup H_{n,r}$ is simply a learning algorithm for the graded space $\bigcup H_n$. The learning algorithm L is said to be *efficiently pac* or *epac* if it pac learns each $H_{n,r}$ and if it does so efficiently with respect to example size, representation size, and confidence and accuracy. More formally, as in the definition of epac learning for boolean spaces, we say that L is epac if

- the running time $R_L(m, n)$ of L is polynomial in m and n;
- the sample complexity $m_L(H_{n,r}, \delta, \epsilon)$ is polynomial in n, r, δ^*, and ϵ^{-1}.

Thus a learning algorithm is epac if in time polynomial in n, r, δ^* and ϵ^{-1} it can produce a hypothesis which, with probability at least $1 - \delta$, has error less than ϵ with respect to a target hypothesis in $H_{n,r}$.

We observed in the previous section that if there is an Occam algorithm L for the space $H = \bigcup H_r$, graded by the size of a representation $\Omega \rightarrow H$, then L pac learns H_r by H and has sample complexity $m_L(H_r, \delta, \epsilon)$ polynomial in δ^*, ϵ^{-1} and r. We say that a learning algorithm for the doubly-graded space $H = \bigcup H_{n,r}$ is *Occam* if the conditions in Section 9.6 hold for each H_n, and with the same value of the constants α and β for each H_n. We have

Theorem 9.7.1 Suppose that L is an Occam algorithm for the space $H = \bigcup H_{n,r}$ and that L has running time $R_L(m, n)$ polynomial in m and n. Then L is an epac learning algorithm for H.

Proof In the proof of Theorem 9.6.1 we obtained the upper bound

$$m_L\left(H_{n,r},\delta,\epsilon\right) \le m_0(H_{n,r},\delta,\epsilon) = \left\lceil \left(\frac{A+B}{\epsilon}\right)^{1/(1-\alpha)}\right\rceil,$$

where

$$A = \frac{4r^\beta}{\epsilon}\lg\left(\frac{12}{\epsilon}\right),\ B = \frac{4}{\epsilon}\lg\left(\frac{2}{\delta}\right).$$

As we noted there, this is polynomial in r,δ^* and ϵ^{-1} and, further, it is independent of n. The result follows on observing that the upper bound $R_L\left(m_0\left(H_{n,r},\delta,\epsilon\right),n\right)$ on the running time of L as a pac learning algorithm for $H_{n,r}$ is polynomial in n, r, δ^* and ϵ^{-1}.   □

We remark that the observations made in Section 6.7 concerning the 'meaning' of epac learning are equally valid here. The notion of epac learning can be regarded as a refinement or as a generalisation of pac learning, depending on the context.

FURTHER REMARKS

Board and Pitt (1990) have given a more general definition of an Occam algorithm for a doubly graded space. An *efficient randomised Occam algorithm* for a doubly-graded space $H = \bigcup H_{n,r}$ is a randomised algorithm L such that for some constant $\alpha < 1$ and some polynomial p of three variables, the following condition holds, for any positive integers m, n, r and any $c > 0$.

> There is a subset $L(m, H_r)$ of H with VC dimension at most $m^\alpha p\left(n, r, 1/c\right)$ such that if L is given as input a training sample **s** for a hypothesis of $H_{n,r}$ then L halts in time polynomial in $m, n, r, 1/c$ and with probability at least $1 - c$ outputs a hypothesis $L(\mathbf{s}) \in L(m, H_{n,r})$ consistent with **s**.

Thus, the algorithm is an efficient randomised algorithm, and the VC dimension of the effective hypothesis space can depend polynomially on n, in addition to being polynomial in r and sublinear in m. With this extended definition, Board and Pitt have shown for 'most' doubly-graded hypothesis spaces that the space is epac learnable *if and only if* there is an efficient randomised Occam algorithm for the space. (More specifically, they have shown that this holds if the space is *polynomially closed under exception lists*, a condition satisfied by many natural hypothesis spaces; see their paper.)

EXERCISES

1. Write a program for the quadrant space learning algorithm described in Example 9.1.4. Is this a memoryless on-line algorithm?

2. Modify the quadrant space learning algorithm to obtain a consistent learning algorithm which makes no use of the empty quadrant.

3. Design a memoryless on-line learning algorithm for the quadrant space which has as initial hypothesis q_v where, for each i, $v_i = large$, some large positive real number. Under what conditions is your algorithm consistent?

4. Prove directly that the algorithm for learning boxes in $\mathbf{R}^2$ has sample complexity at most $4/\epsilon \ln (4/\delta)$. Compare this with the bound that follows from the more general analysis given in Example 9.2.3.

5. Prove that the space B_n of n-dimensional boxes has VC dimension $2n$.

6. Explain why the proof of Theorem 9.4.1 fails in general for infinite real hypothesis spaces.

7. Prove that the space B_1^r of r-fold interval unions has VC dimension $2r$.

8. Using Exercise 7 of Chapter 8, prove that the VC dimension of B_n^r is bounded above by $4rn \lg(3r)$.

9. Prove that if there is an epac learning algorithm for the doubly-graded hypothesis space $H = \bigcup H_{n,r}$ then $\mathrm{VCdim}(H_{n,r})$ is polynomial in n and r.
[Hint: see Theorem 8.5.2.]

Chapter 10: Linear Threshold Networks

10.1 THE BOOLEAN PERCEPTRON

The linear threshold machine with boolean inputs was introduced in Example 2.5.2, and in Chapter 7 we discussed its generalisation, the real perceptron, in which the inputs are allowed to be real, rather than boolean. In this chapter we shall deal with both the boolean case and the real case, and we shall discuss more general networks of 'cells' with threshold characteristics. We shall use the term *boolean perceptron* in place of 'linear threshold machine', and denote (the hypothesis space of) the boolean perceptron with n-bit inputs by BP_n.

We begin with some remarks on the expressive power of the boolean perceptron. The analysis carried out in Section 7.4 applies equally to the boolean case, requiring only the trivial observation that the sample $(o, e_1, \ldots, e_n)$, which is shattered by BP_n, can be regarded as a sequence of *boolean* vectors. It follows that

$$\mathrm{VCdim}(BP_n) = n + 1.$$

Proposition 10.1.1 The number of hypotheses in BP_n satisfies

$$|BP_n| \leq 2^{n^2}$$

for $n \geq 4$.

Proof In the boolean case the example space $X = \{0, 1\}^n$ has cardinality 2^n. For any hypothesis space H defined on X, we have

$$|H| = \Pi_H(|X|) = \Pi_H(2^n).$$

The reasoning is as in the proof of Proposition 7.5.4; the right-hand side is just the number of 'classification vectors' determined by H on X — in other words, the number of distinct functions in H. Applying Sauer's Lemma, in conjunction with Proposition 7.5.3, and observing that $\mathrm{VCdim}(BP_n) = n + 1$, we have

$$|BP_n| = \Pi_{BP_n}(2^n) < \left(\frac{e2^n}{n+1}\right)^{n+1} = 2^{n^2}\left\{\frac{1}{2}\left(\frac{2e}{n+1}\right)^{n+1}\right\}.$$

Now, the sequence $(2e/(n+1))^{n+1}$ is decreasing, and when $n = 4$ the quantity in braces is less than 1. Therefore, for $n \geq 4$, BP_n has cardinality at most 2^{n^2}, as claimed.   □

This result shows that the space BP_n contains only a minute fraction of the 2^{2^n} boolean functions, for all values of n except the very small ones. Even when $n = 2$ we have only 14 of the 16 possible functions, the two which cannot be realised being the exclusive-or function and its complement. (See also Example 10.5.2 below.)

The consistency problem for BP_n can be stated as follows.

LINEAR THRESHOLD CONSISTENCY
Instance A training sample **s** of m labelled n-bit vectors.
Question Is there a linear threshold function consistent with **s**?

If the answer to the existence problem is 'yes', then there remains the problem of finding a suitable linear threshold function. Because the weights α_i ($1 \leq i \leq n$) and the threshold θ are real numbers we need rather different techniques from those discussed previously in this book, even though the inputs are boolean. We shall explain first how the techniques of linear programming can be used.

It is convenient to begin by remarking that there is no loss of generality in taking the threshold value θ to be 1. To verify this, note first that since the example space is boolean, and thus finite, we can alter the parameters of a linear threshold function very slightly without affecting the classification. (Geometrically, this corresponds to the fact that the hyperplane separating the positive and negative examples is not uniquely determined.) In particular, we can always assume that $\theta \neq 0$. Then, by interchanging the positive and negative examples if necessary, we can assume that $\theta > 0$ — this is equivalent to saying that the zero vector o is a negative example. (In practice, we may be unable to tell from the training sample whether the positive and negative examples should be interchanged. However, at worst, this means we should have to run the procedures we describe twice.) Finally, suppose there is a weight-vector $\alpha = (\alpha_1, \alpha_2, \ldots, \alpha_n)$ and a threshold $\theta > 0$ such that the function

$$h_{\alpha,\theta}(y) = \begin{cases} 1, & \text{if } \alpha_1 y_1 + \ldots + \alpha_n y_n \geq \theta; \\ 0, & \text{otherwise;} \end{cases}$$

is consistent with the training sample. Since

$$\alpha_1 y_1 + \alpha_2 y_2 + \ldots + \alpha_n y_n \geq \theta \iff \left(\frac{\alpha_1}{\theta}\right) + \left(\frac{\alpha_2}{\theta}\right) + \ldots + \left(\frac{\alpha_n}{\theta}\right) \geq 1,$$

it follows that we can take a new weight-vector $\alpha' = \alpha/\theta$ and a new threshold $\theta' = 1$, as required. From now on, we shall denote the boolean perceptron with fixed threshold 1 by Θ_n.

Suppose that, for a given **s**, the answer to the *LINEAR THRESHOLD CONSISTENCY* problem for BP_n is 'yes'. Then the answer to the corresponding problem for Θ_n is also 'yes'. If there are no negative examples in **s** then, since we are working in Θ_n, the zero vector o cannot be in the training sample. Thus, if all examples are positive, then they all have at least one 1. In this case the problem of finding a consistent hypothesis in Θ_n is trivial: we can take the weight-vector α to be $(1, 1, \ldots, 1)$. If the training sample **s** contains negative examples, it can be arranged so that the negative examples come first, say

$$\mathbf{s} = (x_1, -1), \ldots, (x_q, -1), (x_{q+1}, 1), \ldots, (x_m, 1).$$

We claim that when $q \geq 1$ a suitable weight-vector can be found by solving q linear programs. Let N denote the $q \times n$ matrix whose rows are the vectors $x_1, \ldots, x_q$, and let P denote the $(m - q) \times n$ matrix whose rows are $x_{q+1}, \ldots x_m$. Since there is a function in Θ_n consistent with **s**, there is a corresponding weight-vector α which (regarded as a column vector) is a solution of the system of inequalities $N\alpha < 1$, $P\alpha \geq 1$. Here 1 denotes an all-1 column vector of the appropriate size, and each component inequality in the first set is strict.

Consider the linear programs $\Lambda(i)$ $(1 \leq i \leq q)$ defined as follows:

$$\text{minimise } x_i\alpha, \quad \text{subject to} \quad N\alpha \leq 1, P\alpha \geq 1.$$

The remarks at the end of the previous paragraph imply that the feasible region for $\Lambda(i)$ is not empty. Thus there is a solution $\alpha^{(i)}$ for $\Lambda(i)$ and, furthermore, it satisfies the ith component N-inequality strictly. It follows that the vector

$$\alpha^* = \frac{1}{q}(\alpha^{(1)} + \alpha^{(2)} + \ldots + \alpha^{(q)})$$

satisfies each N-inequality strictly, and therefore defines a function in Θ_n which is consistent with **s**.

It is known that there are algorithms for linear programming which are, in certain senses, efficient. The simplex algorithm works well in almost all cases, but is not strictly a polynomial time algorithm. Karmarkar's algorithm (Karmarkar 1984) does have polynomial running time, although in practice it may not out-perform the simplex algorithm.

10.2 AN INCREMENTAL ALGORITHM

The learning algorithms described in earlier chapters are all inspired by the principles of formal logic. Each step involves using an example (or examples) to make a significant change in the current hypothesis, based on logical deductions. In the case of linear threshold functions we have already seen that linear programming algorithms, which are based on rather different ideas, can be used to solve the consistency problem. In this section we shall describe another kind of algorithm which can be used to solve the same problem.

The germ of the idea can be traced back to Hebb (1949). Hebb was trying to explain how a network of living brain cells could adapt to different stimuli. He suggested that connections which were used frequently would gradually become stronger, while those which were not used would fade away. This idea was given an explicit mathematical formulation by Rosenblatt (1959, 1962). The procedure may be described as *incremental*, because it operates by making small changes, rather than by bold logical steps. As we shall see, this technique has the desirable features of a memoryless on-line algorithm.

In terms of the boolean perceptron Θ_n with fixed threshold 1, Rosenblatt's *perceptron learning algorithm* may be described as follows. Suppose the perceptron is in the state $\alpha = (\alpha_1, \alpha_2, \ldots, \alpha_n)$, and that the labelled example (y, b) is supplied, where $y = (y_1, y_2, \ldots, y_n)$. If $h_\alpha(y) = b$, the example is classified correctly and no change to the state is made. If the example is negative but is classified as positive (that is, if $b = 0$ but $h_\alpha(y) = 1$), then we make a small reduction in the weights on all the 'active' lines. Precisely, for a given constant $\nu > 0$, we define a new state α' by changing the weights according to the rule

$$\alpha_i' = \begin{cases} \alpha_i - \nu, & \text{if } y_i = 1; \\ \alpha_i, & \text{if } y_i = 0. \end{cases}$$

On the other hand, if $b = 1$ but $h_\alpha(y) = 0$, then we increase the weights on the active lines according to the rule

$$\alpha_i' = \begin{cases} \alpha_i + \nu, & \text{if } y_i = 1; \\ \alpha_i, & \text{if } y_i = 0. \end{cases}$$

The overall effect of these changes can be summarised in a single equation. For each fixed value of the constant ν, we have a learning algorithm L_ν. The action of L_ν is determined by its effect on the weight-vector α: when the labelled example (y, b) is supplied in a state α, the new state $\alpha' = L_\nu(\alpha, y, b)$ is given by

$$\alpha' = \alpha + (b - h_\alpha(y))\nu y.$$

The term $b - h_\alpha(y)$ can take the values 1, -1, or 0. In the first two cases, which correspond to an actual change in the state, we shall say that L_ν is *invoked*.

10.3 A FINITENESS RESULT

In this section we shall investigate the properties of the incremental algorithm described above.

The following technical lemma will be useful. We shall use the angled-bracket notation $\langle \, , \, \rangle$ for the inner product of vectors, and $\| \; \|$ for the Euclidean norm:

$$\langle x, y \rangle - x_1 y_1 + x_2 y_2 + \ldots + x_n y_n;$$

$$\|x\| = \sqrt{\langle x, x \rangle} = \sqrt{(x_1^2 + x_2^2 + \ldots + x_n^2)}.$$

As in Section 10.1, Θ_n denotes the set of boolean functions defined on $\{0,1\}^n$ which are realisable by a linear threshold unit with threshold 1. The function $h_\alpha \in \Theta_n$ corresponding to the state α is given by

$$h_\alpha(y) = \begin{cases} 1, & \text{if } \langle \alpha, y \rangle \geq 1 \\ 0, & \text{otherwise.} \end{cases}$$

Lemma 10.3.1 Given $t \in \Theta_n$, there is a vector α^t and a constant $c_t > 0$ such that

$$t(y) = 0 \implies \langle \alpha^t, y \rangle \leq 1 - c_t;$$

$$t(y) = 1 \implies \langle \alpha^t, y \rangle \geq 1 + c_t.$$

(In geometrical terms, this says that the positive and negative examples of t can be separated by a strip of width $2c_t/\|\alpha^t\|$. See Figure 10.1.)

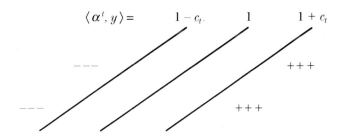

Figure 10.1: Separation of positive and negative examples

Proof It follows from the definition of a threshold unit that there is a weight-vector α^0 such that

$$t(y) = 1 \iff \langle \alpha^0, y \rangle \geq 1.$$

Since the set of negative examples $X^- = \{y \mid t(y) = 0\}$ is finite, there is a constant $c_t > 0$ such that

$$\max_{y \in X^-} \langle \alpha^0, y \rangle = 1 - 2c_t.$$

Let α^t be defined by $\alpha_i^t = \alpha^0/(1 - c_t)$. Then we have

$$t(y) = 1 \implies \langle \alpha^t, y \rangle = \frac{1}{1 - c_t}\langle \alpha^0, y \rangle \geq \frac{1}{1 - c_t} \geq 1 + c_t.$$

$$t(y) = 0 \implies \langle \alpha^t, y \rangle = \frac{1}{1 - c_t}\langle \alpha^0, y \rangle \leq \frac{1 - 2c_t}{1 - c_t} \leq 1 - c_t.$$

□

The next theorem is a version of the *Perceptron Convergence Theorem*, originally due to Rosenblatt (1959), and discussed at length by Minsky and Papert (1969). It provides a bound on the number of times that the algorithm L_ν can be invoked, for a given target function $t \in \Theta_n$. As we shall see, its implications require careful analysis.

Theorem 10.3.2 Suppose we are given a training sample for $t \in \Theta_n$, and L_ν is applied with initial weights all zero. Then, provided ν is small enough, there is a positive integer $I = I(t, \nu)$ such that L_ν is invoked at most I times.

Proof Given t, choose α^t and c_t as in the lemma. Each time L_ν is invoked, the weight-vector α is changed to a new value α' given by

$$\alpha' = \alpha + \eta\nu y,$$

where $\eta = t(y) - h_\alpha(y)$ is either $+1$ or -1. When $\eta = +1$ we have $t(y) = 1$ and $h_\alpha(y) = 0$, that is

$$\langle \alpha^t, y \rangle \geq 1 + c_t \text{ and } \langle \alpha, y \rangle < 1.$$

Thus in the case $\eta = +1$, $\langle \alpha^t - \alpha, y \rangle \geq c_t$. Similarly, when $\eta = -1$ we have $t(y) = 0$ and $h_\alpha(y) = 1$, that is

$$\langle \alpha^t, y \rangle \leq 1 - c_t \text{ and } \langle \alpha, y \rangle \geq 1.$$

Thus in the case $\eta = -1$, $\langle \alpha - \alpha^t, y \rangle \geq c_t$.

These two conclusions can be combined into one statement: for each invocation of L_ν,

$$\eta\langle \alpha^t - \alpha, y \rangle \geq c_t.$$

Now we can calculate the change in $\|\alpha^t - \alpha\|^2$ following an invocation of L_ν, as follows.

$$\begin{aligned}
\|\alpha^t - \alpha'\|^2 &= \|\alpha^t - \alpha - \eta\nu y\|^2 \\
&= \|\alpha^t - \alpha\|^2 - 2\eta\nu\langle \alpha^t - \alpha, y \rangle + \eta^2\nu^2\|y\|^2 \\
&\leq \|\alpha^t - \alpha\|^2 + \nu^2\|y\|^2 - 2\nu c_t.
\end{aligned}$$

Since y is an n-bit vector, $\|y\|^2 \leq n$, and so, provided $\nu \leq c_t/n$, the term $\nu^2\|y\|^2$ is not greater than νc_t. In this case

$$\|\alpha^t - \alpha'\|^2 \leq \|\alpha^t - \alpha\|^2 - \nu c_t.$$

In other words, every time L_ν is invoked, the value of $\|\alpha^t - \alpha\|^2$ decreases by at least νc_t. Initially the value is $\|\alpha^t\|^2$, and it cannot become negative. Therefore the number of invocations cannot exceed

$$I(t, \nu) = \left\lfloor \frac{\|\alpha^t\|^2}{\nu c_t} \right\rfloor.$$

$\square$

Example 10.3.3 Let n be odd, say $n = 2r + 1$. Define the target concept t by

$$t(y) = \begin{cases} 1, & \text{if } y \text{ contains at least } r+1 \text{ ones}; \\ 0, & \text{otherwise.} \end{cases}$$

(This is known as the *majority* concept.) It is easy to verify that t is in Θ_n; in other words, there is a weight-vector α such that $t = h_\alpha$. In fact,

$$\alpha = \frac{2}{n}(1, 1, \ldots, 1)$$

has the required property. Furthermore, all positive examples y^+ satisfy

$$\langle \alpha, y^+ \rangle \geq \frac{2}{n}(r+1) = 1 + \frac{1}{n},$$

and all negative examples y^- satisfy

$$\langle \alpha, y^- \rangle \leq \frac{2}{n}r = 1 - \frac{1}{n}.$$

It follows that, in this case, we can take the quantities α^t and c_t guaranteed by Lemma 10.3.1 to be $\alpha^t = \alpha$ and $c_t = 1/n$. Since $\|\alpha^t\|^2 = 4/n$, the bound for the number of invocations is $I = \lfloor 4/\nu \rfloor$, provided that $\nu \leq c_t/n = 1/n^2$.

Thus, if we consider the efficiency of the algorithm as a function of n, then *for this specific concept* the number of invocations is $O(n^2)$. $\square$

The preceding theorem is essentially a result about the finiteness of the incremental algorithm. It tells us that the algorithm will be invoked only finitely many times, provided that the target function is representable. Without the theorem, it would be conceivable that the algorithm could 'cycle', continuing to make changes forever.

Indeed, this behaviour might occur if the target is not representable by a linear threshold function, and it might also occur if the constant ν is too large.

The proof of the theorem provides an upper bound on the number of invocations required. This bound depends upon the inverse of the 'gap' $2c_t/\|\alpha^t\|$ between the positive and negative examples of the target concept, and need not be polynomial in n (see Littlestone (1988) and Muroga (1971)). We have not, therefore, shown that the incremental algorithm is efficient. But the conceptual simplicity of the Hebbian approach, and the ease of implementation, make this an attractive algorithm in many practical situations.

10.4 FINDING A CONSISTENT HYPOTHESIS

The finiteness theorem for Θ_n shows that the incremental algorithm can be used to find a hypothesis consistent with a given training sample

$$\mathbf{s} = ((x_1, b_1), (x_2, b_2), \ldots, (x_m, b_m)).$$

The idea is simply that we can repeatedly run through the examples until no changes are made.

```
set α = the zero vector;
repeat
    consistent:= true;
    for i:= 1 to m do
        if bᵢ ≠ hα(xᵢ) then
            begin
            consistent:= false;
            set α = Lν(α, xᵢ, bᵢ)
            end
until consistent
```

Each time we run through the training sample there are two possibilities. It may be that a change is made; on the other hand, if no change is made the current hypothesis must agree with the entire training sample. If there is a hypothesis in Θ_n consistent with the training sample, then the procedure will terminate. This is because there is a bound I on the number of changes that can be made, and so after at most I repetitions no more changes are possible.

The running time of this algorithm for finding a consistent hypothesis in Θ_n is therefore proportional to mI. In specific cases we may be able to express this in a more helpful way. For example, in the previous section we showed that, for the *majority* concept, ν can be chosen so that I is $O(n^2)$. It follows that *in this case* the running time is $O(mn^2)$.

10.5 FEEDFORWARD NEURAL NETWORKS

A perceptron contains only one 'active unit', and is consequently severely limited in its capabilities. The idea that more complex assemblies of units may have greater power is an old one, motivated by the fact that living brains seem to be constructed in this way, and it has led to the intensive study of 'artificial neural networks'. In the final sections of this book we shall examine such networks in the context of Computational Learning Theory.

The basic structure is a pair of sets (N, A), where N is a finite set whose members are called *nodes*, and A is a subset of $N \times N$ whose members are called *arcs*. The structure (N, A) is a *directed graph*, or *digraph*, which we think of as a fixed architecture for a 'machine'. For simplicity, we consider only digraphs which have no directed cycles: that is, there is no sequence of arcs beginning with (r, s) and ending with (q, r), for any node r. In the present context this is known as the *feedforward* condition.

In order to present this set-up as a 'machine', in the general sense described in Chapter 1, we require some additional features (Figure 10.2). First we specify a subset J of the nodes, which we call *input nodes*, and a single node $z \notin J$ which we call the *output node*. The underlying idea is that all nodes receive and transmit signals; the input nodes receive their signals from the outside world and the output node transmits a signal to the outside world, while all other nodes receive and transmit along the relevant arcs of the digraph. Each arc (r, s) has a *weight*, $w(r, s)$, which is a real number representing the strength of the connection between the nodes r and s. A positive weight corresponds to an 'excitatory' connection, a negative weight to an 'inhibitory' connection. Another feature is that all nodes except the input nodes are 'active', in that they transmit a signal which is a predetermined function of the signals they receive. For this reason, the nodes in $N \setminus J$ are called *computation nodes*.

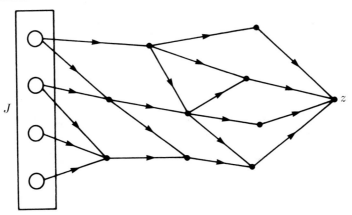

Figure 10.2: A typical feedforward network

To make this idea precise, we introduce an *activation function* f_r for each computation node r. The activity of such a node is specified in two stages. First the signals arriving at r are aggregated by taking their weighted sum according to the connection strengths on the arcs with terminal node r, and then the function f_r of this value is computed. Thus the action of the entire network may be described in terms of two functions $p: N \to \mathbf{R}$ and $q: N \to \mathbf{R}$, representing the received and transmitted signals respectively. We assume that a vector of real-valued signals $y = (y_j)_{j \in J}$ is applied externally to the input nodes, and $p(j) = q(j) = y_j$ for each j in J. For each computation node l the received and transmitted signals are defined as follows.

$$p(l) = \sum_{\{i \mid (i,l) \in A\}} q(i)w(i,l)$$

$$q(l) = f_l(p(l)).$$

The output is the value $q(z)$ transmitted by the node z.

For our purposes it is sufficient to assume that every activation function is a simple linear threshold function:

$$f(u) = \begin{cases} 1, & \text{if } u \geq \theta; \\ 0, & \text{otherwise.} \end{cases}$$

We shall write θ_r to denote the value of the threshold for the node r. (It should be noted that the discontinuous nature of the threshold functions causes some problems if we wish to apply analytical techniques to these models. For example, the usual derivation of the 'backpropagation algorithm' requires that the activation functions be differentiable. However, it is possible that a similar algorithm could be obtained by discrete methods.)

When all the computation nodes are linear threshold nodes, a state ω of the machine is described by the real numbers

$$w(r,s), \quad (r,s) \in A; \quad \theta_r, \quad r \in N \setminus J.$$

The set of all states which satisfy some given rules (such as bounds on the values of the weights and thresholds) will be denoted by Ω. Now we are firmly within the framework developed in the earlier chapters of this book. The function computed by the machine in state ω will be denoted by h_ω, so that $h_\omega(y) = q(z)$. Note that this is a boolean value, because the output node has a linear threshold activation function. The set $\{h_\omega \mid \omega \in \Omega\}$ of functions computable by the machine is the hypothesis space H, and the assignment $\omega \mapsto h_\omega$ is a representation $\Omega \to H$.

We can now look at some very simple examples.

Example 10.5.1 The real perceptron P_n, as described in Section 7.1, is obtained by taking $J = \{a_1, a_2, \ldots, a_n\}$, $N = J \cup \{z\}$, $A = \{(a_1, z), (a_2, z), \ldots, (a_n, z)\}$, and letting

$$w(a_1, z) = \alpha_1, \ w(a_2, z) = \alpha_2, \ \ldots, \ w(a_n, z) = \alpha_n; \ \theta_z = \theta.$$

□

Example 10.5.2 We have already remarked that the perceptron with two input nodes cannot compute the exclusive-or function; that is, there is no choice of α_1, α_2 and θ which represents the function

$$00 \mapsto 0, \ 01 \mapsto 1, \ 10 \mapsto 1, \ 11 \mapsto 0.$$

This is because a state implementing this function would have to satisfy the conditions

$$0 < \theta, \ \alpha_2 \geq \theta, \ \alpha_1 \geq \theta, \ \alpha_1 + \alpha_2 < \theta,$$

which are inconsistent. However, it can be verified easily that the machine depicted in Figure 10.3, with the weights and thresholds shown, does compute the function. □

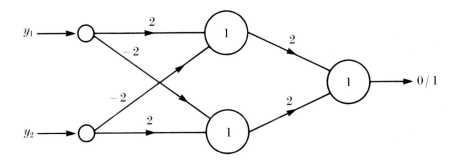

Figure 10.3: A machine which computes the exclusive-or function

Proposition 10.1.1 shows that, in general, not more than 2^{n^2} of the 2^{2^n} boolean functions are computable by the perceptron with n inputs. The preceding example indicates that more complex architectures do extend the 'power of expression' of the model, but the general picture is still far from clear. The old, but very useful, book by Muroga (1971) contains an extensive discussion of 'threshold logic', based on classical techniques of logic and combinatorics. In the next section we shall look at the problem using the VC dimension.

10.6 VC DIMENSION OF FEEDFORWARD NETWORKS

We shall prove a result of Baum and Haussler (1989), which gives an upper bound on the VC dimension of a feedforward linear threshold network in terms of the number of nodes and arcs.

Suppose that we have a feedforward network of linear threshold nodes, with underlying digraph (N, A) and set of states Ω. The feedforward condition allows us to label the computation nodes by the positive integers in their natural order, $1, 2, \ldots, z$, in such a way that z is the output node and $(i, j) \in A$ implies $j > i$. (This may be done by numbering first those computation nodes which are linked only to input nodes, then those which are linked only to input nodes and already-numbered computation nodes, and so on.)

For each state $\omega \in \Omega$, corresponding to an assignment of weights and thresholds to all the arcs and computation nodes, we let ω^l denote the part of ω determined by the thresholds on computation nodes $1, 2, \ldots, l$ and the weights on arcs which terminate at those nodes. Then for $2 \leq l \leq z$ we have the decomposition

$$\omega^l = (\omega^{l-1}, \zeta_l)$$

where ζ_l stands for the weights on arcs terminating at l and the threshold at l. In isolation, the output of a computation node l is a linear threshold function, determined by ζ_l, of the outputs of all those nodes j for which (j, l) is an arc; some of these may be input nodes and some may be computation nodes with $j < l$. We denote the space of such functions by H_l and the growth function of this 'local hypothesis space' by Π_l.

Suppose that $\mathbf{x} = (x_1, x_2, \ldots, x_m)$ is a sample of inputs to the network. (Each example x_i is a $|J|$-vector of real numbers, where J is the set of input nodes.) For any computation node l $(1 \leq l \leq z)$, we shall say that states ω_1, ω_2 of the network are *l-distinguishable by* $\mathbf{x}$ if the following holds. There is an example in $\mathbf{x}$ such that, when this example is input, the output of at least one of the computation nodes $1, 2, \ldots, l$, is different when the state is ω_1 from its output when the state is ω_2. In other words, if one has access to the signals transmitted by nodes 1 to l only, then, using the sample $\mathbf{x}$, one can differentiate between the two states. We shall denote by $S_l(\mathbf{x})$ the number of different states which are mutually l-distinguishable by $\mathbf{x}$.

Lemma 10.6.1 With the notation defined as above, we have

$$S_l(\mathbf{x}) \leq \Pi_1(m) \, \Pi_2(m) \ldots \Pi_l(m), \quad (1 \leq l \leq z).$$

Proof We prove the claim by induction on l. For $l = 1$ we have $S_1(\mathbf{x}) \leq \Pi_1(\mathbf{x})$, because two states are 1-distinguishable if and only if they give different classifications of the training sample at node 1. Thus $S_1(\mathbf{x}) \le \Pi_1(m)$.

Assume, inductively, that the claim holds for $l = k - 1$, where $2 \le k \le z$. The decomposition $\omega^k = (\omega^{k-1}, \zeta_k)$ shows that if two states are k-distinguishable but not $(k-1)$-distinguishable, then they must be distinguished by the action of the node k. For each of the $S_{k-1}(\mathbf{x})$ $(k-1)$-distinguishable states there are thus at most $\Pi_k(m)$ k-distinguishable states. Hence

$$S_k(\mathbf{x}) \le S_{k-1}(\mathbf{x}) \Pi_k(m).$$

By the inductive assumption, the right-hand side is at most $\Pi_1(m) \Pi_2(m) \dots \Pi_k(m)$. The result follows. □

Theorem 10.6.2 Let (N, A) be a feedforward linear threshold network, and let H be the hypothesis space of (N, A) represented by some given set of states Ω. Then, with Π_i as above,

$$\Pi_H(m) \le \Pi_1(m) \Pi_2(m) \dots \Pi_z(m),$$

for any positive integer m.

Proof Suppose an m-sample $\mathbf{x}$ is given. If, for one of the examples in $\mathbf{x}$, two states give different outputs at the output node z then these states are certainly z-distinguishable. Thus $\Pi_H(\mathbf{x}) \le S_z(\mathbf{x})$. By Lemma 10.6.1, $S_z(\mathbf{x}) \le \Pi_1(m) \dots \Pi_z(m)$ for all m-samples $\mathbf{x}$, and so the result follows. □

Corollary 10.6.3 Let (N, A) be a feedforward linear threshold network with z computation nodes, and denote the total number of variable weights and thresholds by $W = |N \setminus J| + |A|$. Let H be the hypothesis space of the network. Then for $m > W$, we have

$$\Pi_H(m) \le \left(\frac{zem}{W}\right)^W.$$

Proof Certainly, $W \ge d(i) + 1$ for $1 \le i \le z$ and so, for each such i and for $m > W$,

$$\Pi_i(m) \le \left(\frac{em}{d(i) + 1}\right)^{d(i)+1}$$

by Sauer's Lemma and since the VC dimension of H_i is $d(i) + 1$. It follows from Theorem 10.6.1 that

$$\Pi_H(m) \le \Pi_1(m) \Pi_2(m) \dots \Pi_z(m) \le \prod_{i=1}^{z} \left(\frac{em}{d(i) + 1}\right)^{d(i)+1}.$$

Now, if α_i $(1 \le i \le z)$ are positive real numbers with $\sum_{i=1}^{z} \alpha_i = 1$ then (Exercise 6)

$$\sum_{i=1}^{z} -\alpha_i \ln \alpha_i \le \ln z.$$

Observing that $W = \sum_{j=1}^{z} (d(j) + 1)$, and setting $\alpha_i = (d(i) + 1) / W$, we obtain

$$\sum_{i=1}^{z} \frac{d(i) + 1}{W} \ln \left(\frac{W}{d(i) + 1} \right) \le \ln z.$$

Hence

$$\sum_{i=1}^{z} (d(i) + 1) \ln \left(\frac{1}{d(i) + 1} \right) \le W \ln z - \left(\sum_{i=1}^{z} (d(i) + 1) \right) \ln W = W \ln z - W \ln W,$$

and so

$$\prod_{i=1}^{z} \left(\frac{1}{d(i) + 1} \right)^{d(i)+1} \le \left(\frac{z}{W} \right)^{W},$$

from which the result follows.   □

Theorem 10.6.4 The VC dimension of a feedforward linear threshold network with z computation nodes and a total of W variable weights and thresholds is at most $2W \lg (ez)$.

Proof Let H be the hypothesis space of the network. By the above result, we have, for $m \ge W$

$$\Pi_H(m) \le \left(\frac{zem}{W} \right)^{W},$$

where W is the total number of weights and thresholds. Now,

$$\left(\frac{2ezW \lg(ez)}{W} \right)^{W} < 2^{2W \lg(ez)} \iff 2ez \lg(ez) < (ez)^2 \iff 2 \lg(ez) < ez,$$

which is true for any $z \ge 1$. Therefore, $\Pi_H(m) < 2^m$ when $m = 2W \lg(ez)$, and the VC dimension of H is at most $2W \lg(ez)$, as claimed.   □

Notice that this bound on the VC dimension depends only on the 'size' of the network; that is, on the number of computation nodes and the number of arcs. That it is independent of the structure of the network — the underlying directed graph — suggests that it may not be a very tight bound. Nonetheless, it is an attractively simple one.

The following result is immediate from the above result and Corollary 8.4.2.

Corollary 10.6.5 Let N be a feedforward linear threshold network having z computation nodes and a total of W variable weights and thresholds. Suppose there is some probability distribution on the set of inputs to the network, and let $0 < \delta, \epsilon < 1$. If a randomly drawn training sample of length at least

$$\left\lceil \frac{4}{\epsilon} \left(2W \lg (ez) \lg \left(\frac{12}{\epsilon} \right) + \lg \left(\frac{2}{\delta} \right) \right) \right\rceil$$

is successfully 'loaded' onto the network then, with probability at least $1 - \delta$, the network will compute a function which has error less than ϵ; that is, it will correctly classify with probability at least $1 - \epsilon$ a further randomly chosen input.   □

We remark that if, as in Baum and Haussler (1989), we substitute the bound of Corollary 10.6.2 directly into the result of Proposition 8.2.3 and use the by now familiar techniques for obtaining a bound on sample length, then we can derive a better bound — one which contains a $\lg (z/\epsilon)$ term, rather than the product expression $\lg z \lg (1/\epsilon)$. (See Exercise 7.)

10.7 HARDNESS RESULTS FOR NEURAL NETWORKS

In Section 5.5 we showed that the consistency problem for a particular kind of 'parallel' machine is hard, in the NP-hard sense. The fact that similar results hold for neural networks was first shown by Judd (1988), using rather complicated constructions. In this section we shall prove a hardness result along the lines of one due to Blum and Rivest (1988), which uses a construction of a linear threshold network very similar to the parallel machine described in Section 5.5.

The machine is illustrated in Figure 10.4. There are n input nodes and $k + 1$ computation nodes ($k \geq 1$). The first k computation nodes are 'in parallel' and each of them is connected to all the input nodes. The last computation node is the output node; it is connected by arcs with fixed weight 1 to the other computation nodes, and it has fixed threshold k. The effect of this arrangement is that the output node acts as a multiple AND gate for the outputs of the other computation nodes. We shall refer to this machine (or its hypothesis space) as P_n^k.

A state ω of P_n^k is described by the thresholds θ_l ($1 \leq l \leq k$) of the first k computation nodes and the weights $w(i, l)$ on the arcs (i, l) linking the input nodes to the computation nodes. We shall use the notation $\alpha^{(l)}$ for the n-vector of weights on the arcs terminating at l, so that $\alpha_i^{(l)} = w(i, l)$. The set Ω of such states provides a representation $\Omega \to P_n^k$ in the usual way.

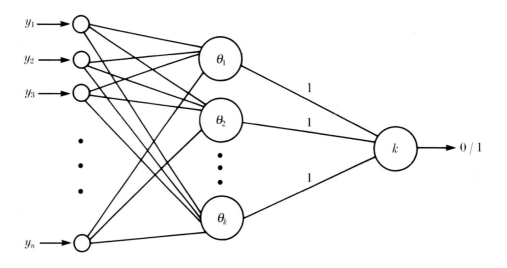

Figure 10.4: The network P_n^k

We shall prove that the consistency problem for $P^k = \bigcup P_n^k$ is NP-hard (provided $k \geq 3$) by a method very similar to that used in Section 5.5. Specifically, we shall reduce the problem to the graph k-colouring problem. Let G be a graph with vertex-set $V = \{1, 2, \ldots, n\}$ and edge-set E. We construct a training sample s(G) as follows. For each vertex $i \in V$ we take as a negative example the vector v_i which has 1 in the ith coordinate position, and 0's elsewhere. For each edge $ij \in E$ we take as a positive example the vector $v_i + v_j$. We also take the zero vector $o = 00 \ldots 0$ to be a positive example.

Proposition 10.7.1 There is a function in P_n^k which is consistent with s(G) if and only if the graph G is k-colourable.

Proof Suppose $h \in P_n^k$ is consistent with the training sample. By the construction of the network, h is a conjunction

$$h = h_1 \wedge h_2 \wedge \ldots \wedge h_k$$

of linear threshold functions. Specifically, there are weight-vectors $\alpha^{(1)}, \alpha^{(2)}, \ldots, \alpha^{(k)}$ and thresholds $\theta_1, \theta_2, \ldots, \theta_k$ such that

$$h_l(y) = 1 \iff \langle \alpha^{(l)}, y \rangle \geq \theta_l \quad (1 \leq l \leq k).$$

Note that, since o is a positive example, we have

$$0 = \langle \alpha^{(l)}, o \rangle \geq \theta_l$$

for each $l = 1, 2, \ldots, k$.

For each vertex i, $h(v_i) = 0$, and so there is at least one function h_f ($1 \leq f \leq k$) for which $h_f(v_i) = 0$. Thus we may define a function $\chi : V \to \{1, 2, \ldots, k\}$ as follows:

$$\chi(i) = \min\{f \mid h_f(v_i) = 0\}.$$

It remains to prove that χ is a colouring of G. Suppose that $\chi(i) = \chi(j) = f$, so that $h_f(v_i) = h_f(v_j) = 0$. In other words,

$$\langle \alpha^{(f)}, v_i \rangle < \theta_f, \quad \langle \alpha^{(f)}, v_j \rangle < \theta_f.$$

Then, recalling that $\theta_f \leq 0$, we have

$$\langle \alpha^{(f)}, v_i + v_j \rangle < \theta_f + \theta_f \leq \theta_f.$$

It follows that $h_f(v_i + v_j) = 0$ and $h(v_i + v_j) = 0$. Now if ij were an edge of G, then we should have $h(v_i + v_j) = 1$, because we assumed that h is consistent with the training sample. Thus ij is not an edge of G, and χ is a colouring, as claimed.

Conversely, suppose we are given a colouring $\chi : V \to \{1, 2, \ldots, k\}$. For $1 \leq l \leq k$ define the weight-vector $\alpha^{(l)}$ as follows:

$$\alpha_i^{(l)} = \begin{cases} -1, & \text{if } \chi(i) = l, \\ 1, & \text{otherwise;} \end{cases}$$

and the threshold θ_l to be $-1/2$. Let $h_1, h_2, \ldots, h_k$ be the corresponding linear threshold functions, and let h be their conjunction.

We claim that h is consistent with $s(G)$. Since $0 \geq \theta_l = -1/2$ it follows that $h_l(o) = 1$ for each l, and so $h(o) = 1$. In order to evaluate $h(v_i)$, note that if $\chi(i) = f$ then

$$\langle \alpha^{(f)}, v_i \rangle = \alpha_i^{(f)} = -1 < -1/2,$$

so $h_f(v_i) = 0$ and $h(v_i) = 0$, as required. Finally, for any colour l and edge ij we know that at least one of $\chi(i)$ and $\chi(j)$ is not l. Hence

$$\langle \alpha^{(l)}, v_i + v_j \rangle = \alpha_i^{(l)} + \alpha_j^{(l)},$$

where either both of the terms on the right-hand side are 1, or one is 1 and the other is -1. In any case the sum exceeds the threshold $-1/2$, and $h_l(v_i + v_j) = 1$. Thus $h(v_i + v_j) = 1$. $\square$

The proof that the decision problem for consistency in P^k is NP-hard for $k \geq 3$ follows directly from Proposition 10.7.1. If we are given an instance G of the graph k-colouring problem, we can construct the training sample $\mathbf{s}(G)$ in polynomial time. If the consistency problem could be solved by a polynomial time oracle, then we could answer the graph k-colouring problem in polynomial time by the following procedure: given G, construct $\mathbf{s}(G)$, and consult the oracle. The Proposition tells us that the answer given by the oracle is the same as the answer to the original question. But the graph k-colouring problem is known to be NP-complete, and hence it follows that the $P^k-CONSISTENCY$ problem is NP-hard if $k \geq 3$. (In fact, the same is true if $k = 2$. This follows from work of Blum and Rivest (1988) — see Exercise 8.)

The work of Chapter 9 shows that if there were an efficient pac learning algorithm for the graded space $P^k = \bigcup P_n^k$ then there should be a randomised algorithm which in polynomial time finds a hypothesis consistent with a given training sample. Under the RP $\neq$ NP assumption, the preceeding discussion therefore proves that there is no efficient pac learning algorithm for P^k ($k \geq 2$).

Thus, fixing k, we have a very simple family of feedforward linear threshold networks, each consisting of $k + 1$ computation nodes (one of which is 'hard-wired' and acts simply as an AND gate) for which the problem of 'loading' a training sample is computationally intractable. This is a rather pessimistic note on which to end our discussion. However, it should be emphasised that the 'non-learnability' result discussed above is a worst-case result and indicates that training neural networks is hard *in general*. This does not mean that a particular learning problem cannot be solved in practice. A number of fairly successful learning algorithms have been devised and neural networks are finding an increasing number of useful applications in fields as diverse as machine vision and financial prediction.

FURTHER REMARKS
Baum and Haussler (1989) have given examples of simple feedforward linear threshold networks with W weights and thresholds for which the VC dimension is $\Omega(W)$. The result of Theorem 10.6.3 gives an upper bound of $O(W \ln z)$. It is unknown whether the factor $\ln z$ is necessary.

Shawe-Taylor and Anthony (1991) have generalised the results of Section 10.6 to feedforward linear threshold networks with more than one output node. This uses a more general framework for pac learning, developed by Haussler (1989), in which the pac learning of functions with values in some arbitrary finite set can be discussed. In his paper, Haussler extends in a number of interesting ways the basic pac learning model and obtains results for feedforward neural networks in which the activation functions are other than simple linear threshold functions.

EXERCISES

1. Show that $|BP_3| = 104$.

2. Using the fact that for $m \geq d > 1$, $\Phi(d, m) \leq m^d$, prove that $|BP_n| \leq 2^{n^2+n}$. (This method is easier than that presented in Proposition 10.1.1, but produces a weaker bound.)

3. Prove that $|BP_n| > 2^{n+1}$.
[Hint: Use Proposition 7.3.3.]

4. Prove that $|BP_n| \geq 2^{n(n-1)/2}$. (This is a result of Muroga; see Muroga (1971).) Note that this result shows $\ln|BP_n| \neq O\,(\mathrm{VCdim}(BP_n))$: refer back to Section 9.4 to see the significance of this.

5. We may define a slight modification of the majority concept as follows. Let $n = 2r + 1$ and take $v = 11\ldots1000\ldots0$ to be the vector with r ones followed by $r + 1$ zeros. Define

$$u(y) = \begin{cases} 1, & \text{if } y \text{ has at least } r + 1 \text{ ones, or } y = v; \\ 0, & \text{otherwise.} \end{cases}$$

Verify that u is in Θ_n, with

$$\alpha^u = \frac{1}{n^2 - 3}(\underbrace{2n + 2, \ldots, 2n + 2}_{r}, \underbrace{2n - 2, \ldots, 2n - 2}_{r+1}),$$

and $c_u = 2/(n^2 - 3)$. Deduce that, for this concept and for an appropriate choice of ν, the number of invocations of the perceptron learning algorithm L_ν is $O(n^4)$.

6. The function $f(x) = x \ln x$ $(x > 0)$ is convex on the positive real numbers; that is, given $x, y > 0$ and $0 \leq \lambda \leq 1$, we have

$$f\,(\lambda x + (1 - \lambda)y) \geq \lambda f(x) + (1 - \lambda)f(y).$$

Use this to prove that for a positive integer z, if $\alpha_i > 0$ $(1 \leq i \leq z)$ and $\sum_{i=1}^{z} \alpha_i = 1$, then

$$-\sum_{i=1}^{z} \alpha_i \ln \alpha_i \leq \ln z.$$

7. As suggested in Section 10.6, use Corollary 10.6.2 and Proposition 8.2.3 to prove that if L is any consistent learning algorithm for a feedforward linear threshold network (N, A) having z computation nodes and W variable weights and thresholds,

then

$$m_L\,(H,\delta,\epsilon) \le \left\lceil \frac{4}{\epsilon} \left(W \lg \left(\frac{6z}{\epsilon} \right) + \lg \left(\frac{2}{\delta} \right) \right) \right\rceil,$$

where H denotes the hypothesis space of the network. Compare this with the bound obtained via the less direct route of Section 10.6.

8. For a positive integer n, let P_n^2 be as defined in Section 10.7, and let $P^2 = \bigcup P_n^2$. Following an argument similar to that given in Section 10.7, prove that the NP-complete *SET SPLITTING* problem, described in Exercise 7 of Chapter 5, reduces to the $P^2 - CONSISTENCY$ problem. Deduce that the consistency problem for P^2 is NP-hard. Thus, unless $RP = NP$, there is no efficient pac learning algorithm for P^2. (This is, essentially, the result of Blum and Rivest (1988), and the details can be found in their paper.)

References

Angluin (1988)   D. Angluin, Queries and concept learning. *Machine Learning*, 2(4): 319–342.

Angluin and Laird (1987)   D. Angluin and P.D. Laird, Learning from noisy examples. *Machine Learning*, 2(4): 343–370.

Angluin and Smith (1983)   D. Angluin and C.H. Smith, Inductive inference: theory and methods. *Computing Surveys*, 15(3): 237–269.

Angluin and Valiant (1979)   D. Angluin and L.G. Valiant, Fast probabilistic algorithms for Hamiltonian circuits and matchings. *Journal of Computer and Systems Sciences*, 18: 155–193.

Anthony (1991)   M. Anthony, *Uniform Convergence and Learnability*. PhD thesis, University of London.

Anthony, Biggs and Shawe-Taylor (1990)   M. Anthony, N. Biggs and J. Shawe-Taylor, The learnability of formal concepts. In *Proceedings of the 1990 Workshop on Computational Learning Theory*. Morgan Kaufmann, San Mateo, CA.

Assouad (1983)   P. Assouad, Densité et dimension. Ann. Inst. Fourier, Grenoble, 33(3): 233–282.

Bartlett and Williamson (1991)   P.L. Bartlett and R.C. Williamson, Investigating the distribution assumptions in the pac learning model. In *Proceedings of the 1991 Workshop on Computational Learning Theory*. Morgan Kaufmann, San Mateo, CA.

Baum (1990)   E.B. Baum, The perceptron algorithm is fast for non-malicious distributions, *Neural Computation*, 2: 249–261.

Baum and Haussler (1989)   E.B. Baum and D. Haussler, What size net gives valid generalization? *Neural Computation*, 1: 151–160.

Ben-David *et al.* **(1989)**   S. Ben-David, G.M. Benedek and Y. Mansour, A parameterization scheme for classifying models of learnability. In *Proceedings of the 1989 Workshop on Computational Learning Theory*. Morgan Kaufmann, San Mateo, CA.

Benedek and Itai (1988)   G.M. Benedek and A. Itai, Learnability by fixed distributions. In *Proceedings of the 1988 Workshop on Computational Learning Theory*. Morgan Kaufmann, San Mateo, CA.

Blum (1990)   A. Blum, Separating PAC and mistake-bounded learning models over the Boolean domain. In *Proceedings of the 31st IEEE Symposium on the Foundations of Computer Science*. IEEE Computer Society Press, Washington DC.

Blum and Rivest (1988)   A. Blum and R.L. Rivest, Training a 3-node neural network is NP-complete. In *Proceedings of the 1988 Workshop on Computational Learning Theory*. Morgan Kaufmann, San Mateo, CA.

Blum and Singh (1990)   A. Blum and M. Singh, Learning functions of k terms. In *Proceedings of the 1990 Workshop on Computational Learning Theory*. Morgan Kaufmann, San Mateo, CA.

Blumer *et al.* **(1986)**   A. Blumer, A. Ehrenfeucht, D. Haussler and M. Warmuth, Classifying learnable geometric concepts with the Vapnik-Chervonenkis dimension. In *Proceedings of the 18th Annual ACM Symposium on the Theory of Computing*. The Association for Computing Machinery, New York.

Blumer *et al.* **(1987)**   A. Blumer, A. Ehrenfeucht, D. Haussler and M. Warmuth, Occam's Razor. *Information Processing Letters*, 24: 377–380.

Blumer *et al.* **(1989)**   A. Blumer, A. Ehrenfeucht, D. Haussler and M. Warmuth, Learnability and the Vapnik-Chervonenkis Dimension. *Journal of the ACM*, 36(4): 929–965.

Board and Pitt (1990)   R. Board and L. Pitt, On the necessity of Occam algorithms. In *Proceedings of 22nd ACM Symposium on the Theory of Computing*. The Association for Computing Machinery, New York.

Chernoff (1952) H. Chernoff, A measure of asymptotic efficiency for tests of a hypothesis based on the sum of observations. *Annals of Mathematical Statistics*, 23: 493–509.

Cormen, Leiserson and Rivest (1990) T.H. Cormen, C.E. Leiserson, R.L. Rivest, *Introduction to Algorithms*. MIT Press, Cambridge, MA.

Duda and Hart (1973) R. Duda and P. Hart, *Pattern Classification and Scene Analysis*. Wiley, New York.

Ehrenfeucht *et al.* **(1989)** A. Ehrenfeucht, D. Haussler, M. Kearns and L. Valiant, A general lower bound on the number of examples needed for learning. *Information and Computation*, 82: 247–261.

Fischer and Simon (1990) P. Fischer and H.U. Simon, On learning ring-sum-expansions. In *Proceedings of the 1990 Workshop on Computational Learning Theory*. Morgan Kaufmann, San Mateo, CA.

Freund (1990) Y. Freund, Boosting a weak learning algorithm by majority. In *Proceedings of the 1990 Workshop on Computational Learning Theory*. Morgan Kaufmann, San Mateo, CA.

Garey and Johnson (1979) M. Garey and D. Johnson, *Computers and Intractibility: A Guide to the Theory of NP-Completeness*. Freeman, San Francisco.

Grunbaum (1967) B. Grunbaum, *Convex Polytopes*. John Wiley, London.

Haussler (1987) D. Haussler, Bias, version spaces and Valiant's learning framework. In *Proceedings of the 4th International Workshop on Machine Learning*. Morgan Kaufmann, San Mateo, CA.

Haussler (1988) D. Haussler, Quantifying inductive bias: AI learning algorithms and Valiant's learning framework. *Artificial Intelligence*, 36(2): 177–222.

Haussler (1989) D. Haussler, Generalizing the PAC model: sample size bounds from metric dimension-based uniform convergence results. In *Proceedings of the 30th IEEE Symposium on the Foundations of Computer Science*. IEEE Computer Society Press, Washington DC.

Haussler et al. (1988)   D. Haussler, M. Kearns, N. Littlestone and M. Warmuth, Equivalence of polynomial models of learnability. In *Proceedings of the 1988 Workshop on Computational Learning Theory*. Morgan Kaufmann, San Mateo, CA.

Haussler, Littlestone and Warmuth (1988)   D. Haussler, N. Littlestone and M.K. Warmuth, Predicting {0, 1}-functions on randomly drawn points. In *Proceedings of the 29th IEEE Symposium on Foundations of Computer Science*. IEEE Computer Society Press, Washington DC.

Haussler and Welzl (1987)   D. Haussler and E. Welzl, Epsilon-nets and simplex range queries. *Discrete & Computational Geometry*, 2: 127–151.

Hebb (1949)   D.O. Hebb, *The Organization of Behaviour*. Wiley, New York.

Johnson (1974)   D.S. Johnson, Approximation algorithms for combinatorial problems. *Journal of Computer and Systems Sciences*, 9: 256–278.

Judd (1988)   J.S. Judd, Learning in neural networks. In *Proceedings of the 1988 Workshop on Computational Learning Theory*. Morgan Kaufmann, San Mateo, CA.

Karmarkar (1984)   N. Karmarkar, A new polynomial time algorithm for linear programming. *Combinatorica*, 4: 373–395.

Karp (1972)   R.M. Karp, Reducibility among combinatorial problems. In *Complexity of Computer Computations* (ed. R.E. Miller and J.W. Thatcher). Plenum Press, New York.

Kearns (1990)   M.J. Kearns, *The Computational Complexity of Machine Learning*. MIT Press, Cambridge, MA.

Kearns and Li (1988)   M. Kearns and M. Li, Learning in the presence of malicious errors. In *Proceedings of the 20th Annual ACM Symposium on the Theory of Computing*. The Association for Computing Machinery, New York.

Kearns and Valiant (1989)   M. Kearns and L.G. Valiant, Cryptographic limitations on learning Boolean formulae and finite automata. In *Proceedings of the 21st Annual ACM Symposium on the Theory of Computing*. The Association for Computing Machinery, New York.

Kearns *et al.* **(1987a)** M. Kearns, M. Li, L. Pitt, L.G. Valiant, On the learnability of Boolean formulae In *Proceedings of the 19th Annual ACM Symposium on the Theory of Computing.* The Association for Computing Machinery, New York.

Kearns *et al.* **(1987b)** M. Kearns, M. Li, L. Pitt, L.G. Valiant, Recent results on Boolean concept learning. In *Proceedings of the 4th International Workshop on Machine Learning.* Morgan Kaufmann, San Mateo, CA.

Li and Vitanyi (1989) M. Li and P.M.B. Vitanyi, A theory of learning simple concepts and average case complexity for the universal distribution. In *Proceedings of the 30th IEEE Symposium on the Foundations of Computer Science.* IEEE Computer Society Press, Washington DC.

Linial *et al.* **(1989)** N. Linial, Y. Mansour and N. Nisan, Constant depth circuits, Fourier transforms and learnability. In *Proceedings of the 30th IEEE Symposium on the Foundations of Computer Science.* IEEE Computer Society Press, Washington DC.

Littlestone (1988) N. Littlestone, Learning quickly when irrelevant attributes abound: a new linear threshold learning algorithm. *Machine Learning*, 2(4): 245–318.

Lovász (1973) L. Lovász, Coverings and colorings of hypergraphs. In *Proceedings of the 4th Southeastern Conference on Combinatorics, Graph Theory, and Computing.* Utilitas Mathematica Publishing, Winnipeg.

McDiarmid (1989) C. McDiarmid, On the method of bounded differences. In *Surveys in Combinatorics, 1989* (ed. J. Siemons), London Mathematical Society Lecture Note Series, 141, Cambridge University Press, Cambridge.

Michalski *et al.* **(1983)** R.S. Michalski, J.G. Carbonell and T.M. Mitchell (editors), *Machine Learning: An Artificial Intelligence Approach.* Tioga Publishing Company, Palo Alto, CA.

Minsky and Papert (1969) M. Minsky and S. Papert, *Perceptrons.* MIT Press, Cambridge, MA. (Expanded edition 1988.)

Muroga (1971) S. Muroga, *Threshold Logic and its Applications.* Wiley, New York.

Natarajan (1988)   B.K. Natarajan, Learning over classes of distributions. In *Proceedings of the 1988 Workshop on Computational Learning Theory*. Morgan Kaufmann, San Mateo, CA.

Natarajan (1989)   B.K. Natarajan, On learning sets and functions. *Machine Learning*, 4: 67–97.

Nigmatullin (1969)   R.G. Nigmatullin, The fastest descent method for covering problems (in Russian). In *Proceedings of a Symposium on Questions of Precision and Efficiency of Computer Algorithms, Book 5*. Kiev, USSR.

Pitt and Valiant (1988)   L. Pitt and L.G. Valiant, Computational limitations on learning from examples. *Journal of the ACM*, 35(4): 965–984.

Pitt and Warmuth (1988)   L. Pitt and M.K. Warmuth, Reductions among prediction problems: on the difficulty of predicting automata. In *Proceedings of the 3rd IEEE Conference on Structure in Complexity Theory*. IEEE Computer Society Press, Washington DC.

Pitt and Warmuth (1990)   L. Pitt and M.K. Warmuth, Prediction-preserving reducibility. *Journal of Computer and Systems Sciences* 41: 430-467.

Pollard (1984)   D. Pollard, *Convergence of Stochastic Processes*. Springer Verlag, New York.

Rivest (1987)   R.L. Rivest, Learning decision lists. *Machine Learning*, 2(3): 229–246.

Rosenblatt (1959)   F. Rosenblatt, Two theorems of statistical separability in the perceptron. In *Mechanisation of Thought Processes: Proceedings of a Symposium Held at the National Physical Laboratory, November 1958. Vol. 1*. HM Stationery Office, London.

Rosenblatt (1962)   F. Rosenblatt, *Principles of Neurodynamics*. Spartan, New York.

Sauer (1972)   N. Sauer, On the density of families of sets, *Journal of Combinatorial Theory (A)*, 13: 145–147.

Schapire (1990)   R.E. Schapire, The strength of weak learnability. *Machine Learning*, 5: 197–227.

Shawe-Taylor and Anthony (1991) J. Shawe-Taylor and M. Anthony, Sample sizes for multiple output threshold networks. *Network*, 2: 107–117.

Shelah (1972) S. Shelah, A combinatorial problem; stability and order for models and theories in infinitary languages. *Pacific Journal of Mathematics*, 41: 241–261.

Sloan (1988) R. Sloan, Types of noise in data for concept learning. In *Proceedings of the 1988 Workshop on Computational Learning Theory*. Morgan Kaufmann, San Mateo, CA.

Utgoff (1986) P. Utgoff, Shift of bias for inductive concept learning. In *Machine Learning: An Artificial Intelligence Approach, Volume III*. Morgan Kaufmann, San Mateo, CA.

Valiant (1984a) L.G. Valiant, A theory of the learnable. *Communications of the ACM*, 27(11): 1134–1142.

Valiant (1984b) L.G. Valiant, Deductive learning. *Philosophical Transactions of the Royal Society of London* A, 312: 441–446.

Valiant (1991) L.G. Valiant, A view of computational learning theory. In *NEC Research Symposium: Computation and Cognition* (ed. C.W. Gear). SIAM, Philadelphia.

Vapnik (1982) V.N. Vapnik, *Estimation of Dependences Based on Empirical Data*. Springer Verlag, New York.

Vapnik and Chervonenkis (1971) V.N. Vapnik and A.Ya. Chervonenkis, On the uniform convergence of relative frequencies of events to their probabilities. *Theory of Probability and its Applications*, 16(2), 264-280.

Wenocur and Dudley (1981) R.S. Wenocur and R.M. Dudley, Some special Vapnik-Chervonenkis classes. *Discrete Mathematics*, 33: 313–318.

Welsh (1988) D. Welsh, *Codes and Cryptography*. Clarendon Press, Oxford.

Wilf (1986) H.S. Wilf, *Algorithms and Complexity*. Prentice-Hall, New Jersey.

Index

accuracy 22–23
    efficiency with respect to 51, 52, 53–54, 61, 65, 66, 108, 119, 120
    parameter 22
active node 71
activation function 132
algorithm 4, 5, 38
    incremental 125
    for long multiplication 39
    running time 38
alphabet 2
approximation of concept 3, 20
arc 131
architecture 131, 132
artificial intelligence 7
artificial neural network 131

B_n 31
backpropogation algorithm 132
binomial
    numbers 36, 79, 80
    distribution 91
boolean
    alphabet 2
    circuit 15
    formula 13, 15, 16, 68
    functions, number of 6, 8
    perceptron 123
Borel set 21
boxes 106
    learning algorithm 107, 110, 122
    VC dimension 110, 122

box union 115, 117, 120
    finding simplest is hard 117, 120
    VC dimension 122

C_n 44
C_n^k 44
    learning by D_n^k 55, 69
$C^k - CONSISTENCY$ 47, 48
$C^2 - CONSISTENCY$ 50
characteristic function 87
Chernoff bound 91, 97
classification
    of examples 2
    of sample 73
    method of 7
    vector 73
clause 14
    learning algorithm 48, 49
closed sets 88, 100
colouring of graph 45, 49, 138
complement
    of boolean function 37
    of hypothesis space 85
        VC dimension of 85
complexity theory 38–39
compression of input 56, 57, 60
computation node 131
concept 2
concept space 3
confidence 23
    efficiency with respect to 51, 52, 61, 65, 66, 68, 108, 119, 120

parameter 22
conjunction 13
conjunctive normal form (CNF) 13
consistent
    hypothesis 4
    learning algorithm 4
consistent-hypothesis-finder 52, 111, 113
consistency problem 44
    restricted form of 44, 48
    hardness of 44–48, 49, 50, 54, 140,
        142
    and efficient pac learning 52–54, 110
constraints
    upon number of examples 31
    upon resources 3
construction, learning by 5, 6, 17
convex
    hull 77, 78
    function 141
    set 77, 78
countable
    hypothesis space 6
    example space 21
cryptographic hardness assumptions 67

$D_{n,k}$ 14, 31, 54, 69
decision lists 32
    and other boolean functions 33, 37
    closed under complementation 37
    evaluating 32, 36
    greedy learning algorithm 64, 70
    learning algorithm 33–34, 35, 36,
        37
    number of 32, 37
    Occam algorithm 64, 70
dimension-based Occam algorithm 117,
    118
directed graph 131
disjunction 13
disjunctions of small monomials 14, 31,
        54, 69
    learning algorithm 14, 15, 18, 55

optimality 114
    running time 40, 43
    number of 14, 17
    VC dimension 114
disjunctive normal form (DNF) 13, 67,
    70
    existence of 17
distinguishable states of network 134
distribution 20
    uniform 21, 53, 87, 96
DNF space 67, 70, 112
doubly-graded space
    boolean 65
    general 120

ϵ-bad hypothesis 29
edge-set 45
effective hypothesis space 118
efficiency with respect to
    accuracy 51, 52, 53–54, 61, 65, 66,
        108, 119, 120
    confidence 51, 52, 61, 65, 66, 68,
        108, 119, 120
    example size 41–43, 51, 52, 54–55,
        65, 66, 108, 111, 120
    representation size 61, 65, 66, 115,
        119, 120
    as generalisation of pac 117
    as restriction of pac 116–117
efficient algorithm 38–39
efficient prediction 48, 67
efficiently pac, *see* epac
elementary function 13
    quadrant 106
encoding 5
enumeration
    of countable hypothesis space 6
    learning by 6, 8, 31, 33, 43
epac learning 65, 120, 122
    as generalisation of pac 67, 121
    as restriction of pac 66, 121
    of decision lists 66

of monomials 66
robustness 69
using Occam algorithm 65, 120–121
epac prediction 68
equivalence query 7
error
during training 26, 27
of a hypothesis 20, 21
sct 21
measurability of 35
Euclidean norm 127
event 20
exact learning 24–26
example 1, 2
negative 2
positive 2
presentation of 2
size of boolean 40
size of real 105
example space 2
exception lists 121
exclusive-or function 18, 124, 133
excitatory connection 131
existence problem 44
and search problem 44
expressive power 71, 74, 123, 133
extension
of potential learnability 36, 103
of *O*-notation 102
of training sample 4

feedforward neural network 131
hypothesis space of 132
VC dimension of 134–136, 140
with multiple outputs 140
finite example space
and exact learning 24–25
and VC dimension 83
finite hypothesis space
is potentially learnable 30
upper bound on VC dimension 76
formula

boolean 13, 15, 16, 68
for monomials 9
framework for learning 1, 3
functional model 26

generalisation 4
generalised
Occam algorithm 121
sample complexity bounds 101
graded by example size 40, 105
learning algorithm 40, 106
graded by representation size 59, 105
graph 45, 49
colouring 45, 138
GRAPH k-COLOURING 47
greedy algorithm
for learning decision lists 64, 70
is epac 66
is Occam 64
for learning monomials 17, 63, 70
is epac 66
is Occam 64
for *MINIMUM COVER* 61–62
performance ratio 62, 64
group action 89, 90, 91
growth function 73
and VC dimension 74, 79
of boolean perceptron 123
of feedforward threshold network 135
of interval space 84
of ray space 73
of real perceptron 84

H-CONSISTENCY 44
half-line 17
half-space 77
hardness of
consistency problem 44-48, 49, 50, 54, 140, 142
finding simplest box union 117, 120
pac learning 54–55, 68, 140, 142
SHORTEST MONOMIAL 57–59
training a neural network 137–140

hyperplane 77
hypothesis 3
    output 5
hypothesis space 3
    effective 118
    graded by example size 40, 105
    graded by representation size 59, 115
    local 134
    non-trivial 100

incremental algorithm 125
inductive bias 7
inductive inference 7
infinite VC dimension 74, 88
inhibitory connection 131
inner product 127
input
    compression of 56, 57, 60
    node 131
    size 38
    to algorithm 38
    to machine 3, 10
interval 27, 106
    learning algorithm 28
    r-fold unions of 115
        learning algorithm 115–116
        VC dimension 116, 122
interval union space 88, 100, 117, 120
    VC dimension infinite 88
invocations of incremental algorithm 126
    number of 128–130, 141

labelled example 3
learning algorithm 4
    for doubly-graded space 65, 120
    for graded space 40, 106
learning by construction 5, 6, 17
learning by enumeration 6, 8, 31, 33, 43
length of sample 3
linear programming 124, 125
    algorithms 125

LINEAR THRESHOLD CONSISTENCY 124, 125
linear threshold machine 16, 71, 123
    representation of 16
linearly ordered space 85, 104
linearly separable 73
literal 9
loading a sample 137, 140
local hypothesis space 134

$M_{n,k}$ 14
machine 1
    for C_n^k 44
    for monomials 9, 10, 12, 17
    linear threshold 16, 71
    parallel 137
    state of 1, 3, 9, 10, 12, 15, 16, 17, 55, 132, 137
machine learning 7
majority concept 129, 130
modification 141
malicious errors 27
measurability 35, 89
membership query 7
memoryless on-line algorithm 6, 11, 19, 26, 64, 122, 126
    running time 41
MINIMUM COVER 57
    and SUBCOVER 58, 70
    and SHORTEST MONOMIAL 58, 70
    greedy algorithm for 61, 120
misclassification error 26
mistake-bounded learning 26
monomials 9
    formula 9
    greedy learning algorithm 17, 63, 70
    machine 9, 10, 12, 17
    monotone 85
        VC dimension of 85
    number of 12

Occam algorithm 63–64
   representation of 16
   smallest consistent 57–59
   standard learning algorithm 11, 12,
      17, 25, 48
     is consistent 12
     is optimal 114
     running time 40, 43
     sample complexity 31, 114
   VC dimension 76
monotone monomial 85
multiple AND unit 10, 44, 137

near-consistent algorithm 36, 103
n-dimensional box union space 115
   representation of 115
n-dimensional quadrant space 106
neural network 131
negative example 2
node 131
non-negative quadrant 105
non-trivial hypothesis space 100
non-uniform pac learning 27, 67
normal form 13
   conjunctive 13
   disjunctive 13, 17, 67, 70
notation
   and terminology 8
   for boolean functions 13–14
NP-complete 39
NP-hard 39
   consistency problem 44–48, 50, 54,
      140, 142
   pac learning problem 54–55

O-notation 38–39
   for real functions 102
observed error 86
Occam algorithm 60, 117, 118
   comparison of boolean and dimension-
     based 119–120
   dimension-based 117, 118
   for decision lists 64, 70

   for doubly graded space 65, 120
     and epac learning 66–67, 120–121
   for monomials 63–64
   for n-dimensional box unions 120
   generalised 121
   running time of 61, 119
   sample complexity 60, 65, 118, 121
Ω-notation 102
optimal sample complexity 113
   disjunctions of small monomials 114
   monomials 114
oracle 26, 47, 48
oracle model 26
output hypothesis 5
   size of 56, 60
output node 131

$P \neq NP$ conjecture 39
P_n^k 137
$P^k - CONSISTENCY$ 140
   consistency problem 138–140
$P_n^2 - CONSISTENCY$ 142
pac learning
   algorithm 22, 23–24
   and potential learnability 30
   and the consistency problem 52–54,
     110
   and VC dimension 94–100
     impossible if infinite 99
   hardness of 54–55, 68, 140
   of functions 140
palindrome 2, 4, 8, 17, 49
parallel machine 131
parity 2, 5, 17, 49
pattern recognition 7
perceptron
   boolean 123
     VC dimension of 123
     cardinality of space 123, 141
   convergence theorem 128
   incremental algorithm 126
     finiteness of 128, 129

learning algorithm 126
real 71, 72–73, 133
  geometrical interpretation 72, 77, 105
  growth function 84
  representation of 72
  graded space 105
  VC dimension 75–76, 77–79, 84
polygonal region 77, 100, 103
polynomial representation size 66, 67, 70
polynomial time algorithm 39
polynomial time learning algorithm 42
polynomially evaluable 49
positive example 2
potential learnability 29–30
  and VC dimension 87–93
  extension to near-consistency 36, 103
  implies consistent algorithm pac 30
  of finite space 30
prediction 48
  efficient 48, 67
  epac 68
pre-processor 1
probability
  distribution 20
    on finite set 24
    on product set 21–22
    uniform 21, 53, 87, 96
  measure 20
  of an event 20
  of training sample 22
  space 20
probably approximately correct 22
probably exactly correct 25
  monomial algorithm 25
product
  probability distribution 21–22
  set 21

query
  equivalence 7
  membership 7
quadrant 105
  n-dimensional 106
  non-negative 105
  space 106
    learning algorithm 106–107, 109, 110, 122
    VC dimension 109-110

Radon's theorem 78
random number generator 52
random sample 22
randomised algorithm 52, 69
  for consistency problem 53–54, 110, 112, 140
  running time of 53, 110
  usefulness of 53
rays 17, 19, 73, 106
  growth function 73
  learning algorithm 19, 20, 27, 106
    is pac 23–24
    sample complexity 24, 27, 96
  potential learnability of 36
  representation of 17
  VC dimension 74, 85
real alphabet 2
real perceptron, *see* perceptron, real
representation 16, 17, 18
  polynomially evaluable 49
  size
    of boolean hypotheses 55–56
    of real hypotheses 105
    polynomial 66, 67, 70
representation-dependent hardness 55
representation-independent hardness 68
restriction
  on hypothesis space 6, 7, 35, 89
  of hypotheses 73
ring-sum expansions 49
RP (random polynomial time) 54
RP $\neq$ NP conjecture 54
running time

of algorithm 38
  for long-multiplication 39
  of learning algorithm 40–41, 51–52, 108
    and sample complexity 42
    of Occam algorithm 61, 119

sample 3
  length 3
sample complexity 41–42
  and potential learnability 42
  lower bound
    consistent algorithms 96–97
    general 97–99, 100–101, 101, 102
  of consistent learning algorithm 42, 52, 94–95, 96–97
  of Occam algorithm 60, 65, 118, 121
  optimal 113, 113–114
  upper bound 42, 52, 94–95, 96, 101, 102
    tightness of 102
  of learning algorithm for finite space 42, 94
SATISFIABILITY 39
Sauer's Lemma 79–81, 83, 89, 95, 104, 123
  tightness of 84
SET SPLITTING 50, 142
search problem 44
  and existence problem 44
  randomised algorithm for 52
SHORTEST MONOMIAL 58
  and *MINIMUM COVER* 59, 70
  hardness of 57–59
shattered sample 74
simplex algorithm 125
size
  of example 40, 105
  of input to algorithm 38
  of output hypothesis 56, 60
  of representation
    boolean concepts 55–57

real concepts 105
smallest consistent monomial 57–59
state 1, 3, 9, 10, 12, 15, 16, 17, 55, 72, 77, 79, 126, 127, 132, 137
subcover 57, 61
SUBCOVER 57, 70
supervised learning 7
swapping group 91
symmetric boolean function 103
  learning algorithm 104
  representation of 104
  VC dimension 104

target concept 4
testing sample 89, 94
threshold 71, 124, 132
threshold logic 133
training 3–5
training sample 3
  determined by sample 22
  representative 4, 5
  unrepresentative or misleading 4, 5, 23
truth table 13

uncountable example space 20
uniform distribution 21, 53, 87, 96
unit ball 2
universally separable space 35

variants
  of learning from examples 7
  of mistake-bounded learning 26
  of pac model
    dependence on distribution 27
    dependence on target 27
    fixed confidence 68
    learning functions 140
    weak learning 68–69
  of standard learning framework 26
vertex 45
VC (Vapnik-Chervonenkis) dimension 71, 74

and efficient learning
   general spaces 108–111
   boolean spaces 111–113
and potential learnability 87–93
and sample complexity 94–96
of boolean perceptron 123
of box space 110, 122
of box unions 122
of complement of a space 85
of disjunctions of small monomials
     114
of feedforward neural networks 134–
     136, 140
of finite hypothesis space 76
of interval space 84
of interval union space 88
of monomials 76
of monotone monomials 85
of quadrants 109–110
of rays 74
of real perceptron 75–76, 77–79, 84
of r-fold interval unions 116, 122
of symmetric functions
polynomial for efficiency 110
when example space finite 83

weak learning 68–69
weighted sum 16, 71
weight-vector 124
weights 71, 124, 131
worst-case running time 38, 40

xor function 18, 124, 133